NO TIDES TO STEM

VOLUME 2

A HISTORY
OF THE
MANCHESTER PILOT SERVICE
1894-1994

BY
DEREK A. CLULOW

The painting on the front cover, entitled
"PASSING WESTON POINT LOCKS OUTWARD BOUND"
was by the late Mr. W. (Bill) Yates, Pilot First Class and
reproduced by kind permission of his wife Mrs. D. Yates

First published 1998 by Countyvise Limited, 1 & 3 Grove Road, Rock Ferry, Birkenhead, Wirral, Merseyside L42 3XS in conjunction with the author Derek A. Clulow

British Library Cataloguing in Publication Data.
A catalogue record for this book is available from the British Library.

ISBN 1 901231 06 2

To

My very dear wife, "Tulip", who for 35 years has suffered silently the unsocial hours of my profession, listened patiently to my endless accident reports, mended willingly my broken body from football, helped unfailingly to "dry" me out from time to time and yet through all this, never stopped loving me.

TO/ RAYMOND

The Author
Manchester Ship Canal Pilot Service
1954 - 1988

SUMMER '98.

Acknowledgements

The longer the task of writing the history of the MANCHESTER SHIP CANAL PILOT SERVICE has been put off, the greater the work of the historian, who will find records get destroyed, the older generation passes on, memories fade and facts blend into legends. In writing this history I found no exception to this rule.

First and foremost, in writing the acknowledgement , I must express my deep sense of gratitude to Mrs. Jean Capper whose unstinting offer to give up her much loved leisure time to transfer my - at times illegible writings in longhand - words to paper by way of the typewriter. Without Jean's help and happy disposition through these long years - five in all - I could not have ever finished this history of the Pilot Service. With no less a sense of gratitude I sincerely thank Adrian Wood and Graeham and Fran Hulbert for their invaluable contribution in editing and correcting the manuscripts a task of no mean feat and gratefully appreciated. A special thank you to Mrs. Yates for her patience and forbearance with me whilst lending me her late husband's (Mr. W. (Bill) Yates, Pilot First Class) voluminous photographic and work records he so painstakingly collected and kept for posterity and for her kind permission for me to use the superb paintings by her late husband of scenes on the Canal especially the one that adorns the jacket of this book.

I shall always be grateful to Miss M. Patch and her staff at the Greater Manchester Council County Records Office for their unfailing courtesy and assistance so readily given to me during my researching at that establishment. To Mr. David Thornley ex. P.R.O. of the old Manchester Ship Canal Company very many thanks for allowing me to browse through the hundreds of photographs in the archives thus preserving an era that has gone for ever. To all the Pilots' widows who so kindly lent me their treasured photographs of their loved ones so that they may be forever remembered in the pages of this book, my thanks to you all.

Finally if I have forgotten to acknowledge anyone from the list below please forgive me, there have been so many and some are bound to be overlooked.

Mr. H.G. Pringle)
Mr. M.E. Warren)
Mr. J.H. Warren } Manchester Ship Canal Pilots
Mr. A.E. Cooke)
Mr. P.K. Rali)
Mr. G. Collins
Mr. J. Southwood River Dee Pilot
Mr. H. Thelwell Ex. Pilots Clerk
Mr G.I.B. Jackson Eng. Dept. Manchester Ship Canal
Mrs. D. Marten)
Mrs. Jan Lemon } Pilots National Pension Fund
Mrs. Sweet)
Mr. Alan Green Liverpool Pilot
Mr. Peter Glamey
Mr. H. Milsom Editor "Sea Breezes"
Mr. A. Potts Privy Council Office Whitehall
Mr. J. Pepper Department of Transport
Mr. B.K. Phillips Public Record Office, Richmond,
Surrey
Mr. J. Allan General Council of British Shipping
Mr. S.K. Conacher General Council of British Shipping
Mr. P. Dunbavand Captain, Manchester Ship Canal Tug Service
Captain D.W. Jones "Dalmor" Nefyn Gwynedd, Inspector,
Board of Trade
Captain R. Kilby-Lennon Ex. Master "Helmsley 1"
Captain G. Cubbins T. & J. Harrisons, Liverpool
F. Armitt and Son Shipping Agents
H.M. Tax Inspectors Head Office, London
British Rail National Railway Museum, York
Whitbreads Brewery
Maritime Museum Albert Dock, Liverpool
Mr. E. Morrison Ex. Pilot Clerk
Arthur Guinness, Son & Co. (Dublin) Ltd.
Mr. R.A. Jamieson Archives Assistant, British Waterways, Gloucester
Central Library, Manchester
Mrs. J.J. Pierpoint
Mrs. J. Lang Currie (Business Equipment) Ltd, Birkenhead
Merseyside Transport Ltd.
Mrs. C. Cartwright
Mr. C. Parsons World Ship Society
John Mills Photography Ltd., Liverpool
Mr. John Young and Family

ALL THAT MANKIND HAS DONE, THOUGHT, GAINED OR BEEN: IT IS LYING AS IN MAGIC PRESERVATION IN THE PAGES OF BOOKS.

THOMAS CARLYLE

THE BEGINNING IS THE MOST IMPORTANT PART OF THE WORK.

PLATO

Contents

1.

THE FIRST ABUSES OF THE ROTARY SYSTEM

In any pilotage working system it will be often pointed out the errors which have existed in its day-to-day management and still do exist. But what pilotage district is there in the world that is wholly perfect in its management or into which, if perfection has been sought, abuses do not creep in? The fledgeling Manchester Pilot Service Rotary System was to be no exception to the rule.

On December 1st 1919, the Manchester Pilotage Committee created a new post in the administration of pilotage affairs - that of a Chief Pilotage Clerk to be based at Runcorn. Mr R Bennion was appointed to this position which he held with great distinction and respect for his equanimity to all Pilots, for 26 years. His was the onerous and often thankless task of ensuring an efficient pilot service, with as little disruption and delay as possible to the movements of vessels in the canal. By placing Pilots on board vessels who required them at the correct time and in their correct order on the Rota, it proved no mean task as events will show.

It must always be kept in mind that not all the pilots agreed or even accepted the Rotary System. Having their freedom of choice to work when they desired removed, coupled with the sharing of the Pilotage Fees they earned, amongst their fellow Pilots - some of whom they regarded as their mortal enemies - went very much against the grain. They became very disgruntled, unco-operative and unwilling to conscientiously work a system that they thought had been forced upon them.

During the discussions for a Rotary System, it became very apparent in the early stages that an adequate and efficient means of communication between the pilots and the pilot clerk at Runcorn, was of tantamount importance towards the successful running of the Pilots' Rota. The provision of a telephone by all pilots at their private addresses was essential towards this end and all pilots were instructed accordingly. Thus the way was opened for the first abuse of the Pilotage Rota. Even in those early days of the Rotary System some pilots had acquired a truly uncanny knowledge of the day-to-day movements of all vessels in the canal requiring a pilot attendance, through either accomplices on the locks, stevedores, tug-masters or shipping agents. The pilots were duty bound to keep in contact at reasonable intervals with the Pilotage Clerk during the day to ascertain their position on the rota; with this information coupled with their knowledge of shipping movements for that day there was every likelihood they could figure out, with a certain modicum of success, when and where they would be required for work.

If after having done all their calculations they then discovered the Pilotage order was not to their liking, e.g. pilotage distance too long; the vessel was large and slow moving or the time of sailing would necessitate their being away from home that night, by not being available to be contacted at the time required through having no telephone at home and by contacting the Pilot Clerk after that time, he would have missed his correct turn on the rota but would remain number one for the next order, usually a shorter distance and at a more convenient time. The next pilot on turn, no doubt having a telephone at home, would have been sent to the vessel originally allocated to the first pilot. There were no penalties for missing a vessel in these circumstances.

By March 1921, all pilots had telephones installed at their private addresses but this did not stop certain pilots abusing the Rota in many devious ways regarding the telephone. I quote one incident :

In May 1921 a senior pilot had his phone disconnected for non-payment of his account. It was reconnected in August on payment

1919

On the port side of the Dock the "Manchester Miller" Grt. 4097 L.360 'B.48' A coal burning vessel of 11 knots with chain and rod steering gear. "The Cormorant" British Continental S.S.Co. on the starboard side completes the picture.

1964

The motor vessel "Manchester Renown" Grt.9300 L.503 'B.62.5' The last of the purpose built vessels for transiting the Ship Canal. She had a service speed of 16 knots with the sophisticated electric steering gear. She lasted seven short years before being sold.

of the outstanding account but shortly after, the telephone developed a fault, the instrument was unreliable in receiving incoming calls and the pilot did not report this fault to the telephone company.

In December of that year, the Pilotage Committee ordered the pilot to take steps to put his telephone into correct working order as he was causing so much disruption and inconvenience to other pilots working concientiously on a strict rota. The fault was corrected on the telephone the following month, but was disconnected again one week later pending a settlement of a dispute with the Post Office over increase of charges and remained disconnected until 23 October 1922. Thus this pilot was without a telephone for nearly 18 months. Was this by accident or design?

Some pilots attended their duties in a manner they thought fit, not always working strictly to the letter of the Rules and Regulations for working the Rota.

On 4 November 1921, four pilots had been detailed for duty at Eastham Locks on tide, to attend vessels arriving from the river from 0947 hrs (four hours to High Water) to 1747 hrs (four hours after High Water) as stipulated in Clause 'A' of the Rules and Regulations. Only one pilot was on station at the correct time and he left Eastham with a vessel for Partington at 1025 hrs. Another vessel arrived at 1100 hrs requiring a pilot, but there was no pilot on station and another pilot was hurriedly called out to attend the vessel.

One of the missing pilots telephoned the Pilot Clerk at 1200 hrs from Liverpool saying he had met with an accident the previous evening, necessitating his attendance at hospital at 1400 hrs. Mr Hindle (pilot's representative) said he knew nothing about an accident to the pilot in question and had been in his company the night previous, i.e. 3rd November and the pilot had only complained of an "aching leg". He did not think that the pilot's explanation for not taking his turn on duty was satisfactory, as he lived close to Eastham Locks and could have telephoned his inability to attend tide prior to his proceeding to Liverpool.

Mr Hindle said in his opinion it was a gross abuse of the Rules and Regulations of the Rotary system and pilots who did conscientiously attend to their duties suffered because of the neglect of others.

The two other pilots absent from duty did not arrive until after High Water and proffered no excuse for the lateness of their arrival. Not one pilot was penalised for their actions because no penalties for such abuse of the Rotary System had been legislated for. One of the greatest abuses and the most frequently used, was the unavailability of pilots to work through sickness, especially during the winter months and more importantly, during the night.

1) A pilot reported to the Pilot Clerk at 1800 hours, 9 December 1921 that he could not attend for tide duty owing to having a cold. High water was midnight but at 10.15 a.m. the next day, said he was ready for work.

2) On Sunday 24 December (Christmas Eve), a pilot reported at 0930 hrs that owing to the death of a grandchild he did not feel able to work, but was told to attend at Eastham for the afternoon tide at 1500 hours, he said he would attend at High Water if required as he lived close to the Locks. He failed to attend at High Water and later reported sick with food poisoning. He was off duty until 27 December. He spent his Christmas at home.

3) On the night of 22 December, a pilot reported he could not attend at Eastham for the morning tide, High Water 0210 hours, as he had contacted rheumatism. He had sufficiently recovered to attend on the afternoon tide the following day. What was this miracle cure?

4) On another occasion, a pilot reported he could not attend at Eastham for the morning tide, High Water 0235 hours, as he was threatened with bronchitis, but at 0730 hours, the same morning, he was on the telephone again asking for orders, duly recovered one presumes.

5) On New Year's Eve, at 1620 hours, a pilot reported to the Pilot Clerk he could not attend the afternoon tide, High Water 1859 hours, owing to having a cold. He resumed work on the morning of 1 January, miraculously cured.

6) A pilot outward bound from Runcorn to Eastham completed the passage at 1830 hours on Saturday night. He was then ordered to return to Manchester for Sunday morning 0730 hours to pilot a vessel for which he was the choice pilot. He refused on the grounds there was insufficient time for him to return to Manchester, but when pressed and told by the Pilot Clerk that in his opinion there

Mr. R.B. Stoker Pilotage Committee
1889 - 1919

Mr. William Browning
Chairman Pilotage Committee
1916 - 1936

Mr. R.B. Stoker (Son) Chairman
Pilotage Committee

Sir Leslie Roberts C.B.E.
Chairman Pilotage Committee
1938 - 1950

was ample time to return to Manchester, he amended his refusal to accept the order by claiming he was ill. A rota pilot was called out to attend this vessel. The Pilot in question telephoned in for orders at 1000 hrs on Sunday morning, saying he felt a lot better and would accept any vessel. It is amazing the recuperative powers of a night in one's own bed.

7) On 8 December (Friday?) a pilot reported he had just arrived home after piloting a vessel to Manchester. He was wet through with rain, going to have a bath and a night in and would report for work the following day. The immediate effect of such abstention from duty is to disturb the working rota and to bring out the next pilot for duty. In this case the pilot next on turn left Eastham with a vessel for Manchester at the same time as the pilot who absented himself from duty and therefore had an equal right to say, if he felt so inclined, that he too was not ready for more work.

Pilots complained about such acts of absenting themselves from the rota and expressed their opinion as to whether a pilot is entitled to withhold his services in this manner unless really ill. If he has, then all order will cease and chaos will reign. With such a depletion of numbers as shown by the foregoing and other cases of suspect illnesses, it was becoming increasingly difficult to carry on the work of a Rotary System satisfactorily. On the weekend of 22/23 December, 22 vessels were piloted on the outward rota by only fourteen pilots; the Pilotage Rota came critically close to breaking down completely. One must wonder if this was an ulterior motive of those pilots who objected to the Rotary System. If it was, then they never knew how close they came to achieving their ambition to abolish the Rota System.

Supposition and speculation too often take the place of hard facts, but the abuses recorded here are undeniably hard facts. Whether the pilots in those early days were genuine in their approach to the working system is a matter of conjecture, but the author has firmly established his own assumptions, having personally witnessed and suffered the many forms of abuse in the Rotary System for 34 years. He can see no viable reason why some pilots then would be any better or different than some pilots of his years. How true it is to say that a "leopard never changes his spots". On the 16 October 1938, Second Class Pilot F Davenport stated that he had given notice

THIS IS THE FIRST PILOTAGE CERTIFICATE TO BE
ISSUED AS OPPOSED TO A PILOTS LICENCE IN 1896

MANCHESTER SHIP CANAL.

Pilotage Certificate No. 1.

This is to certify *that* *Thomas Paul*

aged *forty five* *years of* *9 Victoria Road Runcorn,*

is hereby authorized by the Manchester Ship Canal Company, acting in

pursuance of the Merchant Shipping Act, 1894, to pilot upon the Manchester

Ship Canal, the *S.S. "Maggie Warrington"*

or other *Steamers owned* by *Samuel Hough Esq*
Liverpool.

within the limits of this Canal for a period expiring on the first day of

September next

Granted by the said Company under the hand of its Secretary,

this *25th* day of *January* Eighteen hundred

and Ninety *six*.

Secretary.

for the removal of his telephone as he found he was no longer able to afford its upkeep on his present earnings - he was earning an average of £30 per month. He requested that his orders be given to him by means of telegrams, contending that at the present rate of working his telegram bill would only be £3. p.a. against his telephone bill which amounted to between £7. and £8.

Some discussion followed and reference was made to Minute of the Committee dated 6 April 1920, at which time there were a number of pilots who had no telephones at their homes. The Committee had then informed the pilots concerned that it would greatly assist in the working of the rotary system if they would provide themselves with telephones and since 1920 it had been the invariable practice for all the pilots and helmsmen to be connected by telephone.

The Committee deprecated any departure which might interfere with the satisfactory working of the rotary system. The following month, Messrs J S Ratcliffe and A M Dick found it financially necessary to dispense with their telephones. The Pilotage Ccmmittee sent suitable replies to them to have their telephones reconnected. The question had been raised by a First Class Pilot as to why Mr Pickthall was without a telephone and that it was considered this should be remedied.

A case was instanced of an order for a spirit barge from Stanlow to Manchester - note the length of passage - when Mr Pickthall was first on turn for duty, but as he had not been in communication with the Pilotage Clerk at the time the order required to be given out, the next pilot had to be called out. It was agreed that subject to confirmation of the facts, Mr Pickthall appeared to have been absent without leave and he should, therefore, lose a day's pay. This is the first instance of any disciplinary action taken by the Pilotage Committee over the abuse of the Rotary System. It was suggested that the question of the inclusion in the Byelaws of a suitable provision requiring pilots to install telephones under the powers of Section 17(c) of the Pilotage Act - should be considered. When this was muted all pilots soon had their telephones reconnected. There are no other records of pilots not having a working telephone.

'DRINK NOT THE THIRD GLASS, WHICH THOU CANST NOT
TAME, WHEN ONCE IT IS WITHIN THEE'
GEORGE HERBERT. 17th. CENTURY POET.

'THERE ARE SOME SLUGGISH MEN WHO ARE IMPROVED
BY DRINKING, AS THERE ARE FRUITS THAT ARE NOT
GOOD UNTIL THEY ARE ROTTEN'
DR. SAMUEL JOHNSON.

2.

IMPAIRED PILOTING

It has alway been a popular misconception that Pilots were slaves to the demon alcohol. Unfortunately this totally erroneous assumption has been perpetuated by a few irresponsible pilots who were not averse to taking a glass too many for their or the ship's own good. The history of the Manchester Ship Canal Pilot Service records singularly few incidents of a Pilot being accused of impaired piloting due to the influnce of alcohol. The very first complaint of impaired piloting was recorded at the Pilotage Committee Meeting held on Monday December 7th 1914.

The Chairman reported that a complaint had been received that a Pilot was under the influence of drink whilst in charge of the S.S. "PRENTON" a Birkenhead Ferry (Luggage) boat which was conveying cattle from Birkenhead to Manchester.The Master stated that the Pilot boarded the "PRENTON" at Woodside Landing Stage at 2135 hrs. on Friday November 20th. The night was very dark but there was no fog until the vessel was approaching Eastham Channel. His suspicion of the Pilot's condition was first aroused when entering Eastham Channel and the Pilot mistook the Bromborough Pool lights for the Eastham lights with the result the vessel ran aground. After passing through Eastham Locks at 2315 hrs, the vessel proceed up the canals and struck the port bank of the Canal opposite the

In 1906 the "Prenton" joined three other luggage boats that had been in use for a number of years on the Woodside to Liverpool crossing. She was employed on this service until she was sold, anmd broken up for scrap at Tranmere in 1934. They also regularly carried cattle to Manchester from Woodside.

A Birkenhead luggage boat alongside the Landing Stage as a line of horse-drawn vehicles stands waiting to board the steamer for Woodside, whilst the traffic from the luggage boat makes its way to the floating roadway. In the distance the White Star Liner "Baltic" lies at anchor. The cattle were driven down the same roadway to be herded on to the luggage boat.

Crane Berth in Eastham Basin at 2320 hrs, between that point and Ellesmere Port a distance of some two miles the vessel struck the bank a further five times.

Visibility was fair to good but on reaching Ellesmere Port at 0050 hrs, (Saturday) a thick fog came down and the vessel tied up and remained there till 1330 hours. The Master said he relayed his opinion of the Pilot's condition to the Manager of the Birkenhead Ferries whilst at Ellesmere Port but decided to proceed with the Pilot as he thought his condition was then better than during the passage from Eastham to Ellesmere Port. The vessel arrived at Mode Wheel Lairage at 0850 hours, on Sunday without any further incidents.

The Pilot denied he was under the influence of drink and said that the night was very dark and yellow (?) and navigation in the Eastham Channel was very difficult due to the proliferation of vessels lights leaving and entering Eastham Locks making it confusing with the shore lights. After clearing Eastham Locks the fog came down very quickly, but it had been put to him that the vessel must reach Manchester as quickly as possible. He therefore proceeded in reduced visibility but at slow speed. He was unable, however, to avoid touching the banks of the canal on several occasions and finally decided it would be prudent and seamanlike to tie up at Ellesmere Port. The Pilot stated definitely the darkness of the night (?), the patchy fog, and the vapour arising from the cattle on the vessel's deck (???) were solely accountable for the vessel touching the banks of the Canal.

After a lengthy discussion the Committee arrived at the conclusion that the Pilot was not under the influence of drink. The Chairman told the Pilot that although the Committee did not consider that he had been under the influence of drink they nevertheless found him wanting in judgement in navigating the Canal on such a foggy night. He wished to point out most strongly that should a complaint of a similar nature be brought against him, they would seriously consider suspending or even revoking his Canal Licence.

It was 1922 before the next complaint was recorded of impaired piloting and was thought to be of such a serious nature that the Pilotage Committee ordered a Sub-Committee to be specially convened at the Manchester Dock Office on Wednessday April 12th.

at 11a.m, to consider the complaint of drunkenness coupled with the Pilot's absence from duty.The Committee consisted of:

Mr. W. Browning (Chairman Manc.Pilotage Comm.)
Mr. G.Bowen. (Manc. Steamship Owners Ass.)
Captain Adamson (Canal Superintendent)
Mr. J. Hindle (Pilot's Representative)
Mr. R. Bennion (Chief Pilot Clerk)

The Chairman opened the meeting by stating that a letter had been sent to the Pilot in question requesting an explanation as to why the Pilot did not attend the vessel S.S. "YSRA" on Saturday morning April 1st and for him to attend this Sub-Committee meeting to discuss his letter of reply. Mr. Browning then made the following statement:

That about 10 o'clock on the night of the 31st March the Pilot in question had been arrested by the Salford Police for intoxication and that he had appeared before the Salford Magistrate the next morning and had been fined 10/-s.(50p). In consequence of his being detained by the Police it had been necessary to arrange for another Pilot to take charge of the pilotage of the "YSRA" to Eastham, for which steamer the said Pilot was supposed to be standing by." He asked the Pilot for his explanation of this incident.

The Pilot stated that he had attended the "YSRA" as ordered at noon on the 31st March when he was informed that her sailing had been postponed until the next morning. He therefore left the vessel and went to collect his monthly pay from the Canal Office then to the Bank to cash the cheque. He had no time during the afternoon to get any drink, but admitted, however, that he had had a little whisky on board the ship. In the evening he went to the first house of the pictures but only remained there for about three quarters of an hour because he felt ill. He left the cinema and went to the CLOWES HOTEL where he had a glass of whisky after which he made his way down Trafford Road to the Dock Office to report that he was ill and did not think he would be able to attend the "YSRA" the next morning.

On his way down to the Dock Office he suddenly collapsed and fell on his head. He did not remember very much what next transpired as he was practically knocked senseless and on his being taken by a Police Officer to the Trafford Road Police Station, he had been asked whether he would like to go to hospital but he had said "No". He was troubled about getting word to the Dock Office of his incapacity and thought he would be unable to get word to the Dock Office if he went to hospital.The Pilot also said during the few proceeding days his head had been troubling him and his mistake, as he could see now, was that he should have gone to the Doctor. He reiterated that he was not drunk but that he was seized with an attack of the influenza which together with the small amount of whiskey he had consumed made him very confused.

The Chairman pointed out to the Pilot that in his letter of reply he inferred that he had met with an accident and not told the truth about his being detained by the Police. Had the Pilot mentioned the whole of the facts that would have been in his favour, instead of which he had tried to cloak it, leaving the Committee to assume that he had met with an accident the night before. Mr. Bowen remarked that had the Pilot been able to collect himself together and had asked for the prison doctor to examine him this trouble might have been avoided. Mr. Browning referred to the report in the Press and pointed out it was stated the Pilot had admitted having a drink or two.

The Pilot said he was very confused after being arrested as he had lost a lot of blood and could not remember exactly what took place as he was feeling so ill. He knew it was no use his contesting the case.

The Pilot's statements and letter were fully considered and it was the opinion of the Sub-Committee that the Pilot should be given the benefit of the doubt, it being pointed out that in many cases an attack of influenza had struck a man down. In this case the Pilot had admitted having had some drink which together with the attack of influenza as he stated would make him appear drunk. The Chairman pointed out to the Pilot that the Sub-Committee had considered the case and took a very serious view of the fact that any man in the Manchester Pilotage Service should be found under the influence of drink. There was not any doubt that he was in such a condition, but probably that was assisted by his having an attack of "Flu".

If he had managed to. get to the vessel he might have commenced piloting her down the Canal with perhaps disastrous results in view of the condition he was in. The committee were willing to give him the benefit of the doubt particularly in view of his exceptionally good record in the past, and they hoped that the present would be a severe lesson to him. The Chairman concluded that should a further case come before the notice of the Committee the suspension of his Licence would be seriously considered. Whether any Pilot was standing-by a vessel or in his own time, the Committee would look very seriously at any such complaint as the one under notice. It was a reflection on the whole of the Manchester Pilot Service. The Pilot answered that he quite appreciated the seriousness of the complaint.

It must be recorded that in every complaint against a Pilot brought to the notice of the Pilotage Committee, for whatever reason, if it was at all possible the Pilotage Committee always gave the benefit of the doubt, and recognized his previous good conduct and service. They continued to uphold this admirable and highly commendable tradition until the very last time the Manchester Pilotage Committee convened in 1987.

The following complaint against a Second Class Pilot was quite indefensible even by the Pilotage Committee standards. It must have tried their patience to the very limits, for no matter how they viewed this complaint for impaired piloting they could find no extenuating circumstances to help the Pilot.The Master of the Norwegian vessel S.S. "RYM" lodged the following complaint.

"When I arrived on the bridge of my vessel at approximately 0500hrs preparatory to sailing from Manchester Docks to Eastham I found the Pilot slumped in the corner of the wheelhouse. On closer inspection I concluded that he was under the influence of alcohol. I enquired of the Helmsman if he too thought he was drunk but the Helmsman would not commit himself to an answer. I therefore called my Chief Officer to the Bridge who confirmed my conclusions. He requested a new Pilot for the purpose of sailing to Eastham. The Harbour Master had in the meantime sent for the port Doctor (Mr. J. Goodenough) to examine the Pilot. The Doctor after his examination of the Pilot stated that in his opinion the Pilot appeared to be under the influence of alcohol. I then ordered the Pilot ashore."

At the Pilotage Committee Meeting in October 1937, the Chairman addressing the Pilot referred to the complaint made by the Master and the Chief Officer of the "RYM" that the Pilot was under the influence of drink whilst on board his vessel. The medical report by Dr. J. Goodenough on the Pilot's condition was also referred to. Both these reports had been shown to the Pilot beforehand. Mr. L. Roberts (Chairman) said that due to the seriousness of the complaints if the Pilot wished to consult anyone or to bring witnesses, consideration of this matter would be postponed.

The Pilot stated he was quite willing to continue and proceeded to give the following statement:

"From 0430hrs until 0800hrs when he came ashore from the vessel he could not remember anything, other than telling the vessel's watchman to call the crew and personally calling the Helmsman at 0445hrs. He did not remember telling the Doctor anything. (In the Doctor's report he stated that the Pilot had told him that he was using a drug called Silver Nitrate recommended to him by a student as a method to stop smoking.) He had been awake practically all night and been out on deck several times. As regards alcohol he had had three glasses of beer between 2015hrs and 2130hrs that evening. He reiterated that the conversation with the Doctor was beyond his recollection. The first thing he remembered in connection with the Doctor was the latter's request to give him a final examination."

The Pilot was asked how he accounted for his lapse of memory if he could remember some things so clearly now. The Pilot answered that he could remember what happened before 0430hrs and after 0800hrs and again stated he never slept all night and could remember all that happened during the night even to going to the galley for a cup of coffee. He also said he had not since mentioned this matter to anyone, so that if the Committee wished to verify his statements they could interview the witnesses with the knowledge that he had not coerced them, which he might have easily attempted to do if he had a guilty conscience.

The Committee questioned the Pilot at great length but to all of their questions they received the repetitive reply "I cannot remember anything during those times." The Chairman then asked for any individual views of the Committee members. Mr. J. Warren (Pilot's Representative) said it appeared all very clear to him because the Doctor had definitely stated that the Pilot was under the influence of drink. He said that knowing this matter was to come before the Committee for investigation he had questioned the Helmsman on this incident and had been informed that the Pilot was definitely sober the night before. The Helmsman also remembered the Pilot calling him to stand-by, but later had to look for the Pilot and eventually found him collapsed on the bridge of the vessel. He confirmed the Master's version of the incident. Mr. Warren concluded by saying he would not know where the Pilot could have obtained drink, especially on a Norwegian vessel, unless he had brought it with him.

The Chairman said he knew the Pilot had not been well for some time and might not have been really fit to go to work and had possibly taken some medication and had overdone it and if this was the case a single drink would possibly have this effect. Mr Leigh-Hunt (Manchester Steamship Owners) raised the point with regard to the Pilot supposedly taking Silver Nitrate to prevent his smoking and wondered if this was mixed with alcohol it might bring about a lapse of memory. The question was asked why the Pilot had not called any witnesses if he was satisfied he was not under the influence of alcohol. The Pilot replied that the reason he had not called any witnesses he had explained earlier that he feared the Committee might have thought he had coerced them. He continued to profess he did not really know what had happened and as far as he could remember there had been no conversation with the Doctor in the Doctor's car regarding the taking of Silver Nitrate. The Pilot expresses most forcefully that he had never bought any Silver Nitrate and had none with him. He had never used or obtained any Silver Nitrate. He had never even attempted to stop smoking and if he had told the Doctor about Silver Nitrate he must have made a mistake because he had never used it.

After further discussion the unanimous opinion of the Committee was that the Pilot was under the influence of alcohol whilst on duty. Mr. Roberts then addressed the Pilot:

"The committee have considered your case very carefully and have

1922
S.S. "British Diplomat" GRT:6498. L 420'. B 54'
Courtesy Mrs. W. Yates Collection

1924
S.S. "San Ugon" GRT:5541. L. 412'. B. 53'. Eagle Oil - Esso
Courtesy Mrs. W. Yates Collection

weighed up all the evidence available and have also taken into consideration your recent illness. But at the same time they could not neglect to take into consideration the seriousness of the complaint. This being so they have decided to suspend your licence for one month and I am to give you a very serious warning that if a similar occurrence takes place they will have no alternative but to revoke your Canal Licence".

This was the first time - and happily the last - a Pilot had had his Licence suspended through an over indulgence of alcohol in the Manchester Ship Canal Pilot Service. Sadly it must be recorded that for this Pilot it was the begining of the end of his days as a Pilot. Unfortunately, the Pilot who had so narrowly escaped having his Licenced revoked did not take heed of the dire warnings pronounced by the Chairman in his summing up. The Pilot once again became the subject of a complaint of impaired piloting. At the Pilotage Committee Meeting held on Monday 23rd January 1939 to which the Pilot in question was summoned to attend the following report was read.

"On January 16th at about 1720hrs the vessel S.S. "KAIDA" left Runcorn Docks for Eastham via Runcorn Coal Tip for bunkers. At 1730hrs the vessel ran aground between Runcorn Dock and Bridgewater Lock a distance of less than a quarter of a mile, on the North side of the Canal from Runcorn Docks.The vessel was unable to refloat herself and the assistance of the tug "EASTHAM" was required to refloat her. At 1750hrs the vessel continued her passage to the Coal Tip but sailed past the Coal Tip altogether and between Western Mersey Lock and the Weaver Bend, on the south side of the Canal ran aground once again.The tug "EASTHAM" was again called to the vessel's assistance and on arrival found the vessel was athwart the Canal and partly swung round causing a hazard to the navigation of other vessels in the vicinity who had been warned of the "KAIDA" predicament.

The vessel had run aground at 1803hrs and was refloated at 1858hrs. The Master of the tug (Captain G. Dugdale) had been given orders to inform the vessel to return to Weston Mersey Lock Wall and to remain there with the Pilot until Captain Bennet (Ass. Harbour Master) arrived. The vessel returned to Weston Mersey but whilst going alongside damaged the Lock wall, the weather during this time was recorded as winds westerly, force three, visibility good. Captain Bennet accompanied by a Canal Pilot, Mr. W.H. Roberts, arrived at Weston Mersey Lock at 2050hrs and he immediately questioned the Pilot for not stopping at the Coal Tip and the reasons for grounding the vessel on two occasions. The Pilot made no intelligible or sensible reply. Captain Bennet then interviewed the Master, who said he could not understand the behaviour of the Pilot especially when they went past the Coal Tip and the Pilot said "We have eight miles to go yet". The Master would not say the Pilot was drunk but thought he was drugged with cocaine. Captain Bennet saw the Pilot again and told him in the interest of the Canal Company and his own, he must have a Doctor's report on his condition to which the Pilot raised no objection. Dr. Murphy and his assistant arrived at 2210hrs and made an exhaustive examination of the Pilot and pronounced the Pilot unfit through being under the influence of alcohol or drugs. The Pilot was discharged from the vessel and Mr. W.H. Roberts was placed in charge to complete the passage."

Mr. W. Langley and Mr R. Green said that as the Pilot's representatives on the committee they would like to express their feeling of disgust with the whole affair and on behalf of the body of Pilots wished to disassociate themselves from it. They also stated that the Pilots generally had no sympathy with the Pilot in question. The Chairman remarked that the Pilot had been before this Committee on a previous occasion for a similar complaint and warned of the consequences of a similar incident. Reference was also made to the several cases of accidents which had occurred to vessels while in charge of the Pilot over the past twelve months. After a long discussion the Committee agreed that there were two alternatives in this case. If they found the statements were borne out in evidence they would have no difficulty in finding that the Pilot had been in a state of intoxication, in which case they could suspend or revoke his Licence. On the other hand, was the Committee the most appropriate body to pass judgement; the Pilots Representatives might find it difficult to adjudicate on a complaint of such a nature against a brother Pilot. In that case the matter could be tried in Court on a prosecution instituted under Section 46 of the Pilotage Act by the Pilotage Authority or Shipowners.

The Chairman stated that due to the absence of the Pilot in question through illness they could proceed no further but to summons the Pilot to appear before this Committee when he is fit to do so. The meeting was closed.

It had become abundantly clear to every member of that Pilotage Committee the Pilot had, by his own hand come to the end of his piloting career on the Ship Canal. His past record weighed heavily against him and his own colleagues had publicly disowned him. There appeared to be no alternative but to set a precedent and revoke his licence: a decision they were most loath to take. The Pilot must have been well aware of the inevitable consequences of his conduct and actions. Fortunately for all concerned the Pilotage Committee were not required to make that distressing decision. A letter dated 27th January was received by the Chairman, from the Pilot stating that he wished to relinquish his Ship Canal Licence and resign from the Manchester Pilot Service, to take effect from February 1st 1939. This was unanimously accepted at the Pilotage Committee Meeting held in February, whose members once again showed great leniency towards the Pilots in resolving that, as the Pilot was no longer serving as a Pilot they would not pursue the matter any further. Such was the calibre of the Pilotage Committee in those days.

The last recorded incident of impaired Piloting concerned a report made by Captain Acraman (Harbour Master Manchester) which read as follows:

On Monday morning last the 3rd inst., Mr. G. Green (Senior Pilot) called at this office and stated that he wished to report a second class Pilot for being drunk during tide hours at Eastham, whilst on duty. As I have heard several rumours lately regarding the insobriety of some of our Pilots no doubt you will wish to take this matter further." The Chairman of the Pilotage Committee said his opinion was that the charge made by Mr.G. Green against the Pilot was of such a serious nature that the Committee could not deal with it without an opportunity being given to the Pilot to defend himself. He also stated he had seen the Pilot along with Captain Acraman and he disputed the charge, most emphatically, that he was worse for drink when accused by Mr. Green.

Mr. Young (Pilots' Representative) explained that another Pilot was in the room at Eastham at the time who had expressed his opinion that the Pilot was not worse for drink. He further stated the Pilot had left the room immediately afterwards and had proceeded down to the docks to see if any shifting of vessels was required to be attended to. He had later moved a vessel from the East Dolphins into the Locks and on completion of the service had asked the Captain whether he was under the influence of drink and the Captain had replied "Most certainly not". Captain Acraman said he felt bound to report that he had on certain occasions heard rumours that three or four of the younger Pilots had on various occasions had too much to drink when reporting for duty.

[AUTHOR'S NOTE: In fairness to the young junior Pilot to whom the complaint was levelled at, it should be acknowledged that Mr. C. Green was then the senior First Class Pilot and a lifelong total abstainer, therefore his judgement of when a man is under the influence of drink could have been somewhat questionable.]

After full consideration it was decided that a Sub-Committee should hold an enquiry into the Pilot's case and that Messrs Green and the accused Pilot be instructed to attend together with any witnesses they might require to call on the matter. The Chairman also said that arising out of the recent complaint and rumours he would issue an instruction to the Clerks at Eastham that they were not in future to ring up the Eastham Ferry Hotel or any other Hotels calling for the attendance of any Pilot who was on turn for duty. The Chairman requested the Pilots Representatives to so inform their fellow Pilots.

The enquiry was duly held at Eastham and statements were given by Mr. Green and also by the Pilot in question, who also called Mr. Hughes (Pilot Clerk) and the Eastham Locks Head Gateman Mr. Robinson to speak on his behalf. After much deliberation the Chairman of the Sub-Committee stated that the weight of evidence appeared to be against the Pilot in question and although he did not consider he was seriously under the influence of drink he was of the opinion he had had more than was good for him under the circumstances. The Chairman severely reprimanded the Pilot and informed him the conclusions reached by this sub-committee would be reported to the next full Pilotage Committee. The Chairman thought the Pilotage Committee would allow the matter to rest on the report from this sub-committee but he informed the Pilot that he should be extra careful in future for if another complaint was laid against him regarding drinking in excess it would incur the gravest consequences for the Pilot. It was decided that no further action be taken in this matter.

Considering the Manchester Pilot Service has been in existence for 100 years and the fact that only 5 incidents of impaired piloting were recorded, it proves quite categorically the vast majority of Pilots are and were a most abstemious body of men. The Pilots are certainly a far cry from the popular public view that all Pilots were continually in an alcoholic haze as they went about their duties. I sincerely hope this chapter will go a long way towards alleviating that unfair and totally erroneous judgment of them.

3.

PILOT FAMILIES: THE YOUNG DYNASTY

The Young family is steeped in the traditions of seafaring and pilotage for they have always been closely associated with both these professions, either in Liverpool or Manchester. To trace their history, one must go as far back as 1733, the year the English Colony of Georgia (USA) was founded, when a certain Robert and Grace Young married and settled in Crosby near Liverpool. They had three sons; John, Peter and James, the latter two sons became Liverpool pilots but John who was born on March 17th 1744, sought his livelihood on the many sailing ships that sailed out of the great port of Liverpool during that era.

It is interesting to recall his rather romantic life, for after obtaining a certificate in sail, he left Liverpool for the American Colonies in 1774 shortly before the American War of Independence. There he secured a berth on a two masted schooner sailing out of New York and Philadelphia, a position he held until 1788. He was then hired as a navigating mate on the three masted barque "ELEANORA" under Captain Simon Metcalfe and sailed for the South Sea Islands via Cape Horn.

In 1790, whilst ashore in Hawaii with a Welsh seaman named Isaac Davis they were kidnapped and held captive by the Hawaiian Chief,

Kamehameha 1. These two men, especially John Young, eventually struck up a firm friendship with the Hawaiian Chief, became his advisers and were made Chiefs. John Young was one of the first white men to make his home in the islands - he married a Hawaiian girl and was considered one of the important civilising influences among the Hawaiians. He remained on the islands until he died a wealthy and well loved man in 1835.

John Young had no descendant and all his papers and documents of his life on the islands were destroyed in a great flood in 1885. Although that period of his life is shadowy and undocumented, his gravestone in Honolulu designating him a native of Lancashire, can still be seen to this day. The other two brothers, Peter and James, served with distinction in the Liverpool Pilot Service. They married local girls and settled one in Crosby and the other in Liscard. It was from the lineage of Peter Young that the connection with the Manchester Pilot Service was established. He had two great-grandsons, John and Charles, both boys took to seafaring for a living. John sailed to foreign ports and in due time obtained a Master Mariners' certificate, eventually commanding ships of the Furness Withy Line. When the Ship Canal opened in 1894, he piloted vessels successfully up and down this new waterway, but returned to Furness Withy as Captain just before the Manchester Ship Canal Pilots Service was formed in 1896. He died in February 1919.

Charles Young spent most of his seafaring life trading around the coast of Britain and the continent of Europe. He applied for a first class pilots licence on the formation of the Canal Pilot service in February 1896. The records show that he "passed a highly satisfactory examination in all aspects of canal work. The examining board had no hesitation in recommending this candidate for a first class licence".

Thus the Young dynasty of pilots on the Ship Canal began and lasted for 80 years. He served the pilot service faithfully and zealously through all its embryonic trials and tribulations. This epitaph in the minutes of the Pilotage Committee meeting of January 1922 sums up his dedication to the service so aptly - it read: "On December 19th, 1800 hrs, Pilot C Young reported he could not attend tide at Eastham, due to having a heavy cold. He returned to work

1894 - 1896
Captain John Young

1896 - 1922
Charles Frederick Young
Photograph taken 5.9.21

Both photos by kind permission of the Young Family.

on 23 December for tide duty, high water 1417 hrs, but after shifting three steamers at Eastham, he was forced to return home again at 1600 hrs on 24 December, when he took to his bed with bronchitis and I regret to say, passed away at noon on 30 December". Charles Young was 70 years old - a grand old man of the pilot service.

Charles Young did not die without issue, his son Charles Frederick Young was born in Birkenhead in 1882. He also had a somewhat varied life before obtaining a Canal Pilot's Licence, not as romantic as his ancestor John Young of Hawaiian fame, but nonetheless quite diverse. Charles went to school in Birkenhead, Merseyside and when he was 14 years old, moved with his family to nearby Rock Ferry where he found employment in the butchering trade owned by an uncle for the princely sum of 4/-s.(20p) per week, less 1/-s. (5p) for supplying butcher's apron and washing facilities.

After two years he left his uncle's business and became a clerk with the Co-operative Wholesale Society in Victoria Street, Liverpool, where he stayed for 2 years before leaving to spend a brief spell of 8 months as an Invoice Clerk at Lewis's Store in Ranelagh Street, Liverpool.

Charles was now nearly 20 years old and no doubt influenced by his father, a senior appropriated Manchester Canal pilot, had desire to become a canal pilot. Qualifications to be a successful candidate for the Canal Pilot service had become more stringent since 1896 - one new bye-law introduced was that a candidate must have served at least 2 years in some capacity at sea, on deck. With this in mind he joined the Alexandra Towing Company of Liverpool as an Ordinary Seaman in January 1901. His starting wage was 9/6d (47p) per week and he had to supply his own food, bedding and eating utensils - beer was 2d (1p) a pint, Income Tax 1/-d (5p) in the pound.

In August 1903, he discharged himself from the Alexandra Towing Co and for the purpose of gaining knowledge and experience of the intricacies of the canal (another qualification), he worked with his father for two months steering vessels up and down the Canal. He was then accepted as an official Canal Helmsman in November 1903.

Most families have some mystery in their past - the Young family was no exception. The explanations are often lost in antiquity and one must rely on part supposition and part fact, the supposition in this case is adjudged to be reasonably accurate.

Charles Frederick Young served as a Helmsman for 15 months when on 23 February 1905 he left the service and enlisted in the Denbighshire Hussars Imperial Yeomanry for a binding 3 years. This, incidentally, was not to be the last time he left the service to enlist in the armed forces. In May 1907 whilst still serving in the DHIY, he applied to the Manchester Pilotage Committee to be considered for a position as a Second Class pilot on the Canal.

"Charles F. Young's records presented by him, showed he had steered a great number of vessels over a period of 3 years and having had over 2 years' experience on deck at sea, the young man thought himself sufficiently proficient in the navigation of the Canal to tender his application to the Pilotage Committee for a Second Class Licence. I have made exhaustive enquiries regarding this candidate and have to say that I found nothing detrimental to him as a candidate for the Ship Canal Pilotage. He seems a well behaved and well spoken and respectable looking young man".

Now we move into the realms of supposition - this application for a second class licence which forms the basis of the mystery, does leave room for conjecture. Bearing in mind everyone on the Pilotage Committee that day was fully aware of the local bye-law that stated:

"Every candidate applying for a Pilotage Licence must devote all his time, wholly and only in the pursuit of piloting and if such a commitment is not given, the said candidate would not be granted permission to apply to go before the examining committee".

Therefore, the questions are raised :

1) Just how "exhaustive" were Captain R. Williams enquiries?

2) Could it have been at all conceivable that no one on the Pilotage Committee were aware of Mr C. F. Young's commitment in the Armed Forces?

3) The Pilot's representative on Pilotage Committee, Mr W. Hill, was a long standing friend of Mr Chas Young Senior - would he have not known the circumstances?

4) How did fifteen months become "over 3 years" in the records presented to Captain R Williams by Mr C. F. Young?

It is really of little or no importance to attempt to find an answer to

E.   **CERTIFICATE OF DISCHARGE,**

FOR SEAMEN NOT DISCHARGED BEFORE A SUPERINTENDENT.

ISSUED BY
THE BOARD OF TRADE,
In pursuance of
37 and 38 Vict., ch. 88.

Name of Ship.	Official Number.	Port of Registry.	Registered Tonnage.	Description of Voyage or Employment.
Tug Alexandra & others	—	Liverpool	20	Towing on Mersey

Name of Seaman.	Place of Birth.	Date of Birth.
Charles F. Young	Birkenhead	1882

Number of Fund Ticket (if any).	Capacity.	Date of Entry.	Date of Discharge.	Place of Discharge.
—	O.S.	Jany 1901	August 1903	L/pool

I CERTIFY that the above particulars are correct, and that the above-named Seaman was discharged accordingly.

Dated this 30ᵗʰ day of August 1903

(Countersigned) Chas F Young Jnr Seaman.   Signed WB Bradshaw Jr Master.

Witness John Edward Jones

Address of Witness 1 Langton Pier Head

Occupation of Witness Tug office

NOTE.—One of these Certificates must be filled up and delivered to every Seaman who is discharged otherwise than before a Superintendent.

If this Certificate is lost or mislaid no duplicate of it can be obtained.   Army Form E. 653.

DISCHARGE CERTIFICATE OF AN IMPERIAL YEOMAN.

This is to Certify that (No.) **825** (Rank) Private

(Name) Charles Frederick Young

Denbighshire Hussars, Imperial Yeomanry Regiment, who was enlisted to serve in the Imperial Yeomanry of the County of Denbighshire

on the 14ᵗʰ day of February 1905

has been discharged on the* 22nd day of February 1908

Here state the date and cause of discharge as detailed in the Imperial Yeomanry Regulations.

Time Expired

and that his claims have been properly settled.

His total service in the Imperial Yeomanry is **3** years **2** days, including — years — days embodied service.

Service abroad, viz., — years — days.

Medals, Clasps, and Decorations —

His conduct and character while in the Imperial Yeomanry have been Very Good

(Signature) S. C. Holland Capt Adj ? DYH IY

(Place and Date) Denbigh 22ᵈ February 1908

DESCRIPTION ON DISCHARGE.

		Marks or Scars, whether on the face or other parts of the body
Age	25 ¹²⁄₁₂	
Height	5-8½	
Complexion	Fair	
Eyes	Blue	
Hair	L Brown	
Profession or Trade	Helmsman	

Both photos printed by kind permission of the Young Family.

these questions, for after some discussion it was moved by Captain Waring, senior Canal Superintendent and seconded by Pilot M. W. Hill, that the application be accepted and that Mr C. F. Young be examined as to his proficiency to hold a Second Class licence. The date was set for 24 June. A possible clarification of this situation can be explained thus :

Prior to 1907, there was a strong movement with the Manchester Pilot Service not to increase the numbers of pilots' licences issued. This leads to the supposition that certain people in authority leaked the information that a new pilot's licence was to be issued shortly and George F. Young who received this information, immediately put forward his application for a second class licence. Applications for a Pilot's Licence came from many sources, Masters of Coastal vessels, River Tug boat masters, Canal Tug boat masters and serving Helmsmen. They were never discouraged and all applicants were placed on a waiting list in strict rotation of when the application was received.

When a new Pilot's Licence was issued, the first candidate on the waiting list was not necessarily chosen, it usually went to the one who had the most influence, e.g. related to an existing senior pilot or Pilotage Committee member, preferably both. The situation that also prevailed in 1907 with regards to a candidate's examination, was that he would be allowed three attempts to pass his examination with a suitable time-lapse between each attempt and no other candidate could take his place until he failed at the third attempt.

On 24 June 1907, Mr C F Young was examined for a second class licence and failed - he was re-examined on 23 September 1907 and again failed. He was discharged after completing his three years enlistment from the DHIY on 22 February 1908 and on 25 May 1908 sat his Second Class licence a third time and "passed a very extremely satisfactory examination" as recorded in the Pilotage Committee minutes. Thus, most of the complexities of this application appear to be solved. In that same year, he was married on 15 July and from that marriage a son, George Devonshire Young, was born on 14 May 1909, so ensuring a continuation of the family name in pilotage.

On 21 August 1911, Mr C F Young, passed his first class licence at

1908 - 1942
Captain Charles Frederick Young, Royal Engineers 1916 - 1919

1932 - 1975
George Devonshire Young

Both photos printed by kind permission of the Young Family.

George R.I.

George by the Grace of God of the United Kingdom of Great Britain and Ireland and of the British Dominions beyond the Seas King Defender of the Faith, Emperor of India, &c.

To Our Trusty and well beloved   Frank Frederick Young   Greeting:

We, reposing especial Trust and Confidence in your Loyalty, Courage, and good Conduct, do by these Presents Constitute and Appoint you to be an Officer in Our Land Forces from the Twenty-seventh day of September 1916. You are therefore carefully and diligently to discharge your Duty as such in the Rank of Second Lieutenant or in such higher Rank as We may from time to time hereafter be pleased to promote or appoint you to, of which a notification will be made in the London Gazette; and you are at all times to exercise and well discipline in Arms both the inferior Officers and Men serving under you and use your best endeavours to keep them in good Order and Discipline. And We do hereby Command them to Obey you as their superior Officer, and you to observe and follow such Orders and Directions as from time to time you shall receive from Us, or any your superior Officer, according to the Rules and Discipline of War, in pursuance of the Trust hereby reposed in you.

Given at Our Court at Saint James's the   Twenty-eighth day of   October   1916   in the Seventh Year of Our Reign.

By His Majesty's Command.

Frank Frederick Young
Second Lieutenant
Land Forces

the first attempt. Still being slightly controversial, he once again left the Pilot Service to serve his King and Country by volunteering on 28 October 1916, to join the Royal Engineers. He was immediately commissioned as a Second Lieutenant and on his discharge from the regiment at the end of hostilities, had attained the rank of Captain.

He returned to the Manchester Pilot Service in September 1919 and worked conscientiously as a pilot and at varying times, a pilot's Representative on Committee until he resigned from the Pilot Service on 4 May 1942 aged 60. He died on 1 July 1960 aged 78 years.

Fortunately, he had left a son to carry on the great tradition of the Youngs' piloting on the Manchester Ship Canal. After having served his time as an apprentice with the Furness Withy Line, George D Young entered the Manchester Pilot Service in 1932 and became a first class pilot on 1 May 1948. Like his grand-father and father, he served on various Committees during his lifetime as a pilot and was appointed Choice Pilot for Manchester Liners in 1969, a position he held until his retirement in August 1975. He died in December 1988 aged 79 years.

George D Young was the last of an unbroken line of pilots on the Manchester Ship Canal commencing from its inception in 1895, a period of 80 years. He was the least controversial of the Young dynasty and had the least colourful background, but he was a gentleman through and through during all his piloting life. He upheld all that was good in piloting and the traditions of his forebears who did so much to set the standard of piloting. Their meritorious service over those many years will long be remembered by the Manchester Pilot Service.

4.

THE PILOTS' LEAVE SYSTEM 1920 - 1990

In June 1920 the Pilots commenced to implement their first annual paid leave system of 14 days per Pilot and no more than three Pilots allowed on leave at any one time. This reduced the number of effective Pilots to 23 and when as many as 18 Pilots were engaged on duty on some days, the period of rest between "Turns" was very much curtailed and Pilots were constantly liable to be called for duty rather quickly between "turns". Nevertheless the majority of the Pilots welcomed this innovation realising the benefits to their health of a 14 day rest period especially for the nine Pilots who were over sixty years of age, Mr. W. Marker was 70 years old.

Bereavement leave consisting of three days was granted in 1921 to all Pilots but even this system was abused by a number of Pilots who managed to find unacceptable (to the Pilot Service) amounts of relatives who required them to take bereavement leave. In 1926 the bereavement leave was restricted to three days for immediate family i.e. wife and children and one day for other relatives i.e. mothers, grand-mothers, sisters etc. It appears from the records of Pilotage Committee that a significant amount of Pilots' relatives lived a considerably lot longer after 1926. A "Short Leave" system was also introduced in 1922 whereby a Pilot could request, 24 hours in advance, for one day's leave to cover any emergencies e.g. Doctor's appointments, Dentist appointments etc.etc. on the proviso that he honoured any "Turns" missed while off the Rota or lose the equivalent "Turns" in pay. Throughout the years the Pilots jealously guarded this "Short Leave" privilege.

Three years later, at the Pilotage Committee held in March 1923, Mr. R. Creen (Pilots' representative) said he had been requested to put forward the suggestion that consideration be given to an application on behalf of the Pilots that the leave period should be extended to three weeks. These periods to commence in May and that four Pilots to be on leave at once viz:- two Pilots working inward and two Pilots working outward. The Committee were in favour of this new leave system but the Chairman stated he wished to confer with Mr. Latimer and Mr. Evans of the Pilots Association and report back to the next meeting. This was agreed. At the next Pilotage Committee the Chairman said he had consulted with Messrs Latimer and Evans who agreed with the new leave system and as the majority of the Pilots were in favour of three weeks leave, arrangements had been made to put the new leave system into operation. The first leave Rota can be found in Appendix No. 1. It was pointed out to the representatives by the Chairman that no difficulty was anticipated in allowing four men to be on leave at one time if the general body of the Pilots would co-operate heartily with the Chief Pilot Clerk in the matter. There was still a considerable disturbing influence from certain Pilots.

Ever since the Pilot service was formed, the Pilots never could, nor ever would, agree unanimously to any scheme, resolution or suggestion proposed by their members, and this new leave system was no exception. Certain Pilots intimated that the new leave system had been rushed through a meeting of the Association when the majority of the members were absent and voiced their concern that the Pilots would have great difficulty in carrying out their work with 4 men off the Rota. Because of these objections a special meeting of the Pilots Association was arranged for April 6th, for the express purpose of discussing the leave entitlement once again. In the meantime the Chairman (Mr.W.Browning) of Pilotage Committee had written to Mr. Evans (secretary of the Pilots Association) as follows:

"This morning, Mr. J.G. Green (Pilot First Class) spoke to me over the telephone in regard to the extension of the leave system and stated that a large number of the Pilots were not in favour of the

*same. They do not consider that with the existing number of Pilots
the service could be carried on efficiently. In these circumstances
it might be that the Pilots would agree to continue the old
arrangements for two weeks leave this year,leaving the question of
the extended leave for consideration before the next annual leave
period. I understand a general meeting of the Association has been
called to discuss this situation and if any fresh decision is arrived
at, prompt advice should be communicated to me"*

A reply was received from Mr. Evans: "Your letter was submitted
to the Pilots Association general meeting and I beg to confirm that
the Pilots decided that there should be no alteration in the present
leave system viz:- three weeks duration and four Pilots on leave at
one time."

On April 18th 1923 the new leave entitlement commenced.

In October 1925 Mr. Evans suggested that a scheme of periodical
leave during the Winter months i.e. outside the annual leave periods,
should be arranged. It was proposed that two Pilots one from each
watch might be on leave at one time, two on Sunday and Monday
and another two on Tuesday and Wednessday in each week and the
arrangement should operate from November 1st. to March 31st.
excluding Christmas week. The Pilotage Committee were agreeable
to the trial of the scheme subject to the efficient working of the
Pilot Service and on November the first the scheme commenced
with a certain amount of trepidation. Mr. Bennion gave his first
report on the working of this periodical Leave system at the Pilotage
Committee in December:

*"We have 32 Pilots, 11 of whom are choice Pilots who almost
invariably have "Turns" in hand and are consequently not available
for the Rota, having their respective ships to attend to. Therefore
the periodical Leave system applies to the remaining 21 Pilots only.
Past experience has proved that during the Winter months Pilots
have been required to go on station at Eastham before they have
Docked at Manchester and the same applies when working
outwards, due to the fact that large vessels in their charge have not
been able to transit the Canal in one day: also sickness has to be
taken into account which reduces the manning and when traffic is
moving freely extra pressure is brought upon the Rota Pilots. In my
opinion the scheme only applies to 21 Pilots and the scheme has*

proved during one month's working that instead of the Pilots benefiting by same they have in reality been worked harder due to their numbers being depleted. Therefore this scheme is unworkable with the present number of Pilots available and in the interests of the Pilots and the Ship Canal Company I suggest it should be revoked."

Mr. C.F. Young (Pilots' representative) did not agree with Mr. Bennion's statements. He argued that the adverse weather conditions during November and the high absence of Pilots owing to sickness was the reason for the added difficulties of the Pilotage Clerk and he had not heard any Pilot express dissatisfaction with the scheme. The Chairman remarked that as the scheme had only been in operation one month it was too early to condemn it and it was decided the scheme should be continued but be reviewed every month.

The scheme ran reasonably successfully for three years but in October 1928 Mr. Evans wrote the following letter to the Pilotage Committee:

"The question of the periodical leave system was considered at a recent Association meeting and it was decided that a ballot of the service should be taken on this matter. This ballot has resulted in the majority of the Pilots voting against a continuance of the arrangements during the coming Winter months."

The Pilotage Committee accepted the position and the scheme was phased out.

It would be eight years before the question of additional leave was raised again. On the 11th August 1936 Mr. Evans sent the following letter to the Pilotage Committee:-

" I am instructed to submit to you the following proposal:

"That one weeks leave for the purpose of a rest be granted to each Pilot during the Winter months, one Pilot out of each watch being relieved from duty at noon on each Monday commencing on the last Monday in October and the Rota to correspond as nearly as may be to the Rota approved for annual leave prescribed by bye laws. The Pilots feel that the adoption of this proposal would provide a beneficial break in a long winter's work and would do much to

minimise the absence through sickness which has occurred in recent winters especially if an exchange of leave periods were permitted to be made by mutual agreement,thus making it possible for a Pilot who felt in need of rest to take it at the time when it was most likely to prove beneficial.'

After discussion it was agreed that full consideration should be given to all circumstances before any decision could be made. It was the beginning of a long drawn out saga reminiscent of the negotiations in the 1920's. Once more the stumbling block to all negotiations was the dreaded *Choice Pilots.* It was pointed out that no mention had been made of the opinion of the Choice Pilots and it was quite possible the Steamship Owners who engaged the services of these Choice Pilots might object. If it was the wish of the Pilots generally, the Pilotage Committee stated, that leave be arranged in the winter months, a more definite scheme should be submitted providing for all Pilots' views to be expressed and providing the proper maintenance of the service.

The phrase in the discussion "no mention had been made of the opinion of the "Choice Pilots' was like a "red rag to a bull" to the ordinary Rota Pilots. This differential between "Choice" and Rota Pilots was perpetuated by the steamship Owners and it incensed the Rota Pilots and quite rightly too, because to become a "Choice" Pilot on the Ship Canal it was never what you know as a Pilot in your district but always who you knew. "Choice" pilotage had always been acknowledged as the curse of the Pilots Association right from its inception and continued to be so until it was phased out in 1988. Over the years they had with the acquiesence of the Pilotage Committee and the Steamship owners, placed themselves above the Rota Pilots, even at times above the Pilot Service itself. Nothing,but nothing was to disturb their privileged position even if it was for the benefit of the whole Pilot service, they had become a law unto themselves. This earned them the dubious sobriquet *"The Brahmin Pilots"* or, not as respectful but equally meaningful *"The Sacred Cows"*.

The Pilotage Committee and the Steamship Owners were not slow to exploit this division of loyalties within the Pilot Service, their ideology of 'divided they fall' was superbly demonstrated by the

1910

A Leyland Line Vessel Passing Under Irlam Railway Bridge with the Manchester - Liverpool Passenger Train passing overhead.

1912

Irlam Steel Works Wharf

Both photos printed by kind permission of Mrs. W. Yates

Choice Pilots throughout the long negotiations for a Winter Leave system. In every negotiation the "Choice" Pilots position and views were considered sacrosanct to everything else. A further letter from Mr. Evans dated October 12th 1936 was read at Pilotage Committee. It stated that it was the general desire of the Pilots, including the majority of the "Choice" Pilots that the proposed Winter Leave system should be introduced. The Pilots recognised that objections might be raised by some shipowners to which Choice Pilots were appropriated, but they thought these cases could be mutually agreed. If a "Choice" Pilot elected to attend his company's vessel whilst on leave such turns should count in his turns on the Rota. It was pointed out by the Pilotage Committee that as the "Choice" Pilots generally performed as many or more services than the Rota Pilots the grant of a turn for each service performed during the weeks leave would give no advantage to the Pilot concerned. The matter was deferred for further consideration. It should be pointed out that the "Choice" Pilots did not *have* to be "Choice" Pilots. They accepted this position of their own volition and once attaining this imaginary lofty status proceeded to attempt to dictate to the Pilot Service/Association dismissing any recommendations,with great disdain, if they did not suit their purposes or would in some way disrupt their beloved appropriations. A strange breed of men they were.

The classic phrase "for further consideration" was constantly used by the Pilotage Committee. It was indeed their major stratagem in the procrastination of all negotiations. Whilst the negotiations were still open the Pilots would continue to pursue their claim and not bring to bear any threating action that could damage the profitability of the Canal and bring the Committee into disrepute with the shareholders. At the November Pilotage Committee the Pilots representative (Mr. J.H. Warren) impressed upon the meeting that the proposal for a weeks leave in the winter was of considerable importance and trusted the matter was receiving close consideration with a view to its being put into effect during the coming winter either in its present or a modified form. He stated with the exception of a few Choice Pilots all Pilots were in favour of this scheme.

The Steamship Owners who engaged the services of "Choice" Pilots would not agree to release their particular Pilots in the manner suggested and the Committee said they would approach the Shipowners concerned with regard to the "Choice" Pilot situation. The Committee also felt the present strength of the service was not sufficient to enable it to be maintained satisfactorily, if two pilots were on leave in addition to Pilots performing Dock Pilotage and other Pilots absent owing to illness. The matter was referred yet again for further consideration.

Just how close a consideration was given by the Pilotage Committee for an early settlement to these negotiations is hard to tell. There are no further records of discussions between the parties until July 1938, amazingly two years later, when the Pilots' representative once again requested that further consideration should be given for a week's leave during the winter months, it was further suggested that if the consent of the Shipowners to who "Choice Pilots" were appropriated could not be obtained the Authority should promote a Byelaw giving effect to the proposal. The Pilotage Committee did not think that the present time was opportune to deal with this matter having regard to the fact the Pilotage service was weakened by the prolonged absence of two Pilots through sickness. At the Pilotage Committee in August 1938 the Chairman suggested a trial might be given to a period of three days leave on the understanding that the arrangement would be suspended at short notice if traffic or other requirements necessitated it. There would be ample time in which to make the necessary arrangements to put such a scheme into operation before the coming winter months, *but* arrangements would have to be made between the "Choice" Pilots and the Steamship Owners before any progress could be made. The Ancient Mariner had his Albatross as a cross to bear the Manchester Pilot Service had the "Choice" Pilots as their cross to bear.

The Pilots Association rejected the Committee's proposals providing for a three day's winter leave considering it to be wholly inadequate. The Chairman of the Pilotage Committee appealed to the Pilots to at least give it a trial period. This was also rejected by the Pilots' representatives. History was about to repeat itself, just as in the 1900s, during the long negotiations for a Rotary and Pooling system, war clouds had gathered over Europe and when war was declared in 1914 all negotiations ceased for five years. So it was in the 1930s, the war drums began to beat as Germany went on the march once again. In Septemder 1939, time ran out for the Pilots again with the declaration of war. All hope of a Winter leave system vanished. In June 1940 the Chairman of Pilotage Committee (Mr. Leslie Roberts) referred to the fact that in most industries all holidays had been suspended for the duration of the war and he thought the Pilots should be prepared to forego their leave or at least suspend them if the necessity arose. The Chairman further recommended that Pilots going on leave should be notified that they should be available at short notice and in order that they could be re-called if required they should leave their addresses and telephone numbers with the Pilotage Clerk as to where they could be contacted. This recommendation was unanimously agreed. It should be recorded that the Manchester Pilot Service never relinquished their leave entitlement when all other industries did so during the war.

The Pilotage Committee in March 1942 received the following letter from the Pilots Association:

"Having regard to war conditions it was proposed that the present three weeks annual leave in the summer to be divided into 14 days during the summer and 7 days in the winter"

There was an objection from the "Choice" Pilots who stated that the suggested change was the outcome of a deliberation by 12 men, and did not represent the views of the majority of the Pilots and considered any alteration of this nature should be the result of a ballot. This would ascertain the individual wishes of the Pilots as to how their leave should be allotted. The ten Pilots who were not members of the association should also be balloted.

The result of the ballot was, that in the opinion of the ten Pilots who were not members of the association there should be no change in the present system of leave entitlement. The majority of the "Choice" Pilots sided with the non-members thus the proposal was lost. The Association did request that five Pilots to be on leave at one time instead of four as heretofore. The request was granted. It was not until 1944 that the Pilots again requested one weeks Winter leave and the Pilotage Committee's counter-motion was that the Pilots should once again review the advisability of taking three days only. Six months later the Pilots repeated their requst for a week's Winter leave. The Pilotage Committee could find no further excuses or reasons not to implement this leave and granted the Pilots' request, subject to the understanding that the whole arrangement may be suspended at the discretion of the Harbour Master if the requirements of the service necessitated such action being taken.

It had taken eight years for the Pilots to achieve an additional week's leave, the Pilotage Committee had not lost the art of procrastination one iota, albeit many new members sat on the Committee from the days of the 1920s and 1930s. The leave entitlement over the years changed as follows.

YEAR	SUMMER	WINTER	SPRING
1944-1955	3 weeks	1 week	Nil.
1956-1960	3 weeks	3 weeks	Nil.
1961-1967	3 weeks	2 weeks	1 week.

On July 10th 1960 the Pilots leave entitlement was increased from 42 days to 100 days in an agreement between the Chamber of Shipping and the U.K. Pilots' Unions. The Manchester Pilots agreed to forego 6 days of that leave in return for the continuation of their "*Short leave*" arrangements. Due to the uncertainties that prevailed at the time with regard to the future patterns of shipping in the Canal and the consequent reluctance to appoint too many new Pilots to cover the extra leave, the full leave entitlement was not immediately implemented. It was agreed only to increase the leave to 63 days and the position to be reviewed again after three years. The new leave entitlement was divided as follows:

YEAR	SUMMER	SPRING	AUTUMN	WINTER
1968-1971	4 Weeks	2 Weeks	2 Weeks	1 Week
1972-1988	4 weeks	3 weeks	2 weeks	1 week

The Winter leave consisted of one week in every month of November, December, January, February and March.

The "Short leave" arrangement was phased out in the early 1980s and an additional 20 days leave was granted in lieu of that arrangement, such days to be taken as and when required by Pilots during the annual leave cycle. With the complete re-organisation of the Manchester Pilot Service on October 1st 1990 it naturally followed a complete reorganisation of their leave system. The final leave system still in operation to-day is as follows.

LEAVE SYSTEM FOR 27 PILOTS
THREE WATCHES. NINE PILOTS PER WATCH.
24 Hours on duty.
48 Hours off duty.
This cycle to run for 24 days, then 12 days leave.
 In addition 24 days leave between June and September.

The Pilot service had come a long way since the measely 14 days granted in 1920.

KEEPING THE CANAL CLEAR OF SILTING UP

Two Types of Dredging Craft

Bucket Dredeger M.C.S. "Medlock" with silt barge alongside
Courtesy Mrs. D. Yates collection

Grab Hopper M.C.S. "Bollin"
Courtesy Mrs. D. Yates collection

5.

PILOTAGE TARIFF 1917 - 1918

After the prolonged negotiation in awarding the Pilots a War Bonus on October 1st 1916, a heartfelt plea was received by letter addressed to the Chairman of the Pilotage Committee on 5 May 1917. It was sent from the Secretary of the Pilots' Association and read as follows:

"Dear Sir,

I should be glad if you would allow a discussion at the next Pilotage Committee Meeting regarding an increase in the tariff and the War Bonus allowance. I am told that some of our Pilots are not making a living piloting on the canal and speaking for myself, I certainly am not, unless you consider £8 or £9 per month is enough. I may add that due to hostilities, expenses have greatly increased.

Your obedient servant,

J.A. Hindle."

It was agreed that a discussion for an increase in tariff charges for pilotage in conjunction with a proposed new scheme of a pilotage working system should be placed on the agenda for the next Pilotage Committee Meeting. This was indeed a clever move by the Canal Company and Shipowners. They knew only too well any new scheme for a piloting working system would certainly be a long and protracted affair and thus stave off any hope of an increase in the tariff in the near future.

At the Pilotage Committee Meeting in June, the increase in tariff and War Bonus was duly discussed, the secretary of the Pilots Association pointed out that the earnings of pilots had been reduced considerably recently, owing to the fewer number of vessels navigating the Canal on account of War conditions. The Chairman (Mr Latimer) pointed out that it was not an equitable proposal that tariff charges should be increased in order to compensate the pilots for their loss of earnings, owing to less work being available. The Chairman further expressed the opinion that the present time was inopportune to introduce a proposition for an increase in tariff and/ or War Allowance. The Shipowners' representative, Mr T Baddeley, also intimated as there did not seem any likelihood of all the pilots accepting a proposed new working system and in view of the Chairman's remarks re: the tariff charges, he would not now submit the matter to the meeting of the Shipowners' Association for discussion later that month. This solid re-buff from all sides did not seem to deter the Pilots, for on 29 June 1917 the following letter was received by the Chairman of the Pilotage Committee and was read to the Committee:

"Dear Sir,

The members of the Manchester Ship Canal Pilots Association desire me to call your attention to the fact that pilotage "Fees" are being increased in other ports and to enquire if you cannot do something for the Ship Canal Pilots, the majority of whom are hardly making a living. I enclose a cutting from the "Journal of Commerce" to show what pilots are earning on the East Coast.

To show the injustice of the present tariff, I need only point to the vessel "City of Cairo", draught 27 feet, taking $14^{1}/_{2}$ hours to navigate 35 miles in the canal for a fee of £3.15.0. (£3.75), whilst the same vessel piloted from the Liverpool Bar into Eastham paid a fee of £10.16.0d. (£10.76p), taking $3^{1}/_{2}$ hours, to navigate 25 miles. Vessels nowadays are earning large profits and many owners seeing the Canal Pilotage charges are so low, are supplementing these by giving a bonus ostensibly for assisting in the river, others are paying the travelling expenses of Pilots, a situation we find deporable. I trust you will allow a full and frank discussion on this matter at your next Pilotage Committee Meeting.

Your obedient servant

J.A. Hindle."

1922

Fully loaded cargo vessel S.S. West Cobalt. GRT. 5724 Length. 410' Beam. 54' Inward bound from Modewheel Locks, assisted by the tug Lord Stalbridge. In the background S.S. Cormorant in the floating dry Dock

1922

A windy day at Irlam Locks. Note the smoke from the vessels almost horizontal. The vessels mast are telescoped and scaffolding around the funnel is to enable riggers at the Eastham Crane Berth to remove top half of the funnel and replace it.

The Chairman put before the Pilotage Committee a statement showing the number of Pilots engaged and earnings in total and in average, also the number of services performed during the two periods for the first five months of 1914 and the first five months of 1917 for comparison.

The statement showed that the earnings of Pilots had been well maintained during the first five months of 1917, contrary to Mr J A Hindle's accusations. Mr Latimer pointed out this was due to a reduction in the number of Pilots working and the War Allowance of ten per cent (10%) which had been granted in October 1916.

The Chairman said in reference to the figures for earnings during those two periods that the Board of Trade had sent him a letter on 11 June, asking for particulars of Pilots' earnings at Manchester. They required this information in connection with an application for an increase in Pilotage tariff which had been made to them by the United Kingdom Pilots Association. This information had been duly prepared and forwarded to the Board of Trade. Mr Latimer further stated that until the United Kingdom Pilots Association application for a tariff increase be resolved with the Board of Trade, he could see no point in continuing this dicussion. He also reminded the pilots' representatives that their application for an increase in the tariff must be in conjunction with their acceptance of a new working system.

The Chairman also intimated to the Pilots' representatives that if the pilots were desirous of appointing a deputation to wait upon him to discuss this matter prior to the next Pilotage Committee Meeting, he could and would arrange a convenient date to meet them.

This did not meet with the approval of the Pilots Association and the following letter was sent to Mr Latimer:

"Dear Sir,

At a meeting of the Pilotage Association held at Rock Ferry on 16 July 1917, the following resolution was proposed, seconded and carried unanimously. "This Association having had the amended working scheme put before them, it is agreed that they will not consider it without an increase in tariff".

Also:

"This Association cannot see that any useful purpose can be served by electing a deputation to interview the Chairman of the Pilotage Committee, considering that he is strongly opposed to an increase of tariff, which this Association is equally strong in asking for it.

Your obedient servant,

J A Hindle."

Mr Hindle's letter was read out to the Pilotage Committee on 1 August 1917. The Chairman said he thought the pilots were mistaken in their assumption that he was opposed to any increase in the tariff and it was to be regretted that the Pilots refused to discuss the matter with him, prior to this meeting. Reference was made to the information supplied to the Board of Trade and that a further communication had been sent to the Board of Trade, enquiring what development had taken place in connection with the United Kingdom Pilots Association's request for a tariff increase but no reply had been received to date.

The Secretary of the Pilots Association expressed the opinion that the information given to the Board of Trade did not correctly represent the position; as although the average earnings of Pilots might not have decreased, there had been individual cases where a substantial decrease had taken place. He proposed to communicate with the Board of Trade on behalf of himself and four brother Pilots, putting forward their case for an increase in the pilotage rates payable at the Port of Manchester.

During the remaining month of August and well into September of 1917, a great deal of correspondence flowed between the Board of Trade, the Pilotage Committee and the Pilots Association on the contentious subject of pilotage tariff increase and War Allowance. On 1 October 1917 at the Pilotage Committee, the Chairman placed the following resolution before the sitting members :

"That the Committee approve the proposal that

1) The War Allowance be increased from 10% to 25% subject to authorisation of the necessary byelaw by the Board of Trade.

2) That the maximum amount up to which a pilot shall participate in the monthly division be increased from £35 to £40.

3) That in other respects the method of division of the 25% shall follow the lines of the present division of 10%.

4) That a byelaw be framed to give effect to the increase in pilotage rates by 25% and that sanction be obtained from the Board of Trade in order that if possible, the additional percentage be collected and divided as on and from 1 November next."

The resolution was unanimously adopted. There was one sour note in the proceedings: the Secretary of the Pilots, Mr Hindle, proposed that two first class pilots, Messrs J. Edwards and W. Peacock should not participate in the division of the 25% because they 'did not look for work nor did they want to work'. It was explained to the Pilots' representatives that there was provision made in the memorandum of division dated 2 October 1916 for dealing with pilots who were not continuing to take their proper share of pilotage work.

After hearing the explanation, the Pilots' representatives agreed they would not press the proposal further.

On 14 February 1918 an amendment to the manner in which the War Allowance was distributed was tabled at the Pilotage Committee and read as follows :

"At the last General Meeting of the Pilots Association, it was unanimously resolved that the following division of the War Allowance be put into effect.

1) Divide the present "Suspense" account amongst the first class pilots in equal amounts.

2) All future War Allowance to be distributed as follows :

a) The lowest four pilots to take 25% or £25, at per man £6.5.0d (£6.25).

b) The next five pilots to take 30% or £30 at per man £6.0.0. (£6.00).
c) The remaining twelve to take 45% or £45 at per man f3.15.Od. (£3.75). With the proviso that should any of the War Allowance exceed 50% of earnings, then the excess to be placed in a new "Suspense" account."

The Chairman of the Pilotage Committee said he would have the proposed amendment looked into and if there appeared to be no objection, he would obtain the necessary authority to make the alteration. This was duly granted on 4 April 1918.

1917

The Coaling Crane at Ellesmere Port. It was dismantled in the 1930's

Eastham - Job's Ferry (1509)

1917

Atypical natural draft coal burning vessel outward bound down Eastham Channel.
Note the Pilot Flag flying below the National Flag on the stern.

Photos courtesy of Mrs. W. Yates collection

6.

PILOTAGE EARNINGS: 1918-1919

The pernicious working system described earlier in this book, that had existed as a cancer within the Manchester Pilot Service from its inception, still extended its evil tentacles to encompass the Pilot service even during the war years. Greed is no respector of peace or war; greed has no compassion - nor does greed have a conscience. This was amply illustrated when on the 3 June 1918, the Chairman of the Pilotage Committee (Mr Browning) reported a letter had been received from Pilot J.A. Hindle and read as follows :

"Dear Sir,

I hardly think you or the Pilotage Committee can be aware how the present system of pilotage working operates against certain men. Some of the pilots are making an excellent living - quite as much as before the war; while others, through no fault of their own, are not making enough to keep body and soul together. Take my own case for an example. Through the war the two shipping companies I worked for have had to stop sailing altogether and consequently I now only pilot the occasional Admiralty Chartered Vessel. Last month (May), my total earnings came to £6.12.6d (£6.62p), expenses to be deducted from that amount. This is hardly enough to live on for I have lost the help of my two sons who formerly helped with their financial share to the home - one of whom is seriously wounded and in hospital in France and the other, killed in action a fortnight ago. I earnestly request the Pilotage Committee to attempt to organise a far better working system, whereby all the

54

pilots shall share alike the financial earnings, even some of the Helmsmen are earning more than many First Class Pilots. The rotary system has worked very well with the Admiralty Chartered Vessels and would, I think, work just as well if all vessels were put on the same system, at least until the termination of the war. In the event of the Committee not being willing to do anything for the equalisation of earnings, I should like to ask if they are willing to allow pilots to seek other employment (without forfeiting their Licences) until the end of the war.

I remain your obedient servant

J A Hindle."

The Chaiman was requested to write to Mr Hindle and enquire whether he could give the names of any other Pilots who desired to associate themselves with him in the request to seek other employment without forfeiting their Pilotage Licences until the end of the war.

Fearful of upsetting the status quo of the Master Pilots, the whole matter was referred to a sub-Committee consisting of the Chairman, Mr Browning, Mr Baddeley, Shipowners' representative and Captain Williams, Ship Canal Superintendent. No Pilots were invited to sit on this sub-Committee.

True to form, the sub-Committee reported back to the July Pilotage Committee Meeting. The Chairman of that sub-Committee said they had given this matter careful consideration and recommended that permission should be given to any Pilot who wished to seek other employment until the end of the war, without forfeiting his Licence. The Manchester Ship Canal Company had had the matter brought to their notice and had given authority to the Pilotage Committee to make such arrangements in this matter as were in their opinion, advisable and necessary. But there was to be a sting in the tail of this concession. The Pilot members of the Pilotage Committee were asked to advise their fellow Pilots as to these decisions. It was also pointed out to the Pilots that they would only be allowed to resume pilotage work on the Canal provided that they satisfied the Committee as to their fitness and ability to carry out the work. No mention whatsoever was made regarding the request for a new working system to equalise the work and therefore, equalise the earnings, even in the most horrific war of all time and when fellow Pilots had lost sons in the obscene mud of Flanders, the power and greed of the Master Pilots had stood firm. This insensitivity to their own colleagues' suffering was there for all to see. Again this legacy of insensitiveness would prevail throughout the Pilot service for another 50 years or more.

If you could say nothing else about the Manchester Pilots, at least you would have to admit they were battlers and they never gave up; for at the August Pilotage Committee meeting the Chairman reported he had received yet another resolution adopted by the Pilots' Association from the Secretary of that body whereby certain amendments in the list of Pilotage charges for vessels piloted in the Canal were to be put forward for the consideration of the Committee.

The proposed alterations in the initial fee and mileage charge were as follows :

	OLD	NEW
300 Tons and under	£0.10. 0.(50p)	£1.0.0. (£1)
600 " "	£1. 0. 0. (£1)	£2. 0. 0. (£2)
1,200 " "	£1.10. 0.(£1.50p)	£3. 0. 0. (£3)
3,000 " "	£2.0.0. (£2)	£4. 0. 0. (£4)

All vessels over 3,000 tons - an increase of 10/- (50p) and for every 1,000 tons thereafter; in addition thereto a sum at the rate of 1/- (5p) per mile or portion of a mile for the distance navigated. Vessels in ballast shall pay full initial fee but only half the mileage rate.

It was stated that the Pilots were unanimous in feeling that the increase in tariff should be implemented at once, as they felt the present tariff was inadequate under present day conditions. The feeling was expressed by the Chairman of the Pilotage Committee that the earnings of Pilots had fallen, owing principally to the decrease in vessels entering the Canal and not because the scale of piloting charges was inadequate; because these had been a augmented by a War Allowance of 25% in October 1916.

In these circumstances it was felt that to increase the Pilotage Tariff would be an unsatisfactory way to meet the difficulty as the pilotage returns showed that there was not sufficient work to keep all Pilots adequately employed. The Canal Company, never slow to miss a trick, produced the ace out of the pack or the sting in the tail of the concession granted to the pilots at the last Pilotage Meeting.

The Chairman made reference to his Committee granting two Pilots, Mr Hindle and Mr Lloyd, permission to undertake other work and expressed the opinion that if other Pilots were inclined to follow a similar course during the present exceptional circumstances, the position would be relieved as fewer Pilots could cope with the decreased work.

Then came the real bombshell; the Chairman went on to say that during the present shortage of manpower for enlistment into H.M. Forces, the Committee felt they could not recommend an increase of Pilotage charges to compensate the lack of work and thereby retain the services of Pilots of military age who would not be kept fully employed.

[AUTHOR'S NOTE: The insinuation being that the surplus Pilots all of which were of military age, should go as "gun-fodder" in the "Killing Fields" of France.]

One can but imagine the stunned silence in which the Pilots' representative received that statement - there was absolutely no argument against it. Once again the Manchester Ship Canal Company had proven themselves masters at the art of negotiations when it came to any increase in costs on the Canal which might erode the profitability of the Canal to its shareholders and also proved that they could and always would, out-manoeuvre the Pilots and their representatives in any negotiations.

There was one bright moment in that year of 1918 for the Pilots. On 2nd September 1918, they applied for an increase in the War Allowance on Pilotage charges from 25% to 75%. The Chairman of the Pilotage Committee felt that such an increase could not be justified to the Board of Trade, but intimated that if an application was made for a further increase of 25%, i.e. making a total of 50%, it would receive favourable consideration.

The Pilots' representatives, Mr W.D. Southwood and Mr A. Yates said that they believed the Pilots would be satisfied with an increase of 25%. Mr Baddeley, the Shipowners' representative, was of the opinion that his Association would be agreeable to this proposed increase being made to the Board of Trade.

It was, therefore, resolved that an application be made to the Board of Trade for authority to increase the Pilot charges on the Manchester Ship Canal 50% in lieu of 25% as at present applicable. This proposal was granted by the Board of Trade on 14 October and came into force on 1st November 1918.

Prior to the new War Bonus being implemented, on 14 October 1918, the day the Board of Trade sanctioned the increase, the Secretary (Mr Beckett) of the Pilots Association forwarded a copy of a resolution adopted by the Pilots, to Mr Latimer - it read as follows: "That the nine lowest earning Pilots receive 55% of the total War Bonus equally divided between them and the remaining pilots to get the remaining 45% equally divided between them. The suspense account was to be closed down. The Committee decided that whilst they would not withhold their consent to this method of distribution suggested by the Pilots, they would like to be assured that *all* the Pilots agreed to the proposed alteration. The Chairman (Mr Latimer) said he would have a suitable letter written to Mr Beckett asking for an assurance on this point. If this was forthcoming, the amended method of distribution could be brought into operation with the November earnings which were distributed at the beginning of December.

At the Pilotage Committee meeting on 2 December 1918, the Chairman reported that a suitable letter had been sent to Mr Beckett, Secretary of the Pilots Association, asking them for an assurance on behalf of all the Pilots that the amended method of distribution of the War Bonus was satisfactory to them. No reply or acknowledgment had yet been received.

Reference was made to the application put forward by the Pilots for travelling expenses to be paid in addition to the Scheduled Tariff charges. The Chairman pointed out that at the present time a Pilot was not justified in asking for more than the tariff charges under Pilotage Byelaw No.11. "A licensed Pilot shall not without the Company's consent demand or receive in respect of any services any payment either in excess of or less than the amount which he shall under any resolution or regulation of the Company for the time being in force be entitled to receive." It was also pointed out that the war allowance of 50% had been put into operation in order to meet the increased cost of living. There had been however an increase of 50% in railway fares and after consideration the Committee thought that it would be reasonable to ask the Steamship Owners to make the Pilots an allowance to cover this additional expense.

It is strange to note that whilst Pilots were allowed to deduct 20% from their gross earnings before submitting their annual returns to H.M. Inspector of Taxes, for expenses incurred whilst carrying out their duty as a Pilot, no allowance had ever been granted with respect to travelling expenses. At last this omission was rectified when in December it was proposed and unanimously adopted by the Pilotage Committee to commence on January 1st 1918, that in addition to the pilotage dues a Pilot shall be paid a sum of 5s.0d. (25p) to cover any expense he may incur in travelling from Eastham Pilot Station to join a vessel at or above Latchford Locks or in returning from a vessel at or above Latchford Locks to Eastham. The amount stayed at 5s.0d. (25p) until January 1947 when it was increased to 7s.0d. (35p). Travelling expenses continued to rise and by 1988, by courtesy of inflation they had reached £3.30p.

By way of an historical note, train fares between Liverpool and Manchester were as follows;

YEAR	1st.Class.	3rd.Class.
1894	2s.5$^{1}/_{2}$d. (12p)	1s.2$^{1}/_{2}$d. (6p)
1900	2s.6d. (12$^{1}/_{2}$p)	1s.3d. (6$^{1}/_{2}$p)
1914	2s.7$^{1}/_{2}$d. (14p)	1s.4d. (7p)
1919	4s.0d. (20p)	2s.0d. (10p)
1929	6s.7d. (33P)	3s.11d. (20p)
1939	6s.11d. (35p)	4s.2d. (21p)
1949	6s.11d. (35p)	4s.2d. (21p)
1959	7s.10d. (39p)	5s.3d. (26p)
1990	£6. 30p.	£4.20p

Between 1894 and 1939 there were thirty five train services between Liverpool and Manchester commencing at 0100 hrs. and finishing at 2310 hr. The journey took 40 minutes by express train - two stops only- and 1 hour 43 minutes on the stopping train.

7.

THE PILOTAGE CLERKS 1920 - 1988

On December 1st 1919 a new position was created within the network of the Pilotage Administration, that of a Chief Pilotage Clerk whose mandate was to attend to the following duties:

1) To be soley responsible for the receiving of all orders from Shipowners, Masters, Agents/Brokers etc. for vessels requiring Pilots and Helmsmen.

2) To be soley responsible for relaying those orders to the respective Pilots and Helmsmen.

3) To be soley responsible for the day to day administration and smooth running of the Rota System also introduced on December 1st 1919.

4) To maintain a general discipline of Pilots on the Working Rota.

5) A formal statement was to be made on all aspects of the Pilots' and Helmsmens' work at every monthly Pilotage Committee. This daunting task was placed in the very capable hands of Mr. Richard Bennion.

Mr. Bennion was fortunate in being well aware of the hostility manifestly shown by some Pilots to the new rota and pooling system and that a number of Pilots had not a vestige of respect for authority or discipline. He went about his duties in such a quiet and gentlemanly manner and with such equanimity towards all Pilots he soon gained the confidence and respect of the majority of the Pilot Service. The Pilots Clerks' office was located at Runcorn in a quaintly named area known as "No man's land". The Pilots never quite regarded the Runcorn location as a prestige position for their Pilot Clerk and always felt it would be more in keeping and certainly more convienient if it was located at or near to Eastham Locks.

In 1925 at the age of 16 years Mr. H.(Harry) Thelwell commenced work as a junior Tolls Clerk at Runcorn and over the years he was sent on numerous occasions to the Pilotage Clerks office at Runcorn in the capacity as an assistant to Mr. Bennion. Because of Mr. Thelwells' immaturity in years, whenever Mr. Bennion went on annual leave or was temporarily indisposed due to illness a more senior tolls clerk, Mr. R. Rushton, was appointed temporary Pilotage Clerk. Captain Perry the Runcorn Canal Superintendent was in overall charge of this operation. In 1942, Mr. Thelwell was transferred from Runcorn to Eastham Locks as a full time Tolls Clerk. At the Pilotage Committee in September 1936 the following letter from the secretary of the Pilots Association was read:

"I am instructed to inform you that for a considerable time past a good deal of dissatisfaction has been felt by the Pilots regarding the issuing of orders to Pilots and certain proposals in connection with this matter are now in process of formation by the Pilots and will be submitted for your consideration in due course.

I am further to state that the dissatisfaction felt by the Pilots has been increased by the way in which Mr. Rushton, the Deputy Pilotage Clerk, has carried out his duties during the periods of absence of Mr. Bennion and they feel that Mr. Rushton has not succeeded in getting that grasp of the duties of Pilotage Clerk which is necessary for the smooth and satisfactory working of the service."

Pilots have on several occasions complained to Captain Howard (Harbour Master Manchester) regarding orders received by them which in their opinion were not in accordance with the proper working of the Rota System, but Captain Howard has naturally been reluctant to interfere with an order once it has been issued. The Pilots therefore feel that the attention of the Pilotage Committee should be drawn to this matter".

With regard to the alleged failure of Mr. Rushton to appreciate fully the duties of a Pilotage Clerk, it was pointed out that so far as the Authority were concerned he had handled a very difficult task most

Mr. Richard Bennion 1919 - 1945
THE FIRST CHIEF PILOTAGE CLERK

It was July 1881 That Mr. Bennion commenced his service in connection with the Canal which then was in the course of construction. He worked under the direction of Mr. H.E. Manisty the engineer, whose memory is perpetuated in "artificial mountain" known as Mount Manisty, a well known landmark near Eastham Locks. He had the honour of sailing the length of the Ship Canal when it opened on January 1st 1884 and again on May 21st when he witnessed the official opening by Queen Victoria. From that date he became involved with the interesting and intricate work of the Traffic Department, until 1919, when he was appointed Chief Pilotage Clerk. Mr. Bennion served under no less than five Harbour Masters, Captain Heasley, Acraman, Perry, Bennet and Colebrook. All in all he completed 53 years service with the Manchester Ship Canal Company, a fact that was duly recognised at a presentation ceremony in March 1945.

satisfactorily. Captain Howard stated that only on two occasions had Pilots complained to him. In view of the fact that new rules for the working of the rota system were at present under consideration it was agreed that no action should be taken on this matter. Mr. Rushton was never accepted by the Pilots and they constantly criticised all his efforts to conduct a satisfactory working of the Rota System.

It was not until September 5th 1939 that any serious attempt was made by the Pilots Association to re-locate the Pilots' Clerk's office from Runcorn to Eastham. The Pilotage Committee never renowned for their eagerness to implement changes, even in times of war, were as ever, slow to respond and it was three years later in December 1942 that the Chairman of the Pilotage Committee stated that the location of the Pilotage Clerk at Runcorn was not suitable and as a result of investigation it had been decided to transfer him to Eastham Locks, from where it was hoped he would be able to give more satisfactory service. The change would be made as from the 4th January. It was not known how long Mr. Bennion would be prepared to stay at Eastham - he should have retired in 1940 - but it was hoped it would be sufficiently long to enable a suitable successor to be found. The Pilots representatives acknowledged that there were no Pilots capable of performing the duties of a Pilot Clerk so satisfactorily as Mr. Bennion. The Chairman said he hoped the Pilots would give all the help possible in order that the Authority could decide on the type of man who would be required to succeed Mr. Bennion.

The first Pilotage Clerks office at Eastham was a small one roomed red bricked hut with a slate roof situated on the west side of the 600 foot lock. Two telephone lines were installed one to the main switchboard on the middle island and tne other a direct line to the Liverpool Pilot Office at Canning Dock Liverpool.

The Pilots Association took an inordinate interest in who would be Mr. Bennion's assistant and eventual replacement and it can be explained thus:

The Pilotage Clerk had by now attained a considerable influence at Pilotage Committee level and often his suggestions or recommendations during Pilotage negotiations would be listened

1942
The first Pilots Clerk Office situated on the West side of the 75' Lock.
It had two telephones only, serving 38 Pilots.

1992
The Hi-tec Pilot Clerks Office. A computer and five telephones serving
21 pilots and a lot less vessels.

to sympathetically and acted upon by the Pilotage Committee. The Pilots Association was not slow to appreciate that he who had "the ear" of the Pilot Clerk held a great advantage at the negotiating table and they became determined to install their own man as Pilotage Clerk on the pending resignation of Mr. Bennion. The Pilotage Committee were equally determined to keep the post of Pilotage Clerk under their control. Consequently when the Pilotage Committee announced that Mr. Bennion would be assisted in his duties at Eastham by Mr. R. Jeffery, a Tolls Clerk at Eastham Locks, it brought a swift response from the Pilotage Association who objected to the appointment forcefully on the grounds that his age and qualifications rendered him wholly unsuitable for the position of Pilotage Clerk or Assistant. They also desired to be consulted,in the future, regarding the appointment of Mr. Bennions' successor or assistant. It appears that the Pilots Association had come to the wrong conclusion and had reacted a little too hastily. The Pilotage Committee reply was, that they had no intention of appointing Mr. Jeffery as successor and that he was only called to assist now, because he was already stationed at Eastham. The question of a successor would not be decided without first conferring with the Pilots Association.

Over the next year there was a great deal of speculation and lobbying as each side jostled to place their man in the Pilotage Clerk seat. It was in May 1944 at the Pilotage Committee the Chairman (Mr. L. Roberts) finally announced that Mr. Rushton should be appointed to succeed Mr. Bennion and that he should be responsible for the preparation of the rota etc. Mr. Rushton would be succeeded by Mr. S. (Stan) Evans and he in turn by Mr. Thelwell in the performance of their respective duties at Eastham Locks. Mr Davenport (Pilot's representative) said he understood there was also an application from Mr. S. (Sam) Hargraves, but Mr. Roberts said he had more important duties to perform. [Authors Note: Mr. Sam Hargraves was a good friend and advocate to the Pilots Service]. The Chairman wanted to come to a decision fairly quickly so that Mr. Rushton could commence to take over seriously from Mr. Bennion. The appointment was deferred until the next meeting in order that if the Pilots wished to make any representations they might have an opportunity of doing so.

In June the Pilots considered they had excellent opportunities of forming an opinion as to the suitability of members of the Canal Company's staff who may possibly be candidates for the position of Pilot Clerk and suggested at the Pilotage Committee that the names of Messrs Hargraves and Thelwell should receive consideration. They mentioned that the capabilities of Mr. Hargraves would be well known to the Committee and that Mr. Thelwell had a considerable knowledge of the working of the pilotage system and would prove competent to carry out the duties of Pilotage Clerk. The Chairman stated that all the names mentioned had been under review but he thought it might be advisable to give Mr. Rushton the opportunity of proving himself. A long discussion ensued each side pressing their points in favour of one candidate or another. During the discussion it was agreed that the salary of the Pilotage Clerk should be set in the region of £800 per annum. The Pilots requested a postponement of the appointment in order that they may give the matter further full consideration. The Committee agreed to this request until the next Pilotage Committee.

At the August Pilotage Committee the Secretary of the Pilots Association (Mr. Evans) stated that the Management Committee and a subsequent General meeting of the Pilots Association had given full consideration to the wider aspects of this matter and the Pilots felt the time was opportune for the consolidation into one department of the functions at present exercised by the Pilotage Clerk and those officers of the Company who were at present concerned with the collection and distribution of Pilotage dues. Such a reorganisation would be conducive to the more efficient working of the Pilotage system and would prove more economical than the present methods. The recommendations were as follows:

1. That a separate Pilotage Department be established at Eastham to be manned by an official whose duties would combine those of Pilotage Clerk and Collector of Pilotage Dues. Such official to have the assistance of a Clerk, a typist and possibly a boy.

2. That the principal official and his assistants should be appointed by the Pilots Association by whom their remuneration would be fixed.

3. That the expenses of the Department should be defrayed out of a percentage deduction from the Pilots' gross earnings and other

receipts now credited to the Pilot Fund after payment of the expenses of members attending meetings of the Pilotage Committee and any other expenses of the Authority properly chargeable to the Pilot Fund.

4. That with the consent of the Helmsmen the regulation of their duties shall also be carried out by the Pilotage Department, subject to the contribution of a percentage of the Helmsmens' earnings towards the expenses of the Department.

The Pilots had voted that Mr. S. Hargraves would be suitable to be placed in charge of this proposed new department and the selection of his assistants would be a matter of arrangement. From the very outset these proposals did not have the slightest chance of being accepted at Pilotage Committee.

The Chairman said that in his opinion the duties alloted in the Association's letter to the proposed Pilotage Department could not be efficiently carried out by the staff suggested and the cost would far exceed the amounts charged to the Pilot Fund under the existing arrangements. Moreover, there would be a danger that the important advantages derived from combining the Pilotage Service with the other activities of the Company would be lost. The Secretary of the Pilotage Committee also added that the scheme suggested would not be in accordance either with the letter or the pilotage law as it stands at present. The Chairman then stated that all the considerations given to this appointment had been fully discussed and the Authority had decided to appoint Mr. Rushton as Pilotage Clerk and if the appointment turned out to be unsuitable, contrary to expectations, it would not be irredeemable and the Authority must always reserve the right to make whatever arrangements are, in their opinion, most conducive to the efficient conduct of the Pilot Service. Mr. R. Rushton was duly appointed Chief Pilotage Clerk and took up his duties on January 1st 1945.

From this abrupt conclusion it appears that not a lot of consideration was given to the Pilots Association's recommendations.

It could almost be said that the successor to Mr Bennion was signed, sealed, and delivered in 1942. The Pilotage Committee just toyed with the Pilots efforts to place their man in the position of Pilotage Clerk, and when their patience ran out, steamrollered the appointment through. It was another lesson, learnt the hard way, by the Pilots of the power and influence of the Pilotage Committee. The high esteem in which Mr. Bennion was held by all who came into contact with him during his arduous task as Pilotage Clerk was reflected at the December 1944 Pilotage Committee meeting when the Chairman Mr. L. Roberts referred to the reference in Mr. Bennions' report for the month of November, that this was his final report in a series of 300. Mr. Bennion had been Pilotage Clerk since the inception of the Rotary System of Pilotage in 1919 and he felt sure the Committee would support him in wishing Mr. Bennion the best of health and happiness when he retired from the service on December 31st. All the members of the Committee endorsed the Chairman's sentiments. Mr. Bennion suitably thanked the Committee and the Chairman for his remarks. An era had ended.

Mr. Rushton took up his duties on January 1st 1945 in a purpose built office block alongside the main sluice way of the 75 foot lock at Eastham. He was given one small room, a desk and chair, two telephones and a filing cabinet, but this was luxury compared to where he had been last installed. He worked faithfully, zealously and to the very best of his ability in a none too happy environment created by a very bitter Pilot Service. He continued to keep the high standards of efficiency set by his predecessor but his sojurn as the Chief Pilotage Clerk was far from a happy one. The Pilots made sure of that. Mr. R. Rushton retired nine years later in 1953. There are no records in any minutes of a vote of thanks for his services on his retirement.

After the fiasco of the appointment of the Chief Pilot Clerk in 1945, the Pilot Serrvice never again attempted to promote or influence the Pilotage Committee in their deliberations for a new Chief Pilot Clerk nor did they ever again object to any appointment made by the Pilotage Committee for that position. Mr. S (Stan) Evans had been groomed to be the next Chief Pilot Clerk and in 1952 became the official Assistant Chief Pilot Clerk in readiness for the impending retirement of Mr. Rushton which duly took place in 1953. Here was a Chief Pilot Clerk of a different ilk.

During Mr. Evans working years as a Toll Clerk at Eastham Locks, the many times he had acted as temporary Chief Pilot Clerk during Mr. Rushton's absence through holidays or sickness and the twelve

1952 - 1966
Chief Pilot Clerk Mr. S. (Stan) Evans.

1954 - 1966
Ass. Chief Pilot Clerk Mr. H. (Harry) Thelwell.

months he spent as the Assistant to the Chief Pilot Clerk, he had had ample opportunity to study very closely the machinations of various devious Pilots who attempted to avoid work at all costs. Mr. Evans had made himself more than fully conversant with all the principles in the Pilot Services standing working orders. He was determined to leave nothing to chance when he became Chief Pilot Clerk. It can be truthfully recorded that in all his years as Chief Pilot Clerk, there was not one Pilot who was able to say, with his hand on his heart, he had ever bettered Mr. Evans in an argument regarding his Pilotage Orders or to carrying them out. It was the classic "Greek meets Greek" situation. He maintained this authority until his retirement in 1964. When Mr. Evans died in 1976, aged 71 years only one Pilot attended his funeral.

In 1954 with the ever increasing complement of Pilots and Helmsmen and the boom in shipping using the Ship Canal the Pilotage Authority felt it necessary for the smooth running of the Pilots' Administration to appoint a permanent Assistant Chief Pilot Clerk. Their inspired choice was Mr. Harry Thelwell. The Authority could not have chosen a more contrasting person in temperament to Mr. Evans if they had tried. Mr. Evans was volatile, susceptible to alarming moments of anger or impatience when dealing with errant Pilots. Mr. Thelwell was all peace and quietness, totally unruffled by the malingery of certain Pilots and had all the patience in the world. In their working environment what a foil he was for Mr. Evans, their chemistry worked brilliantly. As in Mr. Evans approach to his position as Chief Pilot Clerk, Mr. Thelwell was equally thorough in his preparation towards the position of a Pilot Clerk. Having observed the dubious working practices of some Pilots since 1925 he was well aware of the knowledge that was expected of him.

In the tranquil world that Mr. Thelwell built around himself the essence of time was of no importance to him. Many were the evenings long after his official time had passed to leave his office and duties behind him and head for home he would be found happily working away, ensuring everything was in order for the next day. He was held in the greatest of affection and respect by all Pilots and Helmsmen and his retirement in 1966 left a gap in the rotary administration of the Pilot Service that could never ever be so uniquely filled again. His beloved wife, Evaline, died in 1969 and Mr. Harry Thelwell died a lonely man in 1988 aged 81 years. It is sad to record there was no representative from the Pilot Service in attendance at the last farewell, to a man who had served them so faithfully and with so much equanimity.

Whilst Messrs Evans and Thelwell held sway as Pilotage Clerks, in 1958 a further addition in manpower was made to that department. Mr. K.(Kevin) Long was appointed as second assistant Chief Pilot Clerk. This appointment was no less inspiring than the previous appointment of Mr. Thelwell, but for entirely different reasons. Messrs Evans and Thelwell were in their mid fifties, deeply set in their individual ways and mannerisms in the running of the Pilots' Rota System. Mr. Long was but a mere youth of some 28 summers and there was speculation as how he would fit in to such an entrenched administration. More to the point how would he be accepted by the Pilot Service who still numbered amongst them. Pilots who were always at variance and highly critical of anything new or youthful. As already stated it was an inspired choice, Mr. Long's youthful enthusiasm and tremendous sense of humour became infectious and soon overcame all prejudices. He became a welcomed addition to the Department.

It was always a real joy to receive a Pilotage order to attend a vessel from Mr. Long no matter what time of day or night it was, summer or winter, wet or dry it was always communicated to you in such a happy mien it was impossible to feel disgruntled. Such was this man's ability to bring a refreshing approach to the Pilotage Department. This happy situation remained until April 1966 when the Pilotage Clerks Department was completely reorganised by the Ship Canal Company. Mr. H. Thelwell was transferred to another department in the Company and a 24 hour manning of the Pilots Clerk Department was introduced. The new staff to man the office were all recruited from the Harbour Masters Department. The original list read as follows:

Mr. Harold Piper
Mr. Edward Morrison
Mr. Raymond Selby
Mr. Shaun Morrissey
Mr. Donald Roberts

1966 - 1983
Mr. H. (Harold) Piper

1966 - 1986
Mr. R. (Ray) Selby

1966 - 1983
Mr. D. (Don) Roberts

1966 - 1983
Mr. E. (Ted) Morrison

1966 - 1983
Mr. S. (Shaun) Morrisey

1986 - 1988
Mrs. Shirley Davies

Mr. K. Long stayed in the Pilotage Clerk office until all the new staff were sufficiently conversant with the workings of the Pilotage Rota System. In 1967 Mr. Long was transferred to another department in the Company. This new system worked extremely well and efficiently for the next 17 years with hardly a change in the staff. The sudden and tragic death of Mr. Harold Piper brought about the only change in staff during that period.

The world of computerisation was beginning to make an impact on the administration departments of the Ship Canal Company and it would only be a matter of time before the inevitable transition took place in the Pilotage Clerk's Department. In February of 1985 the Pilotage Clerk's Department did become fully computerised and the Pilotage Clerks nursed it through its embryonic beginnings knowing full well that in doing so they were at the same time destroying their prospects of work as Pilot Clerks. That they did this without malice and uncomplainingly is a lasting tribute to their dedication to their work and in particular their loyalty to the Pilot Service.

The Pilotage Clerks' Department in 1986 reverted to normal office hours and the soulless self-answering telephone was installed to act as Pilotage Clerk through the night watches. The five Pilotage Clerks were all transferred back to the Harbour Master's Department.

But the greatest calamity of all was about to befall upon that bastion of male chauvinistic ideals, the Manchester Pilot Service. After 90 years as a Pilot Service a female was about to be installed into the Pilots Clerks' Department, with the authority to *order Pilots* to pilot vessels. It was said that in every graveyard in which a Manchester Pilot was buried, he turned over on the day Mrs. Shirley Davies took office as Chief Pilot Clerk in 1986. Mrs. Davies was the first lady Pilotage Clerk in the history of the Manchester Pilot Service and as it transpired she became the last person to hold such a position. In 1988 under the new working system for the Pilot Service the position of Pilotage Clerk was no longer required.

1994

The Modern Day System.

First Class Pilot Mr. F.M.W. Bartlett on duty as Pilot Clerk during his 24 hour watch period. The chemical tanker "North Star" docking at Eastham locks in the background.

1958 - 1967
Mr. K. (Kevin) Long

8.

THE LAMEY STORY

The very name Lamey has always been synonymous with the River Mersey by all the sea going fraternity in the north west of England by way of their fleet of tug boats stationed in Liverpool. They also owned five sailing ships all of which were registered in Devon ports, from where the Lamey family originated. They were well established on the River Mersey in the 1800s and the opening of the Manchester Ship Canal in 1895 seemed a natural progression for the Lameys to establish themselves on this new waterway.

In 1896, James Harvey Lamey, aged 21 years, and living in Onslow Road, New Ferry, was in command of a tug that frequently towed sailing vessels into and out of the Ship Canal, sometimes going up the Canal as far as Runcorn Docks. In May 1901 he applied for a Second Class licence on the Ship Canal. His application was accepted and he duly passed the examination. Mr. J.H. Lamey became the first of five Lameys to hold a Ship Canal licence during the next 70 years. He attained his First Class licence in 1903.

There was a form of choice-appropriated pilot system during those early days when Masters specifically requested a certain Pilot, either through their agents/brokers or by directly contacting the Pilot himself by way of a letter giving an Estimated Time of Arrival (E.T.A.) of his vessel at Eastham. This system did much to generate a great deal of discontentment as you will read in other Chapters of this book. Mr. J.H. Lamey had gained the confidence of a number of Masters as a tug master and now with his piloting expertise, he

MANCHESTER PILOTAGE DISTRICT.

Pilot's Licence No. 7.

The Manchester Ship Canal Company as Pilotage Authority for the Manchester Pilotage District in pursuance and by virtue of the powers given them for that purpose in and by the Pilotage Act, 1913, and of all other powers them enabling having first duly examined Mr. Thomas Lamey of 47 Rockland Avenue, Bebington aged 48 years, height 5 feet 5½ inches, colour of hair Brown, colour of eyes Blue complexion Fresh, and having upon such examination found him to be a fit and competent person, duly skilled to act as a Pilot of the First Class for the purpose of conducting ships navigating within the limits of the Manchester Pilotage District, as defined in the Manchester Pilotage Order, 1920, do hereby appoint and license him to act as a Pilot of the First Class within such limits.

And this Licence (if the same shall not have been revoked or suspended in the meantime, as provided in the said Act and in the Bye-laws made thereunder by the said Pilotage Authority), is to continue in force up to and until the 31st day of August next, after which it shall be subject to renewal from time to time by endorsement hereon as provided in the said Bye-laws.

Given under the seal of the Manchester Ship Canal Company this _____ day of September 19 29 in the presence of

Directors

Secretary

Printed by kind permission of Mr. Peter Lamey

1901 - 1935
Mr. Thomas Lamey

By kind permission of Mr. Peter G. Lamey

was frequently asked to pilot vessels of the Knudsen Line (Danish) and the Thoronsen Line (Norwegian). In September 1919 at the age of 44, he became disenchanted with pilotage and he retired and once again took command of a tug boat in the River Mersey. Mr. William Lamey, brother of Mr. J.H. Lamey, as would be expected had a similar sea-going background, but had been a boy sailor on three mast barques sailing out of Newlyn before coming north to join the Lamey tug fleet as a deck hand in 1898 at the age of 18 years. He soon gained enough experience in the Ship Canal for him to successfully apply for a Second Class licence and one year later passed the examination for a First Class licence. During the 1914-1918 war the Pilotage Committee were actively pursuing a policy of allowing Pilots to leave the service on a temporary basis to assuage the chronic over manning of the Pilot Service due to the decrease in vessels using the Ship Canal during the war conditions. In 1918 Mr. W. Lamey applied and was granted such a leave of absence and he returned to the Lamey tug fleet as Master. He was reinstated as a First Class Pilot in January 1919. He was appointed choice Pilot for Lamport and Holt Line from 1920 to 1932. In 1934 he became the choice Pilot for Mobile Oil Tankers and remained their Pilot until he retired in September 1942 aged 63 years.

The third Lamey to enter the Ship Canal Pilot Service was Mr. Thomas Lamey, a cousin of the two previous Lameys. He joined the Helmsmans' service on June 7th 1901 and steered his first ship on June 9th the S.S. "TONGA" from Partington to Eastham for a fee of £1.4s.0d. (£1.20p). The Pilot of that vessel revered under the name of Mr. Harry Boxer-Jones who lived in Seafield Road, New Ferry, Birkenhead. Mr. T. Lamey steered from June 9th 1901 until September 30th 1905 and in his personal log book a summary of the vessels he steered reads as follows:

For year ending December 31st 1901	22 vessels.
For year ending December 31st 1902	112 vessels.
For year ending December 31st 1903	150 vessels
For year ending December 31st 1904	167 vessels
For year ending September 30th 1905	117 vessels

Total vessels steered 568.

I am grateful to Mr. T. Lamey for keeping such a log for therein is recorded the very first earnings of a Helmsman. One such monthly record is reproduced in the Chapter under the heading "The Helmsman's Service".

Mr. T. Lamey obtained his Second Class Licence in October 1905 and his First Class Licence in September 1908. He became the Choice Pilot for F. Leyland and Company and J. Leete and Sons in 1919 but the latter company was withdrawn because those vessels of that company were all under 1,000 tons gross registered. In April 1934 he began to suffer with a heart condition but continued to work on under this handicap. On May 18th 1935 he had a heart attack from which he never recovered and died the following day aged 54 years.

Mr. Joseph E. Lamey was a second cousin to Mr. Thomas Lamey and also hailed from Devon. He began his nautical career at the age of 13 years sailng in schooners from the port of Bideford, which he always contended was valuable experience and useful discipline training. In 1909 at the age of 18 years he came north and took lodgings in New Ferry, Birkenhead and commenced steering on the Canal. At the outbreak of war in 1914 he was the only Helmsman to volounteer for King and Country and enlisted in the Army. He was sent overseas to Mesopotamia (Iraq) and in 1915 was involved in the first battle for Kut-el-Amara on the River Tigris in which the British Army failed to capture the city. A long siege was held and in 1916 in the horrendous action that led to the fall of Kut-el-Amara Mr. Lamey was severely wounded. He was repatriated and hospitalized for 18 months in the South of England. After hostilities had ended and he had fully recouperated he returned to his position as a Helmsman and in that same year 1919, he married the nurse who had cared for him during the recovery from his wounds.

In 1920 he obtained his Second Class licence and two years later he became a First Class Pilot. He was appointed choice Pilot for the Eagle Oil Company and the Anglo Saxon Petroleum Company in 1922 and served those companies for sixteen years. He was appointed the Choice Pilot for the American Lykes Line from 1938 to 1942. In 1945 he became the Choice Pilot for the Good Gulf Line, a Belgian firm, and remained their Choice Pilot until he retired in August 1957 at the age of 66 years.

The last of the Lameys to hold a Pilot's licence on the Ship Canal was Mr. Thomas William Lamey, son of Thomas Lamey (1901-On

1928 - 1970
Mr. Thomas William Lamey

By kind permission of Mr. Peter G. Lamey

"Irish Minstrel"
*A wooden three masted schooner of 154 Tons. Gross.
She was built at Dundalk, Co. Louth, Ireland in 1879 - Length 100 feet, beam 25 feet*

By kind permission of Mr. Peter G. Lamey

1935). He was without doubt the most cheerful and had the best disposition of all the Lameys who held a licence on the Canal. His command of the English language coupled with his personal restraint was such, that in all the 42 years as a Pilot and a Helmsman he was never once heard to utter a profanity or an offending expletive. Mr. Lamey - Tommy as he was universally known and addressed throughout the Ship Canal - was born in 1905 in Devon. He gained his sea experience as a boy sailor on his uncle's (Mr. William Lamey 1904-1942) sailing ship the "IRISH MINSTREL" and in the Lamport and Holt Line. He commenced steering on the Canal in 1928. In 1939 he obtained a Second Class Licence and in 1942 was promoted to First Class at the age of 36 years.

Like all the Lameys before him his expertise as a Pilot was instantly recognised and his services as a Choice Pilot were much sought after. In 1946 he was appointed Choice Pilot for the Ellerman City Line, a position he held with distinction for twelve years, when they ceased trading to Manchester. His services were soon quickly appropriated for the prestige appointment to Manchester Liners in 1959. Mr. Lamey again acquitted himself admirably in the high standard of piloting that everyone had come to expect from a Lamey. He served the Manchester Liners faithfully until his retirement in 1970 at the age of 64 years.

Mr. T. (Tommy) Lamey was held in the highest esteeem and affection by all his fellow Pilots, Helmsmen and Masters of all the vessels he so ably piloted. He upheld all that was good in piloting and his dress and demeanour aboard a vessel was such that many other Ship Canal Pilots would have done well to copy. He was a credit to the United Kingdom Pilots in general and to the Manchester Pilot Service in particular. He died in 1989 aged 83 years.

The Lameys were the last of the large families who held Pilot licences on the Manchester Ship Canal.

1956
The Lamey Family
Mr. J.E. Lamey, Mr. A. Lamey (Liverpool Tug Owner) and Mr. T.W. Lamey

By kind permission of the Lamey Family

1915
Mr. Joseph E. Lamey aged 23 years. The only Helmsman to volunteer for King and Country in the 1914-18 War.

9.

THE EARLY WORKING OF THE ROTARY SYSTEM 1920-1921

5 January 1920 the Pilotage Committee received the following report on the first month of working the Rotary system, from Mr R Bennion the Chief Pilot Clerk:

"Dear Sir,

I beg leave to report that the Pilotage Rotary Scheme having come into practice as from 1 December 1919, has on the whole worked very satisfactorily and the efficiency of the service - always the main interest - has been adequately maintained. It was perhaps a disadvantage to start the scheme in the month of December, a month of short days, and one which has proved a month of storm and flood, making navigation protracted and full of risks. This has given the pilots at the outset probably the very worst conditions to be encountered and as time advances the service will settle down into a well defined working system and what may have appeared to be initial difficulties and hardships,will gradually disappear. In practice the Rota does not work out absolutely true to turn because it is possible and often happens through delays from unforeseen causes, that one pilot over-runs another, but taking two weeks together this generally rights itself and pilots do an equal number of turns. During the month there have been 244 separate services which is perhaps equal to an average summer month and some of the pilots may have thought turns were punctuated with very short intervals, but most have at all times worked loyally and well to cope with the traffic offering. Of these 244 vessels : 138 have been under 1,000 tons net register; and 106 have been over 1,000 tons register.

There have been 43 'Choice' services and 73 services of moving vessels at Eastham apart from shifting work at Manchester. In practice the manning of the stations at Eastham and Manchester takes up a good deal of the time of the pilots. If it could be arranged for, say, 2 pilots to be reserved for Dock work in Manchester, this would ease the position considerably and the pilots then sent to Manchester could in most cases be ordered direct to the vessel requiring his services. Another point bearing on this question is the one of 'Choice' pilots, because in some cases it has the effect of running a 'Choice' pilot almost entirely clear of station work, thus throwing extra waiting time on the remainder of the pilots. There has been some sickness during the month, Pilot W. Marker having been off duty from December 6th to 31st and has only performed two turns on the Rota. Pilot J Barnes has missed one turn through illness and together this has meant the service being carried on by 24 instead of 25 pilots. A point which the pilots as the wage-earners will no doubt desire to settle is what period a pilot may receive pay for, whilst off duty through a certified illness and whether, if he is only incapacitated for say two turns, he should work these turns up again to bring himself level with the Rota. The 13 Helmsmen authorised by the Company have at the same time worked on a rotary basis, receiving orders in the same manner as the pilots and they have also been very attentive to their duties. I would like to point out that in the supervision of the work of the pilots and helmsmen, I have been at considerable disadvantage in not having a telephone at my home which means that I have to be out at weekends and very often at nights, according as to how the tides run at Eastham Locks, to keep in touch with the work properly. The inherent difficulty of working this scheme from Runcorn has been very much simplified by the loyal co-operation of Capt. Perry, Manchester Canal Superintendent, who has at all times been ready to arrange the pilotage work in the Docks and out from Manchester. Your obedient servant,

R Bennion, Chief Pilot Clerk."

The position of Dock Pilots was quickly resolved by Pilot W Marker (age 69) who wrote the following brief letter to the Pilots' Association: "Since the new Rotary System in the Pilotage Service has come into operation and being the oldest man in the service, I beg to apply to be established as a Dock Pilot".

The Pilots' Association agreed to Mr Marker's application on the grounds of age and living in Manchester. There would be a trial period of one month before the position of Dock Pilot became permanent. It was, however, felt that Mr Marker would not be able to cope with the work himself and that a further pilot living in Manchester be invited to act in conjunction with him.

The name of Mr A.E. Postlethwaite, the only other pilot living in Manchester, was put forward as a likely candidate as Dock Pilot and he readily accepted this duty. At the Pilotage Committee meeting on 2 February it was reported that the performing of Dock Pilotage by Messrs Marker and Postlethwaite had proved highly satisfactory during the first month of its inception. It was, therefore, unanimously agreed that until further notice, they should act as Dock Pilots only. Mr Marker remained as a Dock Pilot until August 1926 when he was forced to retire through ill-health at the age of 75; he died six months later. The Dock Piloting system was phased out in 1923.

On the subject of 'choice' Pilots (appropriated) disruption of the rota, this had always been a contentious issue and would ever remain so until this present day. There never has been, or ever will be, a satisfactory and realistic solution to the constant disruption of 'Choice' pilots work to the Pilotage Rota, but for many devious reasons the 'Choice' pilot system has been supported and perpetuated by the Manchester Ship Canal Company down through the ages. The following was the complete list of Choice Pilots in January 1920 :

T. LAMEY	Age 38	F. LEYLAND & Co
G. CARTWRIGHT	Age 49	MANCHESTER LINERS
J. BAXTER	Age 53	MANCHESTER LINERS
R. SOUTHWOOD	Age 39	MARWOOD AND ROBERTSONS
W. SOUTHWOOD	Age 41	PRINCE LINE
J. HINDLE	Age 60	CLAN LINE
G. DAVIDSON	Age 51	LARRINAGA LINE

W. LAMEY	Age 40	LAMPORT AND HOLT
G. GREEN	Age 65	CUNARD S.S. CO.
E. HANKINSON	Age 62	ELDER DEMPSTER
A. YATES	Age 39	ELLERMAN LINES
J. BARNES	Age 59	ANGLO-AMERICAN OIL CO.

Three more firms had applied for choice pilots but had been refused by the Pilotage Committee on the grounds that their vessels were under 1,000 tons net register. The appointment of Mr J Barnes to AngloAmerican Oil Co. was withdrawn in February, as that company did not feel disposed to paying the pilot the special annual fee of £100 to retain him. From time immemorial, ship-owners have been renowned for their reluctance to remunerate pilots for any special service rendered to their vessels above and beyond the normal pilot service. It is a long-standing adage in any Pilot service, that to separate a ship-owner from his money is likened to that of getting blood from a stone.

At the Pilotage Committee meeting in April, Mr Bennion informed them that 9 Pilots had no telephones at their private addresses and stated this was causing a great inconvenience to contact them when required for work at the correct time and with their correct vessels on the rota. The Chairman of the Pilotage Committee forwarded a letter to the 9 pilots in question pointing out that in his opinion it would greatly assist the efficient working of the rota if they would endeavour to have a telephone installed at their home at the earliest possible moment. Every assistance would be given by the Committee to facilitate the installation should they encounter any difficulty in getting the telephone people to comply with their requirements.

The Pilotage Committee in July heard Mr Bennion report that some Pilots were still without telephones in their homes and continued to take a good deal of the time of the company's staff at Eastham in trying to contact them. He quoted the case of two Pilots who lived in New Ferry, some 6 miles away. Staff at the Lock Office had to travel to their homes to transmit their orders. In other cases, the Pilots who lived further away had to be relied upon to contact the Pilot Clerk from some convenient call box and this did not always synchronize with the issuing out of a Pilotage Order. Mr Bennion thought this position was far from satisfactory.

A further letter was sent to the Pilots in question, stating in no uncertain terms that the lack of attention on their part to keep in contact with the Pilot Clerk was causing serious concern and causing great inconvenience to the satisfactory working of the Rotary System and that they should have a telephone installed in their homes forthwith. It took until March 1921 for all Pilots to be connected by telephone to their homes.

It is interesting to note that the problem of contacting Pilots for work never arose when the old system of "catch-as-catch-can" prevailed and what you earned you kept yourself. There was never any lack of attention on the Pilots' part to keep in touch with the Pilot Clerk; nor was there a necessity for Lock Staff to go six miles to give a Pilot his orders. A Pilot never missed an order in those days.

The new Rotary System had hardly had time to settle down when on 28 June 1920, the Pilot Service voted 17 in favour to 6 against, that a trial be given to a system of half the Pilots working from Manchester to Eastham and half working from Eastham to Manchester. It was agreed at the July Pilotage Committee that this trial system should take place for the two months of September and October.

The greatest fundamental flaw in the Manchester Pilots' Rotary System was that of having had no legislation - rules and regulations firmly laid down; nor were there any penalty clauses to deter any pilot should he attempt to abuse the rules and regulations. The powers to be at that time appeared to rely on the rather naive supposition that all Pilots would conscientiously and fairly work the Rotary System. Unfortunately those two words were not part of some Pilots' vocabulary. In April 1921 a pilot refused to carry out an order to attend a vessel. This immediately highlighted the pressing need for a well defined scale of rules and regulations to be set out for the future working of the Rotary System to be observed by all pilots. The rules and regulations were drawn up, agreed upon by all parties concerned and put into operation on 10 May 1921. They read as follows :

RULES AND REGULATIONS TO BE OBSERVED BY THE MANCHESTER SHIP CANAL PILOTS IN THE ROTARY SYSTEM OF PILOTAGE

A. EASTHAM LOCK PILOT STATION

Each tide to commence with four pilots on the station, the hours for duty being four hours before until four hours after high water at Liverpool. The first pilot who is on turn to be on the locks when traffic is entering the Canal.

B. If two pilots are engaged before high water, the next two pilots will be called out for duty on that tide or as many more as may be required.

C. If a pilot misses his turn through any cause whatever, then he shall go behind all the other pilots on station.

D. Pilots living remotely from Eastham Locks when fifth on turn for duty on night tides or on Sundays, will consider themselves on duty and make their way down to the pilot station in view of the means of transport for getting to Eastham at such times being curtailed.

E. SHIFTING VESSELS TO OR FROM DOLPHINS TO LOCKS

This will be done by the pilots on duty, the first pilot being left free to take his turn should anything enter requiring not to proceed at once. Second-class pilots not to shift vessels over 1,000 tons register if first class are available, the 'Choice' pilots to move their own vessels in all cases unless required for immediate duty elsewhere.

F. TURN AT EASTHAM

The method of deciding the first turn at Eastham shall be the vessel first getting a rope ashore on the pierhead at the outer entrance and if it is night time, this shall be no reason for the pilot not remaining by the vessel for a daylight start unless either of the following conditions apply:

1) If a steamer is proceeding to the Dolphins or Sheer Legs for any work to her masts and/or funnel, or in case of breakdown to machinery, the first pilot to remain behind to take the first ship entering and proceeding on her journey.

2) If during the daytime a vessel has to go to the Dolphins to wait for tugs for any period exceeding 14 hours when the shifting will be done as per Clause 'E'. In the event of such delay causing a steamer to remain at Eastham until the following morning, the pilot first on turn at the conclusion of the tide then in progress to attend to her.

G. Where a steamer has been to the Dolphins or Sheer Legs in connection with work to her masts or funnel or machinery, when she is ready to go forward (subject to tug provision in the case of large steamers) the pilot first on turn will attend to her.

H. Where 1st and 2nd class pilots are on duty together, regard must be paid to the order in which vessels enter the Canal, observing "turn" as far as possible, but so as not to delay any vessel in sight through a 1st Class pilot boarding a ship under 1,000 tons register if his services are required for a larger vessel.

I. The method of half the pilots working up to Manchester and half down to Eastham as commenced on 6 September 1920, to continue, the change over to take place every four weeks on the day tide finishing not later than 5.30 p.m. on the fourth Monday.

J. All vessels moving inwards from Eastham and intermediate points towards Manchester to be treated as on the inward rota and all vessels moving outwards from Manchester or other point towards Eastham as on the outward rota, with the following qualifications :

1. Vessels proceeding to Ellesmere Port, Runcorn or Partington to load coal, salt etc and loading within eight hours, the pilot to remain by her and count one turn.

2. Vessels proceeding from Acton Grange or Warrington Lay-Bye to Partington for bunkers and thence to Eastham, to count one turn.

3. Vessels outward from Manchester going to Partington for coal and afterwards returning to Manchester, will be treated as if the vessel had continued to Eastham and count one turn.

4. Vessels from Manchester going to the Weaver Bend to turn and calling at Partington for coal, to be treated as two turns. NB: 2,3,4, subject in each case to delay at Partington not exceeding 24 hours.

K. Light vessels which may be delayed in starting the journey by stress of weather, the pilot to remain by her for 12 hours, then if the weather still remains the same he may be ordered to another vessel which can proceed, but if a start has been made the pilot to remain by the ship and complete the journey.

L. Shifting at Runcorn or Weston Point to be done by the pilots residing at Runcorn and not to count a turn. Shifting of vessels in dock and below Mode Wheel to be done by the present Dock Pilot (W Marker) assisted by either Pilots Davidson or Postlethwaite, whichever pilot may be working on the outward rota at the time, four such shifts to be calculated as equal to one turn.

M. Pilots to keep themselves informed as to when they are likely to be required for work and immediately after completing a service to send in their card to the Dock Office. These Regulations as agreed were forwarded to each of the pilots for their information and attention. Amazingly, no penalties were included for any flagrant disregard or abuse of these Rules, but as it became abundantly clear that pilots were disregarding and abusing the Rules, especiallyduring tide duty at Eastham Locks, the following additions were made and came into force on 1 December 1921:

a) That failing their attendance at Eastham Locks at tide time in accordance with the Rules and Regulations for working the Rotary System as forwarded to the pilots by Circular Letter on the 10 May 1921, without satisfactory explanation, they may be automatically suspended from further service for such period as the Chairman or Deputy Chairman might determine.

b) That the Pilots must sign on for duty in a book to be in the custody of the Toll Clerk at Eastham Locks.

It was arranged that the system of booking on by the Pilots be put into operation at the earliest moment.

Two other interesting points arose in 1920; firstly, the secretary of the United Pilotage Association wrote to all Pilot Service secretaries asking them to enquire from their Pilotage Committees whether they were in favour of compulsory pilotage in their district. Mr J Hindle, the Pilots' representative, replied that as Mr Latimer, Chairman of the Pilotage Committee was not in favour of compulsory pilotage, the Manchester Pilotage Committee would not be agreeable to pilotage becoming compulsory in the Canal. The subject was never raised again, either at Pilotage Committee or at a Pilots' Association Meeting. Secondly, on a more happier note, on 25 March 1920, Mr R. Bennion (Pilot Clerk) and Captain Acraman (Canal Superintendent) met with Pilots C.Young, J. Baxter and W. Southwood, to formulate the first paid leave system for the Pilots' Service. It took only this meeting to agree :

a) Leave to be taken between April and September;

b) 21 days per Pilot, to run consecutively; and

c) Not more than four Pilots to be on leave, at any one time.

A draw was held for the order in which the holidays should be taken and as a result, Pilots C. Young, G. Green, E. Hankinson and J. D. Shaw, became the first pilots to enjoy paid leave. The twelve Helmsmen or apprentice pilots in the service did not receive paid leave or have a leave rota until 1955, exactly thirty-five years later.

1922

The Runcorn - Widnes Transporter Bridge. One of only two in England. The Ship Canal is in the background behind the retaining wall below the twin support shafts.

1922

An Eagle Oil Tanker passing beneath the Transporter Bridge outward bound.

Photos courtesy of Mrs. W. Yates

10.

THE ABUSE OF THE ROTARY SYSTEM PART TWO

Throughout the history of the Manchester Pilot Service there were always Pilots who abused the Rotary System in one way or another and for one reason or another. In October 1918, Mr. Hindle (First Class Pilot) complained that the Rotary System was being manipulated and discrimination was being shown in regards to certain Pilots, thus abusing the rota of Pilots. He quoted an incident when he was number two on tide station and Mr. R. Southwood was number one. Both Pilots being first class, the S.S. "PURFOL" docked first, followed by the S.S. "BRITISH ADMIRAL", but Mr. Southwood was boarded on the second ship and he was boarded on the first ship, a complete reversal of what should have occurred. In consequence of which Mr. Hindle earned £1.17s.6d (£1.87p) instead of £3.15s.0d (£3.75p).

Mr. Hindle forcefully complained that a man's living was being manipulated as well as the rota and earnestly asked the Pilotage Committee to restore the equanimity of the Rota System. The Pilotage Committee explained that the "PURFOL" arrived without orders where to proceed to, but the "BRITISH ADMIRAL" had orders to proceed to Manchester, The "BRITISH ADMIRAL" was therefore considered first ship to dock. Just how the Dock Master came to this astonishing conclusion is not recorded. The Pilotage Committee did not consider that any case existed for complaint on the part of Mr. Hindle, in the light of the information received from the Dock Master and the matter was closed. One can only draw the conclusion that there must have been some connivance - monetary or otherwise - between the Dock Masters and certain Pilots. On June 7th 1920 Mr. C.F. Young Jnr. wrote to the Pilotage Committee the following letter:

"I beg to bring to your notice an abuse in the Rotary System which took place at Eastham on June 3rd. I was number one Pilot on tide duty and Mr. F. Onion was number two. I enquired from Mr. Onion if there was any vessels in the river for the Canal and he replied "NO". It was a 'leveling' tide and as I watched from the river bank the schooner "NOTRE DAME DE LA MER" with her tug boat go through the locks on the level. Never for a moment did I think she would require a Pilot, until a few moments later I was told that Mr. Onion had boarded her from the Customs Launch. It now transpires that Mr. Onion was in conversation with the Master of that schooner the previous evening and had discovered that the vessel would require a Pilot in the Canal. My main complaint is the lack of comradeship and the breaking of the first principle of the Rotary System viz:- first ship, first Pilot. This whole business is very much a piece of sharp practice on the part of Mr. Onion and I request that some disciplinary action be taken to stamp out this evil practice amongst the Pilots."

 The only disciplinary action taken by the Pilotage Committee was to caution Mr. Onion that a repetition of such an action on his part would be dealt with much more seriously.

The Pilots who worked diligently and kept to the letter of the pilotage working rules must have looked scornfully and with disdain at those who did not. They could never totally dissociate themselves from them as they were, after all, members of the same Pilot Service. Their patience must have been, on many occasions, sorely tried but even these stoical men had limits to their patience with their fellow pilots misdemeanours. This was clearly exemplified in March 1940 when the following letter was submitted to the Pilotage Committee from Mr. A Almond and Mr. W. Musker :

"We the undersigned, wish to make at once a complaint and a request . The request is, that we are moved from the working vicinity of a certain Pilot. While we wish it to be noted that we are willing

to carry out any service at any time, we cannot understand why a man is allowed to draw full pay, criticise all and sundry and then leave the work to those next to him on the rota. After the instance of this weekend, that is the subject of our complaint. We are of the opinion that he receives information as to the class of work in hand, goes off duty under the pretence of sickness till the large vessels are manned by other Pilots, then returns to the rota for some smaller vessel. The Committee have no doubt, more instances on record than this one, but this last instance forces us to refuse to work next to him on the Rota."

The circumstances of the case which had given rise to the complaint were that at 1515 hrs on the 8th March the Pilot in question reported that he was indisposed and would report when he felt better. He eventually reported for work again at 1615hrs on the 9th. March. In the meantime two large vessels, the "SAN AMROSIO" and "MAIHAR" both bound for Manchester entered the canal at Eastham and were attended by the next two Pilots on the Rota Messrs Almond and Musker. The indisposed Pilot took the next smaller vessel, the "WILLIAM BLUMER" on the morning of the 10th. Thus he had a free weekend. Attention was called to the fact that this Pilot had on many occasions over a considerable period been absent when required for duty. It was also understood the exact nature of his absence had not been discovered. Messrs Almond and Musker were refused permission to move from the working vicinity of the Pilot in question but the Pilotage Committee did resolve to keep a strict record of that Pilots absences from the Rota in the future and act accordingly. Their intentions were communicated to the Pilot.

Despite this warning the Pilot continued to ignore the decent and correct behaviour of a Rota Pilot. A letter dated 15th March 1944 from the secretary of the Pilots Association, stating that the continued repeated abuse by this Pilot of the working Rules, which it was understood had been brought to the notice of the Pilotage Committee had not abated. The secretary was instructed to ask the Pilotage Committee if they would take the necessary steps to deal with this matter again. The Chairman of Pilotage Committee suggested that the Pilot should be told his actions were the cause of some concern. It was also agreed that particulars should be taken out of all breaches of the present working Rules in connection with Pilots absenting themselves from duty for the opportunity of the Pilotage Committee to consider and debate this information. This directive was carried out but no conclusive results could be obtained by the Pilotage Committee. To the immense chagrin of many of his fellow Pilots he never changed his working system of abusing the Rotary System throughout his working life as a Manchester Pilot. A letter dated 6th April 1944 from Mr. N. Colvin, reporting what he considered to be a violation of the Pilotage Rotary System by a certain Pilot was placed before the Pilotage Committee. It stated that the S.S. " WESTMOUNT PARK" entered Eastham at 0550 hrs on the 27th April and had remained 15 minutes in the lock for Customs examination. The Pilot ordered to her apparently claimed that the vessel was unable to proceed and boarded a small coasting vessel which had entered the small lock at 0600hrs thus Mr. Colvin did not consider the Pilot's excuse of the delay to the "WESTMOUNT PARK". For customs examination to be a circumstance affecting her readiness to proceed. In addition to breaking Pilot's Working Rule 1(E) the Pilot was also guilty of a breach of the Pilotage Byelaw No. 20 which states " Pilots shall take their regular turn on the Rota for the Pilotage of vessels according to their respective classes." Mr. N. Colvin was a second class Pilot.

The interpretation this Pilot placed on the Pilotage Working Rules regarding the manning of a vessel whilst on tide duty was a blatant abuse of the Rota and he had clearly manipulated the working and wording of this rule to his own great advantage. A genuine delay to a vessel which prevented it from proceeding from Eastham Locks was never ever intended to be construed as a delay due to H.M. Customs being on board and all Pilots knew this. By exploiting this situation he avoided the larger and more exacting service between Eastham and Manchester - possibly two days piloting - in favour of a very much easier service of only some six hours.

The Pilot had been summoned to attend this Pilotage Committee to explain his actions and the Chairman informed the Pilot that the Pilotage Committee had come to the conclusion that Working Rule 1(E) was not capable of the interpretation he sought to put upon it, as he should be aware from his long experience. The Pilot was a senior First Class Pilot. The Pilot in his defence of his action stated that the ship had not been examined by the Customs in the river and the job was therefore likely to take a long time, necessitating the ship's detention at Eastham. It was on account of his long experience as a Pilot that he put the interpretation he did on the Working Rule. He also said that in taking the action he did, he was using his best endeavours to safeguard the interests of the service, and contended that if the vessel had been required to shift to the Lay-bye Dolphins in Eastham Basin, as she would have been if the lock had been required by a following vessel, it would have been clear that it was not his turn.

The Pilotage Committee ruled that the Pilot was at fault and had failed to comply with the rule. The hypothetical circumstances referred to by him would have been distinguishable from those in question for in that case a shifting Pilot would have been required. The Committee decided that the Rule in question was not reasonably capable of the interpretation the Pilot had put on it and that he should have piloted the "WESTMOUNT PARK". The Pilotage Committee's conclusions on this incident has forever remained a major mystery. The Committee's decision was that the Pilot in question must not in the future apply the rule in the way he did on this occasion, but they did not feel however that he acted as he did in order to flout the Working Rules or abuse the Rotary System. It is with the greatest restraint the Author refrains from any further observations on this incident.

The first incident of a Pilot refusing to take his proper turn on the Rota occurred in September 1944, when a Pilot objected to being ordered for duty on tide. It appeared that he and other Pilots were being unfairly forced on duty because of the premature and protracted absence from the rota of several Pilots who were attending a meeting at Ship Canal House. This particular meeting was very important to the future of all Pilots as it was the first meeting to discuss the post-war reorganisation of the Manchester Pilot Service.

The Pilot stated at the Pilotage Committee that he did not consider the Pilotage Committee or the Pilot Clerk (Mr. Bennion) had any right to allow Pilots to be off duty and the same remark applied to the Pilots Association. There was no provision in the Bye-Laws permitting such absence from duty. The Committee hastened to remind the Pilot that a similar request that three Pilots - one of whom was himself - had been allowed to attend a similar meeting and that there had been no objection from him or any other Pilot on that occasion. The Pilotage Committee felt the Pilot had various grievances. Quite apart from the abuse of the Rota, against other Pilots, notably those who attended the meeting, he had taken the action in an attempt to settle some personal difference. The Committee resolved that the Pilot had committed an offence under the Bye Laws for failing to take his regular turn on the rota. As a result of his action a second class Pilot had been required to attend tide, making two second class Pilots on station at Eastham, this was also a breach of the Working Rules. The Pilot was fined £2.00.

It should be noted that the refusal to attend on the rota was over the weekend, a particular period preferred by all Pilots to be free from duty. The Author has only detailed a few various methods that some Pilots used to manipulate or abuse the Rotary System. There were many more and during his 34 years in the Manchester Pilot Service these abuses continued unabated with little or no retribution from any quarter.

11.

RONALD DOUGLAS RICHARDSON 1930-1972

Every once in a while there emerges from the ranks in any profession a character who stands out above all others. It could be because of his expertise in his chosen profession, or his qualities of leadership, or his fearless approach to life, being able to laugh in the face of such adversities that ordinary people would have found insurmountable. Such a person in the Manchester Ship Canal Pilot Service, who encompassed all these qualities and attributes was **Ronald Douglas Richardson**.

He was born on the 20th August 1907, at Rock Ferry, in the Wirral the only son in a family of four. His father was a wine merchant of substantial means residing in the small village of Meols on the Wirral Peninsula in Cheshire. At the tender age of 7 years he was sent away to boarding school at Market Bosworth in Leicestershire about twelve miles west of the county town of Leicester, which to a young boy of 7 in 1914, must have seemed to be at the other end of the world. This bleak, austere and uncompromising institution - adjacent to that famous Bosworth Field of English History were the Royalists in 1485 fought and won a battle that secured the crown of England for Henry VII - was to be his home for the next ten years.

This strict disciplined environment so beloved of that era was to prove invaluable to him in his future life. On leaving school his father immediately indentured him as a Cadet apprentice with the

Ronal Douglas Richardson
1930 - 1972

City of Bombay
GRT 6569 L.464' B.59'
This was the vessel Mr. Richardson served his whole apprenticeship on from 1924 - 1928.

HELMSMANS INCOME TAX RETURNS FOR 1937-1938
MADE BY R.D.RICHARDSON

INCOME.	£316.14.2d.	£316.71p.
LESS EXPENSES.	82. 8.0d.	82.40p.
	£234.6.2d	£234.31p.
PROPERTY + ALLOWANCE	35. 0.0.	35.00.
TAXABLE INCOME.	£269. 6.2d.	£269.31p.
20% ALLOWANCE.	53.17.3d.	53.86p.
	£215. 8.11d.	£215.45p.
PERSONAL + WIFE .	180. 0. Od.	180.00p.
	£35. 8.11d.	£35.45p.
ONE CHILD ALLOWANCE.	60. 0. Od.	60.00p.
MISSED PAYING TAX BY.E	£24.11. 1d.	£24.55p.

TAX WAS PAYABLE AT 2/6d (12½p) IN THE POUND.

The income was from pooled earnings for a full tonnage helmsman.

The expenses £82.8.od (£82.40p) were calculated on the same basis as the Pilots allowances with a few differences and duly deducted before arriving at the taxable figure. The main difference being a Helmsman was only allowed to deduct 15% instead of 25%, from his gross earnings, that was allowed to pilots. A Chief Officer of a vessel of 9,000 Gr,Tons. trading to Manchester was earning £312 per year with none of the Tax allowances granted to Pilots and Helmsmen.

Hall Line Shipping Company, a subsidiary of Ellerman Lines of Liverpool. The only tenuous link with the sea the family had was his great grandfather, Captain Thornton Richardson, who had been a Master in sailing ships in the early 1800s.

On the 6th of September 1924 he sailed from Birkenhead aboard the "City of Bombay" for South Africa and all ports east - see list of voyages- thus commencing another four years of a life of loneliness and strict discipline that was so prevalent on ocean going vessels in the mid 1920s. To quote part of his indentures that he signed,

"The said Apprentice will faithfully and zealously serve his Master his executors, administrators and assigns, and obey his and their lawful commands and keep his and their secrets, nor do any damage nor consent to any damage thereto nor frequent any Taverns or Ale Houses unless on the owners business nor play any unlawful games or frequent houses of ill repute."

HALL LINE LIMITED.

List of Voyages made by RONALD DOUGLAS RICHARDSON - Apprentice.

S/S "CITY OF BOMBAY"

6- 9-24. Left Birkenhead for South African ports; thence to Calcutta; thence to New York; thence to Far East ports, returning to New York; thence to Australia; thence to South and East Africa; thence to U.K.

8- 2-26. Docked Liverpool. Length of voyage. 1year 4 months 2Days.

18- 3-26. Left Swansea for New York; thence to New Zealand and Australia; thence to South Africa; thence to Calcutta; thence to New York; thence to Far East ports; thence to United Kingdom.

3- 6-27. Docked London. Length of voyage 1 year 3 months 9 Days.

23- 6-27. Left Tyne via Continent for Far East ports; thence to New York; thence to New York; thence to Far East ports; thence to United Kingdom.

23- 7-28. Docked Hull. Length of voyage 1 year 1 month.

There was no leave entitlement but Apprentice Richardson was allowed one weeks leave between each voyage at his own expense.

FOR HALL LINE LIMITED

LIVERPOOL,

31st August, 1928.

105

ELLERMAN LINES LTD

HALL LINE, LIMITED.

REGULAR SERVICE OF STEAMERS BETWEEN LIVERPOOL, BOMBAY, KARACHI, MARMAGAO, MALABAR COAST & SOUTH AFRICA.

TELEGRAPHIC ADDRESS
"ALRAD" LIVERPOOL.

TELEPHONE: CENTRAL 3840.

7 ENCLOSURES

Tower Building

Liverpool 31ST August 19 28

WHEN REPLYING PLEASE QUOTE {OUR REFERENCE FP/SS
YOUR REFERENCE

Cadet R.D. Richardson,
    Stirling,
        Forest Road,
            MEOLS
                CHESHIRE.

Dear Sir,

As you have now completed your Apprenticeship in our Service, we beg to enclose herewith your Indentures, duly endorsed as required by the Board of Trade. Attached thereto you will also find your Wireless Watchers Certificate and list of voyages made by you during your Apprenticeship.

Cheque for £50 which was paid on your behalf by the Deputy Public Trustee, Manchester, has been forwarded today.

Further we beg to enclose your wages account which shows a balance in your favour of £4. 9. 4. for which amount we enclose cheque herewith, also your Health and Insurance cards.

We shall be glad to receive your acknowledgment of the various enclosures in due course, and we trust you will be successful in your examination for a second Mate's Certificate.

Yours faithfully,
HALL LINE LIMITED

Director.

Reading those conditions it did not leave an awful lot for a young man of 17 to do especially having spent the last ten years in boarding school. His wages of £1 per month for two years, £2 per month for the third year and £4 per month for his final year did not exactly open the gates to the flesh pots of the world, should he so desire.

On completion of his indentures he passed the examination for a certificate of competency as a Second Officer on October 1st 1928. continued to sail with the Ellerman Lines for a further 18 months as a Third officer, earning £11.10s. (£11.50) per month. On the 5th of April 1930 he became unemployed for the first and only time of his life, like so many men in his profession, when Ellerman Hall Line informed him that due to the slump in shipping they could no longer retain his services in any capacity aboard their vessels. Undaunted by this setback this extraordinary man knowing full well the futility of obtaining work on any vessel at that time - vessels were sailing out of Liverpool with a deck crew all holding Master Mariners certificates - he immediately applied for a position as a Helmsman on the Manchester Ship Canal and at the same time commenced his studies to obtain a certificate of competency as a Chief Officer.

He was successful in both his endeavours and on May 27th. 1930 he steered his first vessel the S.S. "URSA" gross ton 849 for Pilot L. Robinson for which he received the sum of £1.12.3d (£1.61) for his services from Eastham to Manchester. His first full month as a Helmsman was as follows.

June 1930

3rd.	"BRITA"	Reg. Ton. 704	Eastham to Manchester	£1.13.9 (£1.69)
5th.	"EILENEAU"	Reg. Ton. 767	Eastham to Manchester	£1.13.9 (£1.69)
7th	"EILENEAU"	Reg. Ton. 767	Manchester to Eastham	£1.13.9 (£1.69)
10th.	"BRIT.PLUCK."	Reg. Ton. 514	Eastham to Stanlow	£1.13.9 (£1.19)
12th.	"KONIGSAU"	Reg. Ton. 541	Manchester to Eastham	£1.13.9.(£1.69)
13th.	"INVERPOOL"	Reg. Ton. 286	Eastham to Barton	£1.10.3.(£1.51)
16th.	"MOSTYN"	Reg. Ton. 1004	Manchester to Eastham	£1.16.6.(£1.82)
18th.	"MAGNA"	Reg. Ton. 1013	Eastham to Manchester	£1.17.6.(£1.87)
21st.	"KATHOLM"	Reg. Ton. 876	Eastham to Elles.Port.	17.9. (88p)
22nd.	"MARTA SCHO"	Reg. Ton. 343	Manchester to Eastham	£1.13.9.(£1.69)
25th.	"ESTORIL"	Reg. Ton. 969	Manchester to Eastham	£1. 5.3. (£1.26)
27th.	"FLORENTINE"	Reg. Ton. 1031	Manchester to Eastham	£1. 140.(£1.70)

Total. £18.13.9 (£18.69)

Collection Exp. 19.4 (92p)

£17.14.5 (£17.72)

June 28th 1933
*Mr. R. (Ronnie) Richardson, Helmsman on board S.S. San Zeferino from
Eastham to Stanlow fee £2.10od (£2.50) in the background Pilot Mr. W. Milsom
and the Master in white cap top*

1938
*S.S. San Zeferino
GRT. 6430 L.420' B.55'*

No. 7694

United Kingdom of Great Britain and Northern Ireland.

7 AU 24

Certificate of Proficiency as a Watcher in Radiotelegraphy granted by the Postmaster General.

THIS IS TO CERTIFY that, under the provisions of the Merchant Shipping (Wireless Telegraphy) Act, 1919,

Mr. *Ronald Douglas Richardson*

has been examined in Radiotelegraphy and

(a) Is capable of receiving and understanding the Radiotelegraph Distress Signal and the Safety Signal.

(b) Has sufficient knowledge of the apparatus on which he will be required to keep watch, to know by means of a buzzer, or other simple test, that it is in a proper condition to receive signals.

It is also certified hereby that the holder has made a declaration that he will preserve the secrecy of correspondence.

Signature of Examining Officer *J. Cameron Ross*

The holder of this certificate is therefore authorised to perform the duties of a watcher on board a British ship.

Wo it esseine

for the Secretary, General Post Office, London.

7th August 1924 Date

Signature of Holder *R. D. Richardson*

Date of Birth *20th August 1907*

Place of Birth *Rock Ferry, Cheshire*

This Certificate should be carefully preserved. In case of loss through avoidable causes, a duplicate will only be issued on payment of a fee of not less than Five Shillings.

N.B.—This certificate may be endorsed, or withdrawn at the discretion of the Postmaster-General, in the case of misconduct or breach of the Regulations on the part of the holder. Unless so withdrawn it will continue to be valid, so long as the Regulations of the Radiotelegraph Convention concluded in London in 1912 remain in force.

K/515C.
(New 22572/20.)

(2019) Wt 58076/837 3,000 3/24 H & S? Gp 161

Exn. 16. A.   EXAMINATION

IN

FORM AND COLOUR VISION.

ISSUED BY THE
BOARD OF TRADE.   **CERTIFICATE OF EXAMINER.**

Name and Description of Candidate				Insert "Passed," "Failed," or "Not Examined." as the case may be	
Christian and Surname	Age	Birth Place	Rating	Test	Result of Examination
Ronald Douglas Richardson	20	Lg Eny	App	Old Test Letter	
				*New Test	Passed
Height	Colour of Eyes / Hair	Complexion	Personal Marks or Peculiarities (if any)	Lantern	Passed
5'8"	Blue Brown	Fair			

I hereby certify that the particulars contained above are correct.

Dated at ...Liverpool... this ...3rd... day of ...August... 1928.

Signature of Examiner ...G. W. Hart...

Signature of Candidate ...Ronald D. Richardson...

*Failure to pass the new test when the candidate has the option of passing, and passes the old test should not be recorded on this certificate.

7

These two examinations and the one overleaf had to be passed before a candidate was allowed to sit for a Second Mates certificate of competency. In later years a First Aid certificate was added to this list.

C.L.   No. 44577

CERTIFICATE OF EFFICIENCY AS

LIFEBOATMAN.

ISSUED BY THE
BOARD OF TRADE.

Name and Description of Candidate						
Name in Full			Year of Birth	HEIGHT ft. / ins.	No. of Dis. A.	
Ronald Douglas Richardson			1907	5 : 8		
Colour of Eyes / Hair	Complexion		Tattoo or other Distinguishing Marks			
BLUE BROWN	FAIR		- NONE -			

This is to Certify that the above-named seaman was examined on the ...6th... day of ...192... , by an examiner appointed by the Board of Trade, and that he proved to the satisfaction of the examiner that he has been trained in all the operations connected with launching lifeboats and the use of oars ; that he is acquainted with the practical handling of the boats themselves, and that he is capable of understanding and answering the orders given to lifeboat service.

Initials of Issuing Officer }

Office Date Stamp }

One of the Assistant Secretaries to the Board of Trade.

Signature of Seaman R.......

One would have thought being deprived of the close love and affection of his parents coupled with the total lack of a loving family atmosphere during his most informative years - 7 until 21 - that it would have turned him into a morose and bitter introvert for the rest of his life, but to his eternal credit he became the most ebullient and cheerful of persons who endeared himself to all who met him during his 42 years in the Manchester Pilot Service. It was this wonderful disposition that gave him an unprecedented and rapid rise from a small tonnage Helmsman to a full tonnage Helmsman in a remarkable seven months.

He took his first holiday in June 1931. The Helmsmen were working a non-pooling system of earnings in those days and averaging £25 per month. For the privilege of taking fourteen days holiday his earnings were reduced to just £9.4s.0d (£9.20). This system was also used if you could not attend work due to sickness. Many of the less fortunate Helmsmen could not afford to take holidays nor for that matter could they be ill too often. A pooling system for Helmsmen had commenced when he took his next leave in September 1932 when he married his beloved Margery Laurey Lloyd.

In September 1942 he sat and passed the examination to become a Second Class Pilot and four years later on the 19th September 1946 he passed the examination to become a First Class Pilot. In September 1945 he moved from the Wirral to a small farm called Oakley House, in Leeswood, Clwyd, North Wales. He always insisted it was never profitable and he eventually sold out in November 1985 and moved for the final time to Penwortham near Preston. This enabled him to be near to his daughter whom he idolised.

In 1950 he faced the greatest trial of his life when he was struck down with cancer that eventually necessitated major surgery, a colostomy. True to form he bore it with the same fortitude and resoluteness as all his adversities in life and with the same cheerfulness that was beyond the comprehension of ordinary mortals. Even in his last years when he had become diabetic, was forced to have a leg amputated because of circulatory disorders and was virtually bedridden he never lost that indomitable spirit that so typified this man.

Ronnie Rich - as he was always affectionately called - was unbiased in all he did for the Manchester Pilot Service. He was never influenced by mercenary or other unworthy motives so rife within the Manchester Ship Canal Pilot Service. During his years on various committees - as a Helmsman 1934 to 1942 and as a Pilots' representative at Pilotage Committee from 1948 until 1957- he always had that sincere wish to render himself more extensively serviceable to his fellow Pilots. The following is a tribute recorded in the minutes of the February Pilotage Committee in 1972.

"The Pilotage Committee heard officially about your retirement. and the Chairman Mr. Redford, recalled your days as a member of the Pilotage Committee and expressed his appreciation of the excellent record both in that capacity and in general as a member of the Manchester Ship Canal Pilot Service. We all had the greatest admiration for the efficient and good humoured way with which you have gone about your duties in what must have been very trying circumstances."

I think that tribute perfectly sums up the life of one of the Manchester Ship Canal Pilots Service most remarkable men. Ronald Douglas Richardson died, surrounded by his loving family on May 7th 1994 aged 87 years.

12.

THE GUINNESS BOATS

No history of the Manchester Ship Canal Pilots would be complete without a reference to the Arthur Guinness vessels for the inestimable part they contributed to the Pilot Service. A more loyal shipping company to the Pilot Service one would be hard pressed to find. During nearly 65 years of trading to the Canal whether it be to Runcorn or Manchester, through depressions and recessions, they never failed to employ a Pilot in the Ship Canal. Many a newly licensed second class pilot honed his piloting ability from the guidance and suggestions from such friendly Masters as Captains Davies, Meredith, Quirk, Ferris, Whitehead and others.

The vessels were also much in demand by the Helmsmens' Service as ideal vessels to train on during their probationary service of one month. Often as many as three or four helmsmen were on board from Eastham to Manchester. The officers and crew had to keep a careful check on victualling expenses but they were never found wanting when it came to feeding the extra Helmsmen, at times three meals during the day, such was their kindness and consideration.

The hospitality of the Masters at the completion of a passage, especially inward bound was second to none, even if they had had a stressful Irish Sea crossing, through fog or gales with little sleep, they never failed to ensure that the Pilot had a 'glass of stout and a drop of the hard stuff' - usually Black Bushmills- to warm the "cockles of yer heart" before going ashore.

The dear old 'Guinness'- with its open bridge, so dreaded by Pilots young and old, but in those dark, long, and bitterly cold winter passages to Manchester or Eastham Pilots comfort was never forgotten. A never-ending supply of hot buttered toast and steaming mugs of strong sweet tea that a spoon could stand up in, was constantly available. I hope this inclusion in the history of the Manchester Pilot Service will say in some small way, "Thank you Gentlemen"; for the many years we have enjoyed your hospitality and friendship. I personally considered it a great privilege to have shared the fraternity of the sea with you and the immense enjoyment of piloting your ships. All the photographs and information kindly supplied by Arthur Guinness, Son & Co, (Dublin) Ltd.

1931 - 1963

"S.S. Guinness"

Purpose built for Guinness by Ailsa Shipbuilding in Troon. This vessel opened the regular service to Manchester in 1936. An excellent vessel to Pilot in the Canal, good power and steering gear. Service speed 10 knots. Carrying capacity 156,000 gallons or 1¼ million pints.

1954 - 1974

M.S. "The Lady Gwendolene"

The first vessel ever to be designed specially to carry beer in transportable tanks instead of casks - all previous vessels carried the beer in casks. These tanks were made of stainless steel and aluminium, circular in shape, held 504 gallons or 4,032 pints. The holds - as well as that of the "Guinness" - were insulated and air conditioned. Service speed 11 knots. Guinness vessels were good time keepers excellently served by the Cross-Channel Gang formed from the workers at the brewery. One such Cross-Channel man waiting in Dublin in freezing fog for the delayed arrival of a Guinness vessel, who, after hours of disappointment, false hopes and incessant efforts to keep warm, explained with splendid determination "We'll unload this bloody ship whether she comes in or not".

1914 - 1953

S.S. "Clarecastle"

Another converted self trimming collier with similar modifications and speed.

1914 - 1959

S.S. "Carrowdore"

A converted self trimming collier bought from J. Kelly and Sons and fitted with a cooling plant in the holds. Service speeds 7 knots. In July 1941 she was struck by a 550lb bomb from a German aircraft about 15 miles off Dublin. Delivered at low level, the bomb ricochetted off the forecastle into the sea before exploding. The fin caught and held by the deck fittings is retained today at the Head Office in Dublin.

1961
M.S. "The Lady Patricia"
Converted to a bulk tanker in 1973. She carried 205,920 gallons or 1.647 million pints. Service speed 11 knots.

1976
M.S. "Miranda Guinness"
Purpose built tanker for carrying stout. The only vessel now sailing to the Canal. Service speed 15 knots. Carries 234,000 gallons or 1.87 million pints.

13.

"STATION DUTY" AT EASTHAM

One of the most soul destroying and abhorred of all the Pilotage duties was the 'Station Duty' at Eastham. The Rules and Regulations of the Rotary System 1920, stated that four Pilots must be in attendance at Eastham four hours before until four hours after high water at Liverpool and remain in attendance until such time a vessel arrives requiring his services. This could mean a Pilot would often be on 'Station Duty' for three, four, or more tides, a most tedious turn of duty. There were no catering facilities at Eastham Pilot Station in 1920 and this added to the mounting dissension to this onerous Pilotage duty. The first catering facilities at Eastham Pilot Station did not arrive until June 1954 and they were only available between 0800hrs and 1400hrs Monday to Friday.

From the very onset of the Rota System the Pilots failed in their responsibility to 'Station Duty', there were frequent instances of Pilots not being in attendance when on 'Station Duty'. This sorry situation came to the notice of the Pilotage Committee in November 1921 when a complaint was received from Mr. Bennion (Chief Pilot Clerk) which read as follows:

"For your information, I beg to report that Mr. W. Peacock (First Class Pilot) was ordered attend tide ('Station Duty') at Eastham on Sunday morning High Water Liverpool 0703 hrs and in consequence of his non attendance the S.S."NATUNA" which entered the Canal at 0915 hrs was detained at Eastham until 1045

hrs when the next Pilot on turn arrived to take the vessel to Manchester. The S.S. *"PATRICK"* entered the Canal at 1545 hrs and Mr. Peacock had still not arrived so that a second Pilot had to go ahead of him on the rota. The point I am making is that if Pilots are allowed to play fast and loose with the work it might conceivably happen that serious inconvenience would arise through the Pilots not being on Station to handle the traffic as required"

The Pilot in his reply was most non-committal and dismissive:

"Your letter asking for an explanation for not attending tide at Eastham, I have none except that I had been at Eastham two weekends from Saturday until Monday fourth on turn, I risked the third week-end being fifth on turn with the result you name"

For Mr. Peacock's dereliction of duty he was severely censured and warned of his future conduct and responsibility. This incident caused the Pilotage Committee to issue a circular letter on November 7th 1921 to all Pilots reminding them of their responsibility on 'Station Duty' and added two new resolutions.

1. Every Pilot when on 'Station Duty' must sign his name in the Duty Roster Book and the time of his arrival on duty.

2. Every Pilot must sign his name in the Duty Roster Book for as many tides he has had to attend on 'Station Duty' until such time a vessel arrives requiring his services.

On November 15th. Mr. A. Evans (Secretary to the Pilots Association) sent the following letter to the Pilotage Committee Chairman:

"Your circular letter addressed to the Pilots has been considered by the Association and I am instructed to make a protest against the new regulation sought to be laid down, requiring Pilots to sign on for duty at Eastham. I understand that the regulations hitherto in force have worked satisfactorily and that the cases in which Pilots have failed to attend for station duty at the proper time are extremely few. The two cases which occurred last week appear to be isolated cases and the Pilots generally feel strongly that any failure of duty on the part of one or two individuals is no ground for the introduction of a regulation which the Pilots consider both unnecessary and irksome."

The Chairman of Pilotage Committee promptly and succinctly replied.

"It will be necessary for the instruction laid down in the circular letter to be strictly adhered to by the Pilots. The decision was arrived at by the Committee after due consideration of the many complaints which have been before them from time to time in connection with the negligence of some Pilots in attending 'Station Duty' at Eastham. You have been misinformed when you state you understand the regulations hitherto enforced have worked satisfactorily and that the cases in which Pilots have failed to attend 'Station Duty' at the proper time are extremely rare."

Some Pilots chose to ignore the directive given in the new regulation and the following letter was sent to those of the Pilots who were the principal offenders.

"It has been reported that you are not carrying out the instructions contained in the new regulation set out in a circular letter forwarded to you. I am instructed to write to you stating that the Pilotage Committee took a serious view of your conduct and to warn you to strictly adhere to the same in future and not only to sign your name but also insert the time at which you arrive for duty. I would remind you that it is necessary for you to sign the Roster Book for the second or third tide or as many tides as you have to attend before taking a vessel as it has been reported that this is not being carried out."

There was reported a slight improvement in signing the Roster Book.

The 'Station Duty' situation was never satisfactorily resolved and animosity always prevailed. Pilots continued to fail to attend and/ or sign the Duty Roster Book - which was eventually withdrawn in about 1929. Even as late as 1941 the Pilot Clerk reported that the Eastham Pilot Station was on occasion left without any Pilots in attendance, especially at night. In 1940, 'Station Duty' now renamed 'Tide Duty' required only two Pilots to attend and as many more as may be required for known or expected arrival of vessels. The Pilots suggested and it was agreed at Pilotage Committee that Pilots should remain on 'Tide Duty' to a maximum of four tides instead of two as at present and that not more than one second class Pilot should be on 'Tide Duty'.

On February 18th 1956 at 1300 hrs, to the Pilots unreserved delight 'Tide Duty' at Eastham was abolished and the following resolution was passed :

1. When any vessel requiring the services of a Pilot is expected to dock on a tide at Eastham Lock the first Pilot on turn on the Rota shall be booked by the vessel which is expected to complete her passage in the Pilotage District in the shortest time, irrespective of the order in which she may dock and subject to the requisite notice.

2. Any vessel requiring the services of a Pilot docking at Eastham without giving prior or the requisite notice shall wait at Eastham until the arrival of the first Pilot on turn on the Rota.

3. If the vessel requires a Pilot for the purpose of shifting at Eastham then a Shifting Pilot shall perform that service.

4. If the vessel fails to dock on the tide the Pilots service shall be deemed to be completed at 4 hours ebb and a new Rota Pilot booked in the usual manner. If 4 hours ebb is at or after 1630 hrs then Rule 17(b) will apply.

5. These bookings for Pilots for vessel expected to dock on tide at Eastham Locks will be based on the estimated time of arrival of the vessel at Eastham Locks as supplied by the owner, Master or Agent only and will be told off by the Pilot Clerk at Eastham in conjunction with bookings for vessels from all other points in the Pilotage District.

This historic change in the Working Rules of the Pilot Service has always been regarded as one of the major changes ever to be made in the Pilot Service. It was due in no small measure to the foresight and persistence of one man, the then Pilots' representative Mr. R.T. Green, whose father and grand-father had also been Manchester Pilots and also Pilots' representatives in the past.

14.

A PILOTING FAMILY

From time immemorial and of all the Piloting families that served in the Manchester Ship Canal Pilot Service, none could compare in uniqueness or ability to that of the Warren family. They were unique insomuch that they were the first family of a father and two sons to hold Manchester Pilot Licences simultaneously and their ability as Pilots was unquestionable. The patriarch of this family was Mr. John H. Warren who was always affectionately referred to, and ever remembered as,"*Old Jack*". Born into a farming family at Bollington, Cheshire - between Whaley Bridge and Macclesfield on January 30th 1894 he was the last child in a family of five. He never took to the idyllic life of farming and in 1909 was indentured as an apprentice deck officer with Elders and Fyfes, sailing from the Port of Liverpool to the West Indies. By 1918 he had passed all the examinations necessary to obtain a Foreign Going Certificate of Competency as First Mate. During his years at sea he had sailed with various Shipping Companies viz; Court Line, Dalglishes, and Manchester Liners. It was the latter company that brought his attention to the Manchester Pilot Service. In 1919 he applied to join the Helmsmans' Service and on June 14th 1920 a vacancy arose and Mr. Warren started his career on the Ship Canal.

Mr. Warren who in 1916, was married in Altrincham, now had a family of one son and one daughter and he was living in Sale, Manchester. By 1930 his family had increased to seven children. Once again this historian has been fortunate that Mr. Warren had taken the time and the trouble to record his early working life and to preserve, for this age, an insight into the cost of living in those far off days. Mr. Warren's first vessel as a Helmsman was the S.S. "*Sea Victory*" of 1000 net reg tons from Eastham to Manchester for which he received the sum of £1.13s.9d. (£1.69p) for his services.

During the first full year as a Helmsman in 1921, Mr. Warren performed 154 separate steering services and received £381.9s.0d. (£381.45p), not an inconsiderable amount in those days. Had he remained at sea on Foreign going vessels as a Second Officer, with a superior certificate' his corresponding wage would have been £174 per annum. He had made a most fortuitous decision to leave the sea and become a Helmsman. Another notable plus in the fortunes of the Warren family in 1921 was the birth of the first of the two sons who would follow their father onto the Manchester Pilot Service. He was christened after his father John H and for obvious reasons, was always referred to as "*Young Jack*", even after his father had retired.

From the number of services performed by Mr. Warren and his high earnings in 1921, it was abundantly clear that he was never involved in any of the controversial issues of the day that were raging between Helmsmen and Pilots. Within three months of commencing steering the records show that he had been considered sufficiently capable of steering the S.S. "*Mercian*" of 4,066 net reg tons from Eastham to Manchester. The Pilot was Mr. W. Onion a very senior Pilot and one with very strong antagonistic feelings towards Helmsmen. Mr. Warren always conducted himself, during his Helmsmans service, in a quiet and highly capable manner that was to become his hallmark in all the years he held a Pilots Licence.

In August 1926, Mr. Warren was examined and passed for a second class licence. His family had steadily increased and on September 1st 1926 the second son who would follow his father into the Pilot Service was born and christened Michael. E. Warren. His sobriquet the "*Quiet Man*" came from the particular calm and unhurried manner in which he approached all things piloting, so very

1940 - 1975
Mr. J.H. Warren Jnr.

1950 - 1988
Mr. M.E. Warren

1920 - 1958
Mr. J.H. Warren Snr.

1931
S.S. "Ring"
GRT: 1336 L.264' B. 37'

Photos courtesy Mrs. W. Yates collection

reminiscent of his father. The year 1928 saw Mr. Warren purchase a magnificent six bedroom Victorian home named *"Walnut House"* on the Esplanade at New Ferry and moved his family into this most desirable and prestigious location of its day, commanding superb views across the River Mersey. This lovely home is still in the possession of the Warren Family.

On the 3rd February 1930 Mr. Warren was successfully examined for a First Class Licence. During all his years as a Pilot he only once had his pilotage services questioned and this proved totally erroneous. The occasion was as follows:

Mr. J.H. Warren attended the S.S *"Ring"* at Manchester Docks on February 2nd 1932 to Pilot her to Runcorn and that without any reason the Master, Captain Forslund, refused to accept his services. —No explanation or apology was tendered to Mr. Warren by the Master and Mr. Warren naturally felt very aggrieved by the incident, which occurred in the presence of persons who might very conceivably draw wrong conclusions detrimental to Mr. Warren's reputation. Mr. Warren requested the support of the Pilotage Committee in any attempt he may make to obtain redress, or alternatively whether some step might more appropriately be taken by the Pilotage Committee with a view to obtaining an apology from the Master and so avoiding a repetition of the occurrence. Mr. Warren explained to the Pilotage Committee that in July 1931 he piloted the *"Ring"* from Warrington Layby to Manchester. During the manouvering to leave the berth the vessel had bilged i.e. made contact with the Canal bank below water level. The Master fearing grave repercussions from either his owners or the Ship Canal re damage, the Master had made a complaint to him with regard to an alleged wrong helm movement by the Helmsman which had caused the vessel to bilge. Mr. Warren said he had disagreed with the Captain on this point quite strongly and because of his refusal to corroborate the Master's statements he thought this was the reason when he presented himself on board the *"Ring"* on the 2nd February the Master refused his services.

Being the man and the Pilot he was Mr. Warren would never have entertained for one moment any suggestion of proportioning any blame for an accident on to anyone but himself. Such were his high ideals and principles in piloting. Other Pilots, regrettably, often looked for a "scapegoat" as recorded in other chapters of this book. Captain Acraman asked what action must be taken when a Pilot is ordered and whose services are refused when he presents himself aboard ship. The Chairman replied Shipowners understood a Rotary System of Pilotage operated at Manchester and it must therefore be understood that having ordered a Pilot, the Master must either accept the services of the man on turn or Pilot the vessel himself.

The Pilotage Committee on hearing this report unanimously agreed that Mr. Warren's reputation and ability as a Pilot had been unfairly questioned and as they held Mr. Warren's piloting skills in such high regard they would seek suitable redress from the Master. Mr. Warren received a full apology from the Master, and was subsequently accepted by the Master to Pilot his vessel.

One of Mr. Warren's greatest attributes was his ability to listen and immediately distinguish fact from fiction in all discussions, arguments or negotiations relating to Pilotage. This enviable ability was recognised by the Pilots Association when they appointed him their senior Pilots' representative in 1936. When Mr. Warren retired from that position in November 1941, his distinguished contribution as a Pilots representative was accorded this unique tribute from the Chairman of Pilotage Committee, Mr. L. Roberts. The Chairman wished to place on record the unanimous appreciation of the Pilotage Committee of the valued assistance and high standard of professionalism as a negotiator Mr. Warren had shown during his term of office as the Senior Pilots' Representative. It has been a pleasure and a privilege to have sat on Committee with him. The remarks were endorsed by the whole of the Pilotage Committee. This was the very first time a Pilots' representative had been acknowledged for his work on Pilotage Committee.

In December 1937 Mr. Warren's skills were recognised by F.C. Stricks and Co., and they appointed him their Appropriated Pilot until July 1941, when due to wartime conditions most appropriations were cancelled. He was reappointed in 1946 and served them with great distinction until his premature retirement from the Pilot Service in 1958. Mr. Warren had been in ill health in the latter years of his piloting life and wisely he retired at the age of 62 years. In 1968 at the age of 72 years Mr. J.H. (*Old Jack*) Warren died and one of the "Greats" of the Manchester Ship Canal Pilot Service was no longer among us.

Fortunately, he had left two sons to carry on the piloting traditions of the Warren family. They were highly regarded just as their father was, having inherited many of his finest attributes. Their ship handling could not be faulted and their constant consideration for everyone who assisted them during their pilotage - Tug Boats, Helmsmen, Lock Masters etc. became legendary throughout the length of the Manchester Ship Canal.

Mr. J.H. (*Young Jack*) Warren entered the Helmsman's service in 1940 aged 19 years after having spent four years sea going. He passed his second class licence in 1953 and twelve months later successfully obtained his first class licence. Mr. Warren Jnr. made his own unique contribution to the chronicles of the history of the Pilot Service. On October 1st 1955 he was appointed much to the consternation of all the Senior Pilots, First Class Appropriated Pilot for the Prince Line (now known as Furness Ship Management) one of the most prestigious and sought after appropriations of its day. He was the youngest First Class Pilot, in age and in experience, to have ever acquired an appropriation. It shook the very foundations of the Pilot service old boys system and its reverberations were felt in every four ale bar on the Ship Canal.

In 1975 the enjoyment and satisfaction of piloting which was the very adrenaline of his life, was slowly fading, mainly due to the enormous changes in the working life and system of pilotage that had taken place over the years. In that year he decided to retire from the Pilot Service at the age of 54 years. Here again the Warrens made themselves unique and had set a precedent once again. Mr. Warren Jnr. became the youngest First Class Pilot to retire of his own volition in the history of the Manchester Pilot Service. Mr. Warren Jnr. remained a bachelor and is still living in the family residence of "*Walnut House*".

Mr. Michael E. Warren entered the Helmsman's service in 1950, after spending eight years at sea. At the age of 29 years he successfully attained a Second Class Licence in 1954 amongst a welter of criticism. The senior Pilots - who had steered for ten years or more - were of the opinion that having steered for only four years that person was totally incompetent to Pilot a vessel of any tonnage, even if he did hold a Pilot's licence. They described it as a recipe for disaster and could only see it leading to the total

A WEEKS HOUSEKEEPING IN NOVEMBER 1922

THE J.H.WARREN FAMILY

Thursday 2nd.

Little Womens Green Grocery	3s.3d.	*(16p)*
3 Loaves	7½d.	*(3½p)*
Cakes.	1s.7d.	*(7½p)*
Beef. 3Lbs.	1s.2d.	*(6p)*
Herrings. (6)	7d.	*(3p)*
Scots Oats 5Lbs.	1s.4d.	*(6p)*
2 Gas Mantles.	1s.3d.	*(6p)*
Burner and set.	10½d	*(4p)*
Coal (6 Bags)	£1 0s. 0.	
Total	£1.10s.8d.	(£1.53p)

Friday 3rd.

Fresh fruit.	1s.2d.	*(6p)*
Butter 2 lbs.	7½d.	*(3½p)*
Nestles Milk and Biscuits.	2s.2½d.	*(11p)*
Total	4s0d.	(20p)

Saturday 4th.

Little Womens Green Grocery	2s.2d.	*(11p)*
Washing and Insurances.	2s.9d.	*(14p)*
Pork	7s.8d,	*(44p)*
Apples cooking/eating	1s.2d.	*(6p)*
Custard Powder.	1s.3½d.	*(6p)*
Bread.	7½d.	*(3½p)*
John Williams Tea Sugar etc.	9s.5d.	*(47p)*
Sponge Cake.	1s.2d.	*(6p)*
Kiddies Club.	3s.6d.	*(17½p)*
Total	£1.9s.9d.	(£1.48p)

Monday 5th.

Cakes and twists.	1s.4;d.	*(6p)*
Coal (3 Bags)	10s.0d.	*(50p)*
Eggs. (2 Dozen)	1s.0d.	*(5p)*
Total	12s.4½d	(62p)

Tuesday 6th.

Black Puddings.	8d.	*(3½p)*
Bacon (2Lbs)	1s.9d.	*(9p)*
Total	2s.5d.	(12p)

Wednesday 7th.

Fish and Apples.	1s.11d.	*(10p)*
Chops	1s.2d.	*(6p)*
Cakes.	1s.0d.	*(5p)*
Coal (2 Bags)	5s.8d.	*(28p)*
Tomatoes and Kippers	1s.6½d.	*(9p)*
Pram Tyres (?)	6s.10d.	*(39p)*
Gas Meter	2s.0d.	*(10p)*
Total.	£1.0s.1½d	(£1.01p)

Total for week

£4.0s.4d. (£4.02p)

By kind permission of the Warren Family

destruction of the Manchester Ship Canal along with the Docks, the locks and to any vessel who had the effrontery to employ one of these *"four year wonders"*, as they were so contemptuously referred to by their so called senior colleagues and mentors.

They shared their views with all and sundry especially the Masters of vessels who looked upon this new breed of Pilots with grave suspicion and sometimes in abject terror. Fortunately the Masters soon began to realise and appreciate - despite the tales of woe from the senior Pilots- the consummate ease with which these new Pilots handled their vessels often far exceeding the skill of many of the older Pilots. Mr. M. Warren obtained his First Class Licence in 1956 and immediately became a member of that elite group of six Pilots who became First Class Pilots in a record time of six years starting from the commencement as a Helmsman. It had never been achieved before nor was it ever achieved again. Those six Pilots were indeed unique. Mr. Michael. E. (*The Quiet Man*) Warren is married with two children and a grandchild. He retired in 1988 and is living happily, enjoying the fruits of his piloting years.

1932

H.M.S. "Wallace"

Lead vessel of flotilla's first visit to Manchester. Pilot Mr. J.H. Warren seen left on top open bridge whilst passing through Bowaters Cutting.

By kind permission of the Warren Family.

15.

OF THIS AND THAT: ALIEN PILOTAGE

The following correspondence was exchanged between the Board of Trade (Harbour Department) and the Manchester Ship Canal Company on April 27th 1905.

" I am directed by the Board of Trade to request that you will favour the Board at your earliest convenience with the particulars specified below relating to Pilotage within your jurisdiction.

1) How many Pilotage Certificates (if any) held by Foreign subjects were in force on the 31st March 1905 and in respect of what vessels.?

2) What is the nationality of each of such subjects?

3) In how many cases have applications for the grant or renewal of certificates to Foreign Subjects been refused or withheld?"

The letter was signed by Mr. Hyde Jekyll, a name so ominous that it could not help but strike fear into any enquiries into alien pilotage!

The Manchester Ship Canal replied that regarding questions one and three no pilotage certificates are held by foreign subjects , and in answer to question three, no application has ever been received from any Foreign subject for a Pilotage Certificate on the Ship Canal. Could these enquiries be construed as a form of racism?

On April 22nd 1919 another letter, bearing the overtones of racial discrimination, was received from the Board of Trade which read:

" I am directed by the Board of Trade to state for the information of the Pilotage authority that it has been suggested by the Lord Commissioners of the Admiralty that it would be desirable in the

Licensing of Pilots to apply the rule established by the recent regulation under the Defence of the Realm Act under which the Master of a British vessel must be British born and the son of British subjects. The Board of Trade concur in this suggestion and will be glad to learn that the Pilotage Authority will adopt this rule for the licensing of all Pilots under your jurisdiction. The regulation referred to was as follows.

"37D A person shall not unless specially authorised for the time being by the Admiralty or Board of Trade act in the capacity of Master or person in charge of a British Merchant vessel unless he is a natural born British Subject and the son of parents both of whom were at the time of his birth either natural born British subjects or British subjects by naturalisation, and if any person acts in contravention of this regulation he shall be guilty of a summary offence against these regulations"

This matter was considered by the Pilotage Committee and it was decided that the recent Regulation under the defence of the Realm Act as quoted above should be strictly adhered to by the Committee when issuing future licences and certificates.

AGE FOR LICENSING PILOTS

In 1907 the Manchester Ship Canal Company passed the following resolution;

"That no application for a Manchester Ship Canal Licence shall be entertained from persons under 24 or over 45 years of age."

A NICE COSY NICHE

The Chairman of Pilotage Committee reported in December 1914 that Mr. A. Postlethwaite (First Class Pilot) had been appointed and was now acting as Officer in charge of the German vessel *"Hornsund"* berthed in Manchester Docks. Pilotage work on the Canal had become very limited owing to numerous steamship services being discontinued on account of the war and in view of the exceptional circumstances now existing the Committee approved

"OK Pilot, so you have proved a Manchester Liner will steer on wet grass, so lets get back into the canal". - Tug Captains quote!

1954
Dining Saloon "Manchester Regiment". The food served on these vessels was by far the best in the United Kingdom including Cunard.

the Chairman's action. This same Pilot, who lived in Old Trafford, Manchester had been credited walking along the Ship Canal Banks from Eastham to Manchester and vice-versa on a number of occasions prior to 1914, thus saving his travelling expenses.

PILOTS AND THE MILITARY SERVICE (No 2) ACT 1918

In June 1918 Lord Haig and his donkey like generals had led the young lions of Great Britain and her Commonwealth almost to extinction on the fields of slaughter called Flanders. Under the above act the military age had been raised to include men between the ages of 41 and 51. In consequence two Pilots Mr. G. Davidson (aged 50) and Mr. G. Cartwright (aged 48) had been brought within the scope of the Act. The Canal Company were making application to the Manchester Port Labour Committee for exemption certificates in favour of the Pilots in question in order that their services could be retained. The application proved successful.

OLD PILOTS NEVER DIE

At the Pilotage Committee in April 1927, the Chairman (Mr. Browning) referred to the report from the Pilotage Clerk that Mr. E. Hankinson (First Class Pilot) had been absent through sickness during the whole month of March and the doctor's note stated:

"Mr. Hankinson has not recovered from the after effects of his attack of influenza and is still unfit for duty. He is still subject to attacks of giddiness and is yet still somewhat debilitated".

The Chairman said that in view of the reports which he had received from the Canal Superintendents as to Mr. Hankinson's physical condition and taking into account his advanced age (he was believed to be in excess of 75 years) he was strongly of the opinion that the time had arrived when the Committee should say that Mr. Hankinson was physically unfit to carry on the duties of a First Class Pilot on the Ship Canal. The Pilot's representatives said that Mr. Hankinson's condition had been discussed at the Pilot Association meeting but they had decided not to make any suggestions and would leave his case for the Pilotage Committee to deal with at their discretion. Mr. Bowen (shipowners representative) also agreed a definite step should be taken in this matter especially as the Pilot had reached the age when he should be debarred from acting as a Pilot coupled with his physical condition.

Reference was made to No. 6 and 7 of the Pilotage Byelaws. Duration and Renewal of Licences.

"6. The Pilotage Authority may at any time suspend or refuse to renew a licence if they find that the holder is suffering from any physical infirmity or any defect of hearing or sight, rendering him unfitted to carry out the duties of a Pilot.

7. The Pilotage Authority may refuse to renew a licence at any time after the holder has attained the age of 65 years."

Mr. Bowen pressed for the matter to be dealt with forthwith and after considerable discussion it was unanimously resolved:

That in view of the advanced age of Mr. E. Hankinson and his present physical disability, his licence be suspended until further notice and that he must report to the Chairman of Pilotage Committee should he sufficiently recover from his present illness to consider himself fit again to follow his employment.

The Pilot's Representatives said they appreciated the Pilotage Committee's time in considering this matter so fully and indicated they had no doubt that the Pilots would consider favourably the continuance of the Sickness Payment for a period not exceeding six months. The following letter dated April 17th from Mr. Hankinson was read to the Pilotage Committee:

" With reference to my suspension I wish to keep up my contribution to the Pilot Benefit Fund if this is in order. I am sorry I am not fit for work yet, I am still under the Doctor and my head still gets dizzy but it is getting better slowly. I will inform you immediately I am fit to return to Piloting Duties."

Mr. Hankinson was still very determined to return to work undaunted by his age or physical condition. Unfortunately his health did not improve sufficiently for him to take up his piloting duties again and he retired on August 30th 1927. He died the following year.

AGE OF RETIREMENT

In September 1927 the Manchester Steamship Owners Association informed the Pilotage Committee thus:

"At the monthly meeting of the Association I was instructed to inform you that a resolution was unanimously passed to the effect that in the opinion of this Association the time has arrived when the Pilotage Authority of the Port of Manchester should seriously consider the advisability of exercising their power under Byelaw 7, to retire pilots on attaining the age of 65 years."

It was not until 1930 that this directive was acted upon when all Pilots were retired on attaining 65 years of age if their birthday fell before the commencement of the pilotage year on September 1st, otherwise they would be allowed to serve an additional year. It was quite amazing how many Pilots chose to serve another year knowing full well that their life expectancy in retirement, from previous records, was extremely short.

SOUNDING OF SHIPS SIRENS/WHISTLES IN THE WARRINGTON DISTRICT

The Chairman of Pilotage Committee stated that a leader had appeared in the Warrington Guardian on Saturday the 16th August 1931, to the effect that complaints had been made of the noise made by the sounding of sirens or whistles on vessels in that district. The leader contended that the complaints were fully justified on the ground that the use of the sirens/whistles was largely unnecessary, especially at night. The Chairman said that there were many small vessels not in charge of Pilots navigating the Canal and possibly they were to blame to some extent. It might be, however, that Pilots could prevent unnecessary sounding of sirens/whistles and he hoped the Pilots' Representatives would mention the matter to their fellow Pilots with a view to obviating as far as practicable any cause for complaint. One can only presume it would be far more suitable for the pilot of a vessel to collide with the swingbridge in endeavouring to awake the bridge master in order for him to operate the controls to open the bridge and allow his vessel to pass through rather than disturb the sleep of the worthy citizens of Warrington by using the

The Schedule hereinbefore referred to :-

SCHEDULE OF SIGNALS.

I. SOUND SIGNALS.

The following signals shall be given :—

    (i) by steam vessels, on the whistle or siren ;
    (ii) by other vessels, on the foghorn.

Number of Blasts.	Meaning of Signal.

1. One Long. ... ...
(When inward bound)
 	
One Long and One Short. ...
(When outward bound)
	To call attention generally, *e.g.*, when
	  i. Approaching or overtaking another vessel in the Canal.
	 ii. Approaching or passing a lock.
	iii. Approaching a swing bridge which is required to be opened.
	 iv. Approaching a bend in the Canal.
	  v. Navigating the Canal in fog, mist, or falling snow.

2. Two Long and One Short. ...	(To vessel overtaking in the Canal)—" Am in a position to be passed."
3. One Long and Two Short. ...	(To stern tug)—" Pull on port quarter."
4. One Long and Three Short. ...	(To stern tug)—" Pull on starboard quarter."
5. One Short.	(To forward tug)—" Ready, go ahead." (To stern tug)—" Cancel last Signal."
6. Three Short.	(To stern tug)—" Go astern."
7. Four Short.	(*a*) (To tugs)— " Hold ship in position." (*b*) " Am holding ship in position."
8. Succession of Short Blasts. ...	" Vessel temporarily out of control."

9. (By Tugs at Ellesmere Port)—
One Long and One Short. ...
    followed by :
One Long and One Short. ...
One Very Long (8 to 10
    seconds duration). ...
	" About to round-up craft."
	
	" Have completed rounding-up of craft."

10. One Long, One Short and One Long.	(To stern tug)—" Am about to pass another vessel."

The following signals shall be given by means of mouth whistle :—

Number of Blasts.	Meaning of Signal.
11. One Long and Two Short. ...	(To forward tug)—" Pull on port bow."
12. One Long and Three Short. ...	(To forward tug)—" Pull on starboard bow."
13. One Short.	(To forward tug)—" Cancel last signal."

vessels sirens or whistles. This complaint has always been a bone of contention between vessels and residents living close to the canal and always will be.

CHOICE/APPROPRIATED PILOT FEES

The following letter was read to the Pilotage Committee in November 1931 from Messers Herbert Watson and Company:-

"We beg to advise you that we have received an instruction from the United States Shipping Board, London, that they desire to discontinue their arrangements with the Manchester Ship Canal Company in respect to the Appropriated Pilots Messers Lloyd and Onion, for the three lines viz:- ORIOLE, DIXIE and MOBILE; OCEANIC, and desire to terminate such arrangement on 31st December 1931. Whilst fully appreciating the value of the appropriated Pilots they are of the opinion that the service rendered does not warrant such a high retaining fee. According to our understanding, the retainer of £100 per Pilot (set in 1895) is not governed by the Pilotage Bye-laws and therefore is a matter which is controlled by the pilots themselves. AUTHORS NOTE:- This statement was not strictly correct, the amount of the APPROPRIATED FEE was established in 1895, as a result of discussions between the Pilots and the Pilotage Authority who limited the fee to a maximum of £100.

We presume, however, that your committee do have a certain amount of control in regard to sanctioning or otherwise the engagement of appropriated Pilots and therefore we are in order in submitting this notice to your committee. We shall be glad if you will kindly pass on to the proper quarter a suggestion we have to make viz:- that Messers Lloyd and Onion continue the service of Appropriate Pilots of the three lines at a reduced fee of £50 per annum. If they agree to this, we can persuade our Principals to continue their services as Appropriated Pilots"

It was the feeling of all Steamship Companies that some reduction should be made in the appropriation fee. This particular case brought about many applications for a reduction of appropriation fees.

The Pilots refused to accept a reduction in their appropriation fees and consequently Messrs Lloyd's and Onion's services as Appropriated Pilots were discontinued.

PROMOTION OF SECOND CLASS PILOTS

On the 8th May 1934 Mr. C. G. Killender (Second Class Pilot) ,having served the requisite period to qualify for a First Class Pilot's Licence, applied for permission to sit for the examination to be passed as a First Class Pilot.

The Secretary of the Pilots Association stated that as Mr. Killender's application had the necessary support of two thirds of the Pilots, his promotion should not entail any increase in the present number of First Class Pilots! It was agreed that Mr. Killender be allowed to take the examination, but consideration of the question as to when a First Class Licence should be granted, if he satisfied the examiners, was deferred until a future date. The Senior Pilots, as ever, were still keeping a tight hold of the monetary reins.

DRAFT OF VESSELS ENTERING THE CANAL AT EASTHAM

The vessel S.S.*"Comet"* entered the Ship Canal on May 25th 1934 with 13,000 tons of motor spirit bound for Stanlow Oil Refinery and her draft was 29 feet forward and 29 feet 3 inches aft. It was necessary for this vessel to be lightened (part discharged) at Eastham before she could proceed. In consequence of communications passed between the Mersey Docks and Harbour Board and the Manchester Ship Canal Port Authority the following notice was issued to all Mersey Pilots:

"A Pilot must not take a vessel into the Eastham Channel of a greater draft of water than 28 feet 6 inches until he is handed a written authority to do so signed by the Harbour Master of the Manchester Ship Canal or by his representative at Liverpool. This ruling still stands."

A MERRY-GO-ROUND

It had been the practice since 1931 to charge the service of piloting a vessel - mainly Prince Line vessels - to Partington Basin and back to Manchester after bunkering if within 24 hours, as a "Point to Point " service with half initial fee plus mileage plus detention. In 1939 a claim was made for two separate services i.e. Manchester to Partington and Partington to Manchester charging two half initial fees, plus mileage, plus swinging fee but no detention charges. It was agreed that in future two ship services mileage and swinging fee would be charged. The bunkering usually took more than $4^1/_2$ hours to complete, therefore two Pilots were required and this obviated the need of a Pilot to be aboard such a vessel for nearly 12 hours or more.

WAR PENSIONS AND DETENTION ALLOWANCES (MERCANTILE MARINE) SCHEME 1939

There appeared to be some doubt as to the extent the above scheme could be applied, because it might be contended that the Manchester Pilots were not on board a vessel for the purpose of taking her or assisting to take her into or out of Port in the British Islands within the meaning of Section 4 of the governing Act. Reference was made to the fact that Merchant Navy Badges had not been issued to the Manchester Pilots although some of them felt they were entitled to wear them. The Manchester Pilots never ventured outside the safety of their Lock Gates during the war and therefore were excluded from any of the War Benefits under the Mercantile Marine Scheme 1939.

BOBS LANE FERRY, CADISHEAD DISASTER

APRIL 14th 1970

A REPORT ON THE CORONER'S INQUEST HELD AT THE ECCLES TOWN HALL ON THE 25TH AND 26TH JUNE, 1970.

In his summary of the evidence heard at the inquest the Coroner, Mr. Leonard Gorodkin commented as follows :

1)   It was known that the six men died as a direct consequence

of the fire on the Manchester Ship Canal in the vicinity of the Bobs Lane Ferry.

2) That the material which caused the fire was almost certainly that same material which had overflowed from the petroleum barge "*Tacoma*" berthed at No. 4 berth Partington, some $2^1/_2$ to 3 hours earlier.

3) That is was not known what had ignited the material, but that he hoped that this would not prevent a verdict being reached.

4) That "papers" in this case have been sent to the Director of Public Prosecutions and he considers there is insufficient evidence to bring manslaughter charges against any person.

5) That no person involved in the loading of the "*Tacoma*" could be said to have been recklessly negligent and that this being so a manslaughter verdict was out of the question. Verdicts of death by misadventure were then returned on all six deceased.

The Coroner then added:

"Throughout this inquest we have heard a most horrifying story and although a deep tragedy has occurred it could have been far worse - a local disaster, with shore installations and habitations involved. It is to be hoped that a serious lesson will have been learned: that safety regulations are not just pieces of paper but are meant to be complied with to save life and property. Where human beings are concerned mistakes can happen but it is to be hoped that in the future if such a spillage occurs, however large or small and whatever the consequence to the people involved, they will not, as in this case remain silent but will bring it to the notice of the Authorities".

I feel that having reported as above I could well let the matter rest were it not for the fact that the operations of "*Tacoma*" in particular and Low Flash Petroleum carrying vessels in general have been and indeed still are a matter of real concern to the Pilot service, special emphasis being put on the safety in navigation aspect. It is a common belief among Pilots that the most likely way that inflammable material can find its way into the Canal in any significant quantity is as the direct consequence of a navigational accident. The Authority have been made well aware of the Pilots' views on the subject and are agreed that a better system of traffic guidance is desirable for the future.

Regretfully however no mutually satisfactory system has been agreed for the present or near future, although negotiations have been promised. The matter of safety in navigation being for the time being still left to the individual discretion of Duty Harbour Master, Ship Master and or Pilot where employed.

The Pilots have been consistently advised that their fears with regard to the dangers involved in the handling and carriage of inflammable materials are groundless and in particular that the normal safety precautions are adequate to meet all the demands ever likely to be made on them. In other words the Bobs Lane Ferry tragedy could never happen! *It did though!* and consequently I must offer the following comments.

(i)   That the death of six men is proof enough that the danger is real and that the Pilots' fears are not groundless.

(ii)   That the evidence produced at the inquest proves that the normal safety precautions are not always adequate to the needs and certainly not when allied to admitted human failings.

(iii)   That the short comings of the Mate and 2nd Engineer of the *"Tacoma"* so patently revealed by the enquiry must permit of the gravest doubt being entertained as to the ability of that vessel to be safely navigated at all times as required by Bye Laws and etc. Further even than this, one can now feel entitled to enquire "is any such vessel being safely navigated when those in charge lack the extensive specialised local knowledge that is required to cope properly with the traffic problems frequently arising and a full appreciation of all the Regulations?

(iv)   That we as Pilots and indeed as responsible members of society should both heed the Coroner's warning and also have the courage of our own expressed convictions and insist that the Authority agree with us the conditions necessary for maximum safety in the navigation of such vessels in the Canal.

(v) That not even our own self-interest must be allowed to interfere with the establishment of such a safe system.

In conclusion may I say that having sat through the whole of the Inquest and having heard all the evidence, I personally shall need a terrible amount of convincing that there is no need to worry about the ability of the "system" to operate safely and it will certainly be my intention to do my bit in the future.

(signed)

ROBERT S. BOYLES

YOU JUST HAVE TO SMILE

On a more lighter note, the United States Line complained forcibly about the candle power of the few leading lights just after the end of the war - 1939 to 1945. In reply to this complaint of the lack of intensity of light emanating from these globes the Manchester Ship Canal Engineers Department - cut to the quick at any disparaging remarks regarding their beloved lighting system - quickly replied that a marked improvement had been made in the strength of the lighting by introducing a wider wick and a change from standard paraffin oil to the new and highly improved Esso Blue Paraffin. I wonder how that went down at head office in New York ?

1924

An Ellermen Line Vessel leaving the Sheer Legs (Crane Berth) after having the top part of the funnel replaced. In those days the majority of Coal Burning Vessels were "Natural Draft" that necessitated a very tall funnel for the efficient burning of the coal in the boiler furnaces. In order for these vesels to proceed to Manchester and avoid hitting the many overhead railway and road bridges. That traversed the canal, the top half of the funnels had to be removed, hence the crane at Eastham. The recommended height for masts/funnels was 70' above the water line.

Photo courtesy of Mrs W. Yates collection.

16.

PILOTAGE TARIFF 1919-1920

When the final stages in the negotiations for the new pilotage system of working was being reached, a new Pilotage Tariff which the Pilots had always insisted should be inextricably linked with any new working system was being formulated. At a meeting of the Pilotage Committee held on 7th July 1919, the Pilot's representatives presented the following suggestions for an increase in the Pilotage Tariff.

1)   An initial fee shall be paid for each vessel when requiring pilotage service entering or leaving the Canal according to the nett registered tonnage:-

1 to 300 tons:	£1. 0. 0.
300 to 600 tons:	£2. 0. 0.
600 to 1200 tons:	£3. 0. 0.
1200 to 2000 tons:	£4. 0. 0.
2000 to 3000 tons:	£5. 0. 0.

and £1 per 1000 tons or portion of 1000 tons and in addition ls.6d (7$^1/_2$p) a mile for the distance navigated. Vessels in ballast shall pay the full initial fee but only half the mileage fee. Increases in the fees for moving vessels within the Dock area and within the Canal limits, detention fees, and Eastham shifting rates were also included in this manifesto. A number of very important and much desired additions in the administration of the Pilot service were also presented to that Pilotage Committee meeting. The most important

being:
1) All oil tankers to be treated as loaded ships.
2) All Pilots' travelling expenses to be paid.
3) Pilots' earnings to be divided amongst the Pilots at the rate of
    a. $^1/_3$ share to each First Class Pilot.
    b. $^3/_4$ share to each Second Class Pilot.
4) A Superannuation Scheme to be inaugurated as soon as possible and to be managed by the Pilots Association.
5) The retiring age of a Pilot is to be not less than 60 years of age.
6) All Pilots who retire at the age of 65 years to be entitled to receive not less than £52 per annum. Pilots who retire before that age owing to sickness or accident to be treated as may be decided by the Committee of the Pilots Association who manage the fund.
7) Any Pilots unable to work through sickness to receive one months full pay and then half pay for six months and after that to be dealt with by the Superannuation Committee.
8) The penalty for missing a turn through any fault of the Pilot shall be a fine of 10s. 0d. (50p) for the first offence and £1 for a second offence or any subsequent offence and the Pilot to make up that turn missed.
9) The responsibility for the arrangements of the pilotage shall rest with some official chosen by the Pilots Association and approved by the Canal Company.

The Chairman of the Pilotage Committee, Mr. Latimer, stated he had discussed the whole scheme with the Pilots representatives and Mr. Beckett (secretary of the Pilots Association) and had reported same to the Directors of the Manchester Ship Canal Company who now had the subject under consideration. In order that a co-ordination of the new working system and the tariff could be created, he would arrange further meetings with the Pilots representatives as soon as possible to iron out any misunderstandings or objections. Between July and September, four meetings were held between deputations of the Pilots and the Pilotage Committee, to specifically discuss this very contentious subject of a new tariff and administration changes, without any apparent agreement being reached between the two parties. At the Pilotage Committee meeting in September 1919 the Chairman was requested to prepare a statement showing the earnings of the pilots for the months of May and August of that year on the tariff suggestedby the Pilots and on a tariff which he would prepare. On October 14th 1919 at the Pilotage Committee Mr. Latimer reported he had met a deputation of Pilots on October 9th and the new tariffs proposed by the pilots and his proposals had been fully discussed.

Following that meeting a further communication had been sent to Mr. Beckett which set out the basis of the proposed new scheme as regards remuneration. The letter read as follows:-

"Dear Sir,

I am now able to give you additional particulars so that you may have before you at your next meeting with the Pilots the figures which were referred to in our discussions. This statement gives you particulars of the present initial fees with the War Bonus included the rates proposed by the Pilots Committee and the rates proposed by the Company".

There followed a very comprehensive calculation, covering three pages, of Pilotage earnings for the forthcoming 12 months encompassing all the relevant charges that would be made. e.g. Collection charges, Pilot Clerks' salary, upkeep and maintenance of Pilot Stations and Pilots travelling expenses. The letter ended:

" It will be clearly seen that at the present tariff the earnings for May were £867 and August £1,087. On the basis of my figures the earnings would have to be £1,000 per month, against which on the basis of May the earnings at the proposals of the Pilots would be £1,114 and for August £1,389. compared with the earnings at the Company's proposals of £998 and £1,253 for the respective months

Yours faithfully

E. Latimer."

The Chairman now suggested to the Pilots' representatives that if the new scheme was to be put into force as desired on November 1st it was essential that the Pilots should have a meeting at the earliest possible moment to discuss the proposed tariff changes put forward by him. On October 20th the following letter was received by Mr. Latimer from Mr. Beckett.

"Dear Sir,

At a General meeting of the Pilots Association held on October 17th, by a majority, they agreed to the tariff put forward by you, subject to the increases for other services. They expect the new tariff and byelaws to be implemented as soon as possible. I would also like to know your arrangements regarding choice of appropriated Pilots about which the Association is very firm. In this connection the Association insist that Shipowners requiring appropriated Pilots should guarantee to the fund a sum equal to a First Class Pilot.

Yours faithfully

R.Beckett"

The relative Bye-Law was duly published and on December 1st. 1919 along with the new Rotary System it came into force. The new tariff for vessels entering or leaving the Canal loaded or in ballast the following initial fees were to be charged, according to net. reg. tonnage.

Up to 300 tons	£0.17.6.	(87p)
Over 300 tons up to 600 tons	£1.15.0.	(£1.75)
Over 600 tons up to 1200 tons	£2.12.6.	(£2.62)
Over 1200 tons up to 2000 tons	£3.10.0.	(£3.50)
Over 2000 tons up to 3000 tons	£4. 0.0.	(£4.00)
Over 3000 tons up to 4000 tons	£4.10.0.	(£4.50)
Over 4000 tons up to 5000 tons	£5. 0.0.	(£5.00)
Over 5000 tons up to 6000 tons	£5.10.0.	(£5.50)
Over 6000 tons up to 7000 tons	£6. 0.0.	(£6.00)
All over 7000 tons.	£6.10.0.	(£6.50)

and in addition thereto a sum at the rate of ls.6d. (7^1/$_2$p) per mile or portion of a mile for the distance navigated when loaded and 9d (3p) per mile or portion of a mile when in ballast.

All the other fees for extra services had also been increased in line with the Pilots' demands. Although the rotary and pooling system commenced on December 1st a lot still had to be legislated for, to ensure the smooth running and financial stability of the Pilot Service. It was quickly perceived that the utmost urgency should be given to implementing a Sick Pay Allowance. On February 2nd. 1920 a Sick Pay scheme was adopted, but a number of anomalies came to light which had to be corrected during the first year. Accordingly a new Sick Pay allowance was proposed, adopted and commenced on March 1st 1921 and remained in practice for the next 25 years. It read as follows:

'When a Pilot is absent from duty on account of accident or illness he may at the discretion of the Pilotage Committee receive from the Pilotage earnings a sick allowance as follows.

1)   A period of absence not exceeding three days. No Allowance.

2)   Exceeding three days but not exceeding three months. The Pilot shall produce a Doctor's certificate of incapacity from time to time and on production of such a certificate he shall be entitled to receive during incapacity an allowance at the rate of two thirds of his monthly earnings for a period or periods not exceeding in the aggregate, three months in any period of twelve months.

If exceeding three months but less than six months the rate is reduced to one third his monthly earnings. Exceeding six months each case shall be specially considered by the Pilotage Committee.

A great deal of credit must be given to Mr. Bennion, the new Pilot Clerk, who devised the whole of the Sick Pay Scheme. Once again Mr.Bennion's influence prevailed when the Pilots eventually agreed to his proposals to receive their monthly earnings in a manner similar to that adopted in a well tried and trusted system carried on by the Liverpool River Pilot Service viz:

1)   Monthly earnings to be paid at a standard rate of £35 for a First Class Pilot and £25 for a Second Class Pilot.

2)   All surplus earnings to be shared equally between Pilots quarterly. At the same time it was proposed and resolved that the annual payment of £100 to Choice Pilots as their retainer fee should also be paid quarterly. Mr. Bennion continued to keep a keen and watchful eye on all aspects of procedure during the early months of the Rotary System.

THE HELMSMAN SERVICE
1894 - 1988

THE HELMSMEN, THAT WONDERFUL BODY OF MEN, WHOSE GLORIOUS SENSE OF HUMOUR AND ABILITY TO ALWAYS SEE AND APPRECIATE THE HILARIOUS SIDE OF PILOTING, HAS ENRICHED MY LIFE IMMEASURABLY.

IT ALWAYS HAS BEEN A GREAT PLEASURE AND PRIVILEGE TO WORK WITH THEM - MY SINCERE THANK YOU TO YOU ALL.

D.A.C. 1995

THE MAN BEHIND THE WHEEL

HE DESERVES A HERO'S MEDAL
FOR ALL THE TIME HE'S SAVED
AND UPON THE ROLL OF HONOUR
HIS NAME SHOULD BE ENGRAVED
HE DESERVES A LOT OF PATIENCE
 FOR THE WAY HE STANDS THE STRAIN
FOR THE PILOTS HE HAS TO STEER FOR
WOULD DRIVE A MAN INSANE.

WHEN YOU WALK ON TO THE BRIDGE
 HE WILL GREET YOU WITH A SMILE
BE YOU PILOT DRESSED FOR A DISCO
OR A CAPTAIN DRESSED IN STYLE
BE YOU RUSSIAN, GREEK OR FRENCH
 IT DOESN'T MATTER WHAT
HE WILL TREAT YOU LIKE A GENTLEMAN
UNLESS YOU PROVE YOU'RE NOT.

IT MATTERS NOT THE WIND AND RAIN
AND HARDSHIPS HE ENDURES
 HE DOESN'T TELL YOU HIS TROUBLES
THOUGH YOU ALWAYS TELL HIM YOURS
AND IF THE WEATHER'S GALE FORCE NINE
OR TURNS FROM RAIN TO SNOW
ITS THE PILOT WHO HAS TO TELL HIM
HE'S NOT SUPPOSED TO KNOW.

BUT TIME MUST COME WHEN HE
MUST SHUFFLE OFF THIS MORTAL COIL
HANG UP HIS WHEEL AND OILSKINS
NO MORE THIS EARTH TO TOIL
WHEN ST. PETER SEES HIM COMING
 HE WILL SET THE BELLS TO PEAL
FOR HE KNOWS HE'S HAD HIS HELL ON EARTH
 HAS THE MAN BEHIND THE WHEEL.

The Author.

YOU CAN MANIPULATE SOME OF THE PILOTS ALL OF
THE TIME
YOU CAN MANIPULATE ALL THE PILOTS SOME OF
THE TIME
AND WITH A LITTLE GUILE YOU CAN MANIPULATE ALL
THE PILOTS ALL OF THE TIME

Helmsman's Axiom.

17.

THE HELMSMANS SERVICE 1894-1914

The History of the Manchester Ship Canal Pilot Service would not be complete without recording the immeasurable contribution the Helmsmen's Service made through the ages towards the Pilot Service. It is unequivocally true that they became an integral and important part of piloting a vessel safely in the Canal and without a Helmsmen's Service being operative for over 90 years there would not have been a Pilot Service as it is known to-day. That they were treated so shamefully for their dedicated and willing service by a Pilot service that was so ungrateful, truculent, greedy and jealous and also suffered the petty whims of some self opinionated Pilots is indeed hard to understand, let alone believe.

Before the establishment of a properly constituted Pilot Service in 1896 and for some years after, it was the custom for Canal Pilots to select from the vessels they were piloting a crew member to act solely as the Helmsman. They chose him because of his ability to steer the vessel steadily in the Canal and usually the Pilot had experience of the crew member's capabilities on a previous passage in the Canal. Other Pilots in charge of vessels large enough to have to employ tug boats to assist their passage in the Canal chose the First Mate of one of the tug boats as a Helmsman, either having previouly experienced his ability to steer a vessel or by the recommendation of the Captain of the Tug boat. There was also a growing practice for Pilots to employ friends or relatives as Helmsmen. These people inevitably had no sea going experience whatsoever and were usually unemployed or unemployable.

The Pilots attempted to train these Helmsmen on board smaller coasting vessels and when the Pilot was sufficiently satisfied with their competence, he would duly engage them to steer the larger ocean going vessels. In the two latter categories of employing Helmsmen, the Pilot would make a charge to the Captain or Shipping Agent for a certain fee, usually half the pilotage fee, for the Helmsman's service. The Pilot would then recompense the Helmsman what he thought was a fit and proper percentage of that fee. The percentage being judged on the ability of the Helmsman to steer the vessel and the state of the Pilot's liver on that particular day. In no circumstances did that percentage exceed 25% and could drop as low as 10%. It was quite a profitable side-line for a Pilot,but more to the point, the Pilot could keep the Helmsmen under his complete control.

The first unofficial Helmsman tariff was as follows:

"For each vessel entering or leaving and navigating the Ship Canal and requiring a Helmsman an initial fee shall be payable according to the net tonnage of the vessel:

For a vessel not exceeding 300 tons	5s.0d. (25p)
Exceeding 300 tons but not exceeding 600 tons	10s.0d. (50p)
Exceeding 600 tons but nto exceeding 1200 tons	15s.0d. (75p)
Exceeding 1200 tons but not exceeding 3000 tons	£1.0s.0d. (£1.00p)

For a vessel exceding 3000 tons an additional fee of 5s.0d (25p) shall be paid for every 1000 tons net or part thereof above 3000 tons. A vessel in ballast (no cargo) shall pay full initial fee but only half the mileage rate. The mileage rate shall be 6d ($2^1/_2$p) a mile or portion of a mile, for the distance the vessel has been steered. A service rendered.to a vessel but not leaving or entering the canal half initial fee plus mileage shall be charged.

The first mention of Steersmen occurred on March 2nd. 1896.

[*Author's Note:* The word Helmsman did not come into the Pilotage vocabulary until April 11th 1904, when the Pilots demanded to change the name Steersman to Helmsman as the connotation of the word Steersman was like the Scandinavian word Styreman meaning officer. The very thought of a Helmsman being referred to as an officer was totally abhorrent to the Pilots].

HELMSMANS NIGHTMARES

S.S. "Inverpool" GRT. 680 L. 169' B. 31'
Because of the bridge being so well forward these two vessels could only be correctly steered by looking aft to check the check the position of the vessel in the canal

S.S. "Elmol" GRT. 1170 L. 210' B. 35'.
A 1914 - 1918 Naval Bunkering Craft. Speed 8 knots with the fenders inboard and with tyre fenders outboard trailing in the water. Speed 5½ knots.

Both phtographs courtesy of the World Ship Society

155

A HELMSMANS MONTHLY EARNINGS DECEMBER 1902

Mr. THOMAS LAMEY.

DATE	VESSEL	NET.TONS	FROM-TO	PILOT	FEE.
3 .12.02.	SPIND	623	East.-Manc.	G.Frederick	£1.12.0(£1.60p)
5 .12.02	FOREST BROOK.	1729	Latchford-Manc.	D.Jones	£1.7s.0(£1.35p)
6 .12.02	GREENBRIER	1819	MANC.-EAST.	E.Taylor.	£1.17.0(£1.85p)
7 .12.02.	EXMOORTH	2499	Manc.-East.	C.Young	£1.8s.6(£1.42)
10.12.02	DRAUPNER	1869	East-Manc.	F.Penney.	£1.17.0(£1.85)
12.12.02	FOREST BROOK	1729	Manc.-East.	B.Whitehouse	£1.8s.6(£1.42)
13.12.02.	DRAUPNER.	1869	Manc.-East.	F.Penney	£1.8s.6(£1.42).
14.12.02.	BANGOR	2202	East.-Latchford.	J.Ellis	£1.10.6(£1.52p)
15.12.02.	NANNA	700	East. -Manc.	C.Cave.	£1.12.0(£1.60)
16.12.02.	STADT SCHLESWIG	336	East.-Manc.	R.Iddon	£1.7s.0(£1.35p)
18.12.02.	CONCURRENT.	510	Weaste-East.	W.Marker	£1.7s.0(£1.35p)
20.12.02.	LINCLUDEN	1764	Manc.-East.	A.Waterworth	£1.8s.6(£1.42p)
23.12.02.	BIRMINGHAM	1541	Manc.-Partington.	B.Whitehouse	£.13s.0(65p)
23.12.02.	BIRMINGHAM	1541	Partington-East.	B.Whitehouse	£1.14.0(£1.70p)
24.12.02.	TELEGRAF.	452	East.-Manc.	C.Cave	£1.7s.0(£1.35p)
29.12.02.	SALUS	1393	Manc.-East.	G.Batty	£1.7s.0(£1.35p)

Total for the month £22.16s.0d. (£22.80p)

A pint of beer cost 2d.(1p) and a glass of whiskey 3d. (1½p). Income tax
was 1s.3d. (6p) in the pound but after allowances Mr. Lamey had no Tax to
pay. A Master of a deep sea vessel would be paid approximately £18 per month.
Mr. Lamey's total earnings for 1902 were £ 120.9s 0d there was no pooling
system in 1902. Mr. Lamey only worked for 102 days (3½ months) as a helmsman
in 1902 therefore one must presume he had alternative employment elsewhere.

When the secretary of the Pilotage Committee reported that the number of Pilot Licences had reached the fixed limit of sixty, it was resolved:

1)   That no further Piloting Licences be issued, but any applicants who may satisfy the examining committee that they are competent, and who have acted as a steersman under a First Class Pilot, will be preferred when vacancies occur. (This method of appointing Pilots was hardly ever practised).

2)   That before a steersman can become eligible he must have made twelve passages upwards in the Ship Canal and twelve downwards in the Ship Canal as a steersman. Twelve such passages must be made on an ocean going vessel transiting the full length of the Canal. The aforesaid passages must be certified by the Captain and Pilot of the vessel, upon which he has acted as Steersman. (These qualifying passages were not entitled to payment).

3)   Pilots holding a second class licence on the Ship Canal will be allowed to act as steersmen of any vessel in the charge of a First Class Pilot.

There was another more sinister reason for these three proposals put forward by the Master Pilots on the Pilotage Committee. They already held sway over many other Pilots on this Ship Canal and now saw a possible threat to this dominance with uncontrolled Steersmen eventually becoming licensed on the Canal. However, with these resolutions passed, any steersman objecting to any of the practices carried out by the Master Pilots e.g. "farming out", percentage charge of fees etc.or deemed unsuitable for any other reason the Master Pilots could easily make it almost impossible for a steersman to complete his compulsory twelve services up and down the Ship Canal. To cover themselves should a short fall of steersmen occur due to steersmen leaving through the actions of the Master Pilots the resolution to allow Second Class Pilots to act as steersmen, bridged that gap admirably. The Second Class Pilots were already servitors to the Master Pilots and they would be only too willing to co-operate with them.

The Master Pilots continued, albeit in a roundabout way, to choose the men they wanted as steersmen, rather than have men imposed upon them. Often sons, brothers or relatives of the Pilots were given Steersmen positions which in turn led to bitter feuds between warring families. This dominance and control over the steersmen was to continue for another sixty-five years.

A regular and properly organised steering service was not constituted until March 1913, up until then it appears that any person could justifiably call himself a Steersman and act in that capacity and no one seemed to know what a steersman could do or could not do. In the June of 1902 the following letter was read out to the Pilotage Committee from the secretary of the Manchester Ship Canal Free Pilots Society stating:

"It had come to the knowledge of some of their members who were licensed Canal Pilots that men who are not members of the ships crew or licensed Pilots, are in the habit of boarding vessels and acting as helmsmen up and down the Canal without a licensed Pilot being in charge"

The Chairman of that Pilotage Committee stated the only case of the kind which had come to the knowledge of the Committee was the S.S *"Alsen"* and this had been suitably dealt with. He instructed the secretary to inform the Pilots Society that if they would send particulars of any other cases they would be thoroughly investigated.

Not all the Pilots, albeit very much in the minority, were in agreement with the system of employing Helmsmen, as described earlier in this chapter, nor were they in agreement with the manner in which some of their colleagues piloted the vessels they were in charge of. At the Pilotage Committee Meeting held on April 10th 1902 the Chairman (Mr. Latimer) submitted and read the following letter from Mr. B. Whitehouse (Pilot) representing a number of Pilots:

"We wish to draw your attention to several of the Pilots when in charge of vessels on the Ship Canal as Pilot are acting as steersman also and possibly to their advantage pecuniarily but to the disadvantage of other men who earn their living steering and also to Pilots who attend to pilotage alone. We do not object to a Pilot steering for another Pilot but when in charge of a ship as Pilot on the Canal we think he has quite enough to do to look after the safety of the vessel in his charge without accepting the dual

responsibility of steersman also; besides in case of an accident on the Canal which might possibly have to come before the Law Courts to be settled what would be the position? and how would it affect the underwriters of the vessel if insured? The consequences could be very serious and we would like you to stop this practice as soon as possible before serious complications arise."

The Pilotage Committee were not going to get involved in any legal complications and neatly side-stepped the issue. They expressed their opinion that the interests of both Shipowners, the Canal Company and the Pilots would best be served by leaving the question of steering vessels along the Ship Canal to the discretion of the Pilot in charge. It was considered that he ought to be the best judge of what steering assistance was required from himself personally to enable him to conduct the vessel to her destination safely without damage to any vessel or property. The secretary was informed to reply to Mr. Whitehouse the findings of the Committee. It could not have been more helpful to the Master Pilots. They had been virtually given an offical licence to control the steersmen as they wished.

In June 1907 the following letter from Mr. G. Green (Pilot) respecting the practice of Pilots steering vessels which they piloted on the Canal was read:

"I wish to call the attention of the Pilotage Committee to a very dangerous practice which now exists on the Ship Canal that is to say Pilots are steering their own vessels. On several occasions I have been passing vessels where the Pilot has been steering, it has been extremely dangerous and in particular with regard to those vessels which now have wheel-houses. The Pilot inside steering his vessel certainly cannot see to navigate in a proper manner. In one case to avoid a collision I had to keep to my own starboard side so close, that my vessel's bilge rubbed the Canal Bank. I am sure that the Pilot could not judge his distance for passing, from the wheelhouse. I have also observed Pilots when steering their own vessels leave the wheel and go to the side of the bridge when passing another vessel to see if all was clear to pass. I am sure you will agree with me this is not a prudent action for a Pilot and I think it is detrimental to the safe navigation of the vessel as well as being

detrimental to the Pilot Service.

I know of no better way than to train young men as steersmen to become Pilots on the Ship Canal than behind the wheel of a vessel, but if the pilots and particularly the older ones are allowed to continue this most dangerous practice, there will be very little inducement for practical young men to take up the Ship Canal Pilotage by way of acting as a steersman. I would make the suggestion that no Pilot should be allowed to steer the vessel upon which he is acting as a Pilot but to employ a second class pilot or a steersman so that at least it will give one an insight to handling larger vessels and the other a chance to learn the intricacies of piloting. Hoping that you will take immediate steps to stop this growing and dangerous practice etc.

A conversation ensued during which the opinion was expressed that in some cases it was necessary for pilots to steer vessels because it was very often the case that no member of the ship's company was thoroughly capable of steering vessels in narrow waters. Ship owners refused to bear the expense of engaging steersmen and Pilots considered there was less risk of an accident if they steered the vessel themselves than if they obtained the services of one of the crew who was not familiar with the Ship Canal.

After further consideration of this matter it was resolved that Mr. G. Green be informed by letter of the findings of a previous complaint of this nature in April 1902. The matter was considered closed. Mr. G. Green was a senior Pilot having been one of the original Pilots licensed in 1895. The practice of Pilots steering vessels that they are in charge of continues even to this day.

The haphazard manner of employing steersmen by the Pilots did not escape the notice of the Pilotage Committee. On April 11th 1904 it was reported :

'A number of the Canal Pilots were in the habit of employing persons to act as steersmen outside the crews of the vessels they were engaged on and to whose ability and knowledge of the Ship Canal to enable them to satisfactorily perform their duties, the Pilotage Committee had no information.

It was pointed out that should an accident occur to a vessel which was being steered by an incompetent person provided by a Ship Canal Pilot it might seriously prejudice shipowners against trading in the Ship Canal. Captain Waring (Canal Superintendent) proposed the following resolution:

"No person other than members of the Ship's Crew, or riggers acting as such, or Ship Canal licensed Pilots be allowed to undertake duties of a steersman on vessels navigating the Ship Canal without first having obtained a permit from this committee to perform such service generally or from a Superintendent of the Ship Canal for any specific vessel on any voyage".

Due to legal complications that might ensue the matter was postponed to a future meeting. On October 4th 1904 Captain Waring stated at the Pilotage Committee that he had recently observed persons acting as steersmen on vessels navigating the Canal of whom the Superintendents had no knowledge and some of whom in his judgment were inexperienced and incompetent to act as steersmen on such narrow waters as the Ship Canal. The Chairman remarked that some such system of controlling the steersmen engaged to steer vessels along the Canal should if possible be put into force. He was somewhat doubtful whether this Committee or the Canal Company had the power to issue permits or licences to persons to act as steersmen on the Canal and also whether the Masters of vessels were not within their rights in employing anyone they thought proper to steer their vessel on the Ship Canal. He asked that this question might be deferred for further consideration and this was agreed upon.

Many suggestions were put in writing for the consideration of the Pilotage Committee but all to no avail. The Master Pilots still wished to keep overall control of the employment and use of Steersmen on the Ship Canal. They vetoed any attempt to undermine their authority over the steersmen by pronouncing every new suggestion as 'unworkable'. The prospect of a properly organised Steermans' Service, officially recognised by the Pilotage Committee and the Pilots' Association, did not seem likely to be established in the foreseeable future. It would be five years before any significant progress was made. In the meantime the steersmen were exploited shamelessly. In September 1909 the Chairman of the Pilotage Committee said a question which from time to time had been discussed by the Committee as to whether all Steersmen other than Pilots who were engaged to steer vessels on the Ship Canal should not in some way be registered by the Canal Company and after passing some kind of examination be granted a permit to allow them to act as steersmen on the Canal.

A scale of the charges to be made for such work should be fixed and authorised by the Pilotage Committee. Some discussion ensued, after which the Chairman's suggestion regarding the steersmen, was agreed and Captain Williams was asked to make enquiries and as far as possible prepare and submit to the next meeting a list of the men who were at present engaged as steersmen on the Ship Canal. Captain Williams reported to the October Pilotage Committee Meeting that he had seen all the men (15 in number) who are regularly employed steering vessels on the Ship Canal under the Pilots licensed by them and submitted the names, particulars and qualifications of those men.

HELMSMANS' SERVICE LIST 1909

M. Green	J. E. Lamey
C.F. Young Jnr.	W.D. Southwood
H. Limb	W. H. Roberts
R. Lloyd	F. Onion
T. Lamey	J. Heath
J. Lamb.	W.P. Dudley
E. Southwood	W. Mackenzie

The general opinion was expressed that all steersmen should in some way be under the jurisdiction of the Pilotage Committee, be licensed or certificated and a fixed schedule of charges for their services implemented. The Pilots' representatives proposed no applicants should be eligible for a licence or certificate to steer unless he had the minimum of two years service at sea. In the time honoured fashion of the Pilotage Committee they referred this matter once again for further consideration. They say the wheels of justice grind slowly onwards. They ground even slower where the Pilotage Committee were concerned. Four more years were to pass before this matter was successfully concluded.

Since the establishment of the Pilot Service in 1896, Pilot Licences were granted to persons who could show they had experience navigating the Ship Canal and passed a suitable examination. The necessity of having been a steersman was not an automatic qualification for a Pilots Licence.

In October 1907, Mr. John William Klahn , Chief Officer with the Donald Currie Line, a firm of regular traders to the Canal, was successfully examined for a second class licence and in February 1908 a barge Captain Mr. J.D. Shaw applied for a second class licence and he too successfully attained a licence. In 1909 during a discussion at Pilotage Committee on an application from a Tug Boat Master, Mr. E. Hankinson, for a First Class licence, it was pointed out that there were now young steersmen on the Canal whose age and experience would soon qualify them for Pilotage work. The question was whether, the vacancy for a Second Class Pilots licence arose the Tug Boat Captain be given priority over Steersmen.

Certain members of the Committee did not think sufficient encouragement was given to young and promising steersmen. They suggested that some rule might be adopted so that a young man taking up the work as a steersman should know what to expect in respect of being granted a Pilots Licence. It was resolved to put on record that the Pilotage Committee thought it was desirable that Pilots in the future (other than Appropriated Pilots) should be appointed if possible from those acting as steersmen on the Ship Canal. It should also be made generally known to those acting in that capacity that in the event of vacancies arising, their claims, if they cared to put them forward, would be favourably considered. Their claims would be further strengthened if they possessed active sea service over two years. It was a very weakly worded resolution. Mr. E. Hankinson was examined and passed for a First Class Licence; no steersmens' applications were considered. So much for the high sounding resolution.

Further evidence of flouting the resolution can be seen when an application for a second class licence had been received by Mr. Matthew Green, son of Mr. George Green one of the original Pilots on the Canal. The application was duly recommended by three members of the Committee and the particulars on the application form showed him to be 24 years old and to have been a steersman for 4³/₄ years. There was no mention of sea service. The Committee considered the necessity to incease the present number of licences that now stood at 34 - the limit was set at 40 licences - as the limit had not been reached during the last five years. The Pilot representatives did not think there was work for any more Pilots substantiating this statement by saying that recently a Pilot had only managed to obtain one pilotage service in four months and had been forced to return to seagoing - how much this was the result of the "farming out" system is a mute question. It was finally decided that the application could not be entertained at this present time but his application would be duly considered when the appointment of an additional Pilot was decided upon. The sting in the tail of this resolution came in the final sentence which read," but he must not infer that the fact of having made an application would give him priority of turn over other applicants", a complete contradiction of the resolution passed earlier in the year.

The non-committal resolution full of ambiguities did nothing to help a steersman to gain a licence or make the steersmen's service recognised as an Association, by all concerned. Indeed, Pilots licences continued to be granted to persons ahead of those steersmen working on the Canal. It was not until 1913 that this subject was once more placed before the Pilotage Committee. A member of the committee expressed the opinion that as an alternative to issuing a permit to steersmen the Committee might approve the issue of an instruction to all Pilots holding Ship Canal licences that only such steersmen were to be engaged as were mentioned on a official list which would be enclosed with such instructions. In the event of any of these steersmen not being available, the steering shall be undertaken by a member of the vessel's crew only.

The qualifications of the steersmen now employed on the Ship Canal were then examined and after all the names had received individual consideration, three steersmen who were employed were not approved and deleted from the list. The revised list of steersmen was sent to all Pilots with the instructions that only steersmen mentioned thereon be engaged to steer vessels of which such Pilots are in charge. On March 17th 1913 the first officially approved

Helmsmen's list -from that date they became referred to as Helmsmen- was published, and an official schedule of charges for their services was also implemented. (Appendices II)

J. Unwin	J.H. Packwood
E. Barnes	J.E. Lamey
W. Marshall	R. Lloyd
M. Green	W. Dudley
R. Green	F. Onion
A. Limb	R. Fleming-Jones
A. L. Robinson	

Further appointments to the list of approved Helmsmen as required would only be made at the discretion of the Chairman of Pilotage Committee and Captains Williams and Acraman (Canal Superintendents). It was also resolved that the lack of sea service, other matters being equal, would prejudice such Helmsmen's applications. One such application was received from a Helmsman, Mr. J. Unwin, aged 40 years, who had been a Helmsman since 1898 and was the senior Helmsman at the time. The Pilotage Committee granted his request to be examined for a second class licence in March 1914. Unfortunately Mr. Unwin died tragically one week before he was examined.

At last there appeared to be some advancement towards the recognition of an authorised Helmsmen's Service. Not all the Pilots agreed with this approved list of Helmsmen. They took great exception to what they saw as an intrusion into their private arrangements with Helmsmen, some of whom were not on the approved list. Five letters of objection were received by the Pilotage Committee from the Pilots. On April 14th 1913 the Chairman replied to those letters stating:

"That no Pilot is debarred from undertaking the steering of a vessel himself if such steering can be done without interference with his duties in the capacity of a Pilot, also that the system previously prevailing in regard to the employment of Helmsmen will continue, except that only such Helmsmen as are on the approved list should be engaged."

It is interesting to note the subtle phrasing '*should* be engaged' as opposed to '*must* be engaged'. When one really studies this closely, made by the Pilotage Committee to form an approved Helmsmens Service you can see how pathetic it was - no firm statements, no strict conditions and no penalty clauses for not observing the rules of the resolution.

It did not change the Helmsmans' position one iota, nor did it give them security of job or guarantee a Pilot licence. The Pilots still had control over them and they were still open to abuse in respect of extra remuneration for Pilots. The only concession to this resolution was that at least it was a start in the right direction towards a fully approved Helmsmans Service. But many years were to pass before this became a reality, it had taken them nearly fifteen years to reach this point.

The Pilots continued to ignore any directive from the Pilotage Committee regarding the steering of vessels themselves as surely the Pilotage Committee realised they would, under such a lack lustre resolution. In June 1913 two cases of accidents were reported to the Pilotage Committee in both of which the Pilot in charge was at the wheel of the vessel when the accident occurred. It was pointed out that as increasing numbers of vessels were being built with a wheelhouse a Pilot was unable to see clearly ahead and would not be able to give the proper attention to the pilotage whilst steering the vessel himself. In such cases, the Committee considered that Pilots should not undertake the steering of the vessel themselves but obtain the services of a Helmsman from the authorised list, or failing that employ the services of a crew member. The Committee resolved that these observations should be sent to all Pilots with a warning that in the future if an accident of a similar nature occurred when a Pilot was in charge of the wheel, a more serious view of the incident would be taken. This letter was treated with the usual disdain by the Pilots, reserved for these missives and continued to steer vessels whatever the circumstances and still do even to-day, in 1990.

18.

THE HELMSMEN'S SERVICE 1915 - 1920

Pilots still tended to ignore the directive from the Pilotage Committee to employ Helmsmen only from the authorised list. Such a case arose in September 1915 when a Pilot was asked to submit a report explaining why the vessel he was in charge of ran aground in the Ship Canal between Partington and Latchford Locks. His reply was as follows:

"I ordered my Helmsman 24hrs ahead but he did not appear when the vessel was ready to sail and though I tried to get several others I could not do so. The crew were two men short and all foreigners and had not been in the canal before and also had sufficient drink. The person I engaged I knew as a 'rigger' for some years and chose him in preference to any of the crew. This person managed very well down to Partington but while the vessel was bunkering he apparently obtained some strong drink which I did not notice until recommencing the passage. The vessel began to wander all over the Canal and eventually touched the Canal Bank. Seeing his condition I immediately sent him from the wheel and the second officer steered the vessel to Eastham. I hope this explanation proves satisfactory"

During the discussion it was revealed that although the Pilot had requested a Helmsman (Mr. G. Richardson) to be in attendance he had not taken the trouble to find out if he was available; Mr. Richardson was engaged at that time with another vessel. The Committee were of the opinion that the Pilot did not realise the importance of engaging Helmsmen from the approved list and a letter was sent to him pointing out the necessity of doing so. Mr. G. Richardson was one of the three Helmsmen not approved by the Pilotage Committee when the first official list was published.

The first world war was twelve months old, the first battles of Marne, Mons and Ypres had been fought with horrendous casualties, the second battle of Ypres was being fought when poisonous chlorine gas was first used by the Germans and the Cunard Liner *"Lusitania"* was torpedoed and sunk off the west coast of Ireland. The earth shattering news from the Ship Canal amongst all this carnage in Europe and at sea was a complaint from the Secretary of the Pilots Association to the effect that owing to the shortage of Helmsmen many Pilots had been obliged to steer vessels themselves. (Not without a private fee being charged, I am sure - *Author*).

Furthermore owing to the shortage of Helmsmen they (the Helmsmen) were in a position to choose what vessel they would steer and sometimes would not accept a vessel if it was deep draughted and making a full transit of the Canal. How the Helmsmen must have revelled in this situation. It was almost the reverse of the "Turning Down System".

The Chairman replied that there were 15 approved Helmsmen of which six had enlisted - no doubt they felt that trench warfare was infinitely better against the Germans than the canal warfare against the Pilot - leaving nine available Helmsmen plus three Second Class Pilots who were available to act as Helmsmen. The six who enlisted were:

> Matthew Green 25
> H. Limb 32
> R. Lloyd 27
> H. Hill Jr. 34
> C.F. Young Jr. 31
> W.H. Roberts 38

All returned safely with the exception of Mr. Limb who died on active service in France in January 1918.

At that same Committee meeting it was confirmed that there were certain Helmsmen who refused to steer for certain Pilots. It was resolved that Captain Williams (Canal Superintendent), should contact them either personally or by letter and make it clear they must take whatever work was offered to them irrespective of the Pilot or the vessel of which he was in charge. This would not be the last time Helmsmen refused to steer for certain Pilots because they either objected to part of their earnings being paid to the Pilot or the Pilots ungentlemanly conduct towards them. It was obvious that this situation could not be tolerated. For the few months that it did, it must have brought immeasurable pleasure to Helmsmen to be able to choose the vessel they worked on and more importantly the Pilots they wanted to work with. The wheel had indeed turned full circle [No pun intended! *Author.*]

Captain Williams' stern rebuke to the Helmsmen and reminding them of the State of Emergency that existed in the country in consequence of the war with Germany, however, soon had a normal Helmsmen's Service in operation again.

It had left an indelible mark on a number of Pilots, who sought recriminations with a vengeance in the years ahead.

During the next four years the Helmsmen dutifully went about their work without acrimony. They continued to apply for Pilot Licences but on every occasion were rebuffed. On November 4th 1915 Mr. A.L. Robinson, a Helmsman of six years standing, applied for a second class licence. He was refused on the grounds of reduced tonnage using the Canal due to war conditions but on the resumption of peace the necessity to increase the licences would arise and his application among others would then be considered.

In July 1919 Mr. T.N. Gorst Helmsman, aged 28, applied for a second class license and stated:

"I have now been steering up and down the Ship Canal since the beginning of 1914 for various Pilots, but principally under the tuition of Mr. George Cartwright. Trusting you will give my application your kind and careful consideration and I hope to hear further from you".

The rather naive wording 'principally under the tuition', should have read 'under Mr. G. Cartwright's patronage'. Some Pilots had adopted the practice of employing only one Helmsman of their choice to steer all the vessels they piloted. It had certain dubious

"Helmsley I" GRT:1178. L. 216'. B.35'
Another 1914 - 1918 Naval Bunkering vessel and equally awkward to steer.

Captain Roy Kilby-Lennon
Master of "Helmsley I" always sympathetic towards Helmsmen.

advantages but the biggest disadvantage - other than the retaining fee paid yearly to the Pilot-was if the Helmsman's pilot patron was unable to work, through illness, suspension of licence, or even taking a holiday, the helmsman would find himself similarly indisposed because other Pilots, out of a fit of pique, would refuse his services whilst his patron was off duty. Mr Gorst's application had no chance of being approved and was deferred for later consideration. One interesting anomaly occurred in August 1919 when a Second Class Pilot, Mr. J.W. Lamb, was informed by Pilotage Committee that they could not renew his licence as he had done no pilotage services since June 1917. Bearing in mind that Second Class Pilots were allowed to steer vessels for First Class Pilots, he replied that he was not desirous of holding a second class licence as he was making a very good living as a Helmsman. Mr. Lamb had started as a Helmsman in 1896 and was therefore well known and experienced in steering on the Ship Canal. He became a permanent Helmsman for three Appropriated Pilots thus ensuring a plentiful supply of good paying vessels although he had to pay a percentage of his earnings to the three Pilots who employed him.

It was because of just this sort of situation that the Helmsmen, as a body, wished to bring in a Rotary and Pooling System, to prevent one or two Helmsmen coveting the larger vessels which paid the largest renumeration, to the detriment of the Helmsmen's Service as a whole. On the 23rd March 1919 the Pilotage Committee received a letter signed by nine Helmsmen - out of a possible twelve - asking them to support an application for an increased tariff and suggesting a rotary and pooling of earnings system. The Committee decided to defer the same until a decision had been arrived at in connection with the application of the Pilots Service for a similar system.

At the Pilotage Committee held on July 7th. 1919 the Chairman stated that arising out of the discussions with the Helmsmen's Committee it had been reported that several First Class Pilots had steered vessels along the Ship Canal, although a Helmsman had been available. The Chairman referred to the minutes of October 1918, whereby permission was given to First Class Pilots until further notice, to act as Helmsmen in order to supplement the services of the Helmsmen then available. Several of the Helmsmen had now been demobilised from H.M. Forces and had resumed steering on the Ship Canal, bringing their strength up to the agreed level of 15 men. After discussion it was unanimously agreed that a letter should be sent to all First Class Pilots informing them that the permission previously granted to undertake steering is now withdrawn. For any vessel requiring a Helmsman the Pilot must obtain the services of one of the registered Helmsmen.

Many Pilots chose to completely ignore this resolution and continued to refuse to employ a Helmsman on certain vessels. This practice continued for the next seventy years. Certain Pilots were still angered by the Helmsmen's refusal to steer for them in 1914 and this action was the first of many in their long war of attrition against the Helmsmen. It also upset the Pilots because they saw a reduction in their incomes.

Very often they would be paid a portion of the Helmsman's fee for their services of steering the vessel. This would be done privately by either the Master of the vessel or the Shipping Agent. The Pilots' negotiations for a Rotary and Pooling System was settled in November 1919 and on the 29th of that month the Chairman announced to the Pilotage Committee that the formation of a scheme to bring the Helmsmen's Service into a Rotary System only would be put into operation on December 1st 1919.

Unfortunately the rotary system did not fulfil the high expectations of the Helmsmen. The equitable distribution of work was sabotaged by some vindictive Pilots as a retribution for the Helmsmen's mini revolt of 1914 and the personal family feuds that were constantly being conducted. The Pilots always had the power to make or break a Helmsman financially, while the Helmsmen did not pool their earnings by-the insidious practice of refusing his services colloquially known as "turning down.", thus forcing him to "leave the service." A Pilot could and would refuse the services of any Helmsman for any trumped up reason without having to explain that reason to the Pilotage Committee. Here is an example how the "Turning Down" system worked:

Two vessels order a Pilot and Helmsman for the same sailing time 0800hrs. One vessel proceeding from Eastham to Manchester has a net tonnage of 1,505 tons, the Helmsman's fee £2.1s.3d. (£2.07). The other vessel proceeding from Eastham to Ellesmere Port net tonnage 499 tons, the Helmsman's fee 10s.0d(50p). The Pilot of the larger vessel would refuse the services of the Helmsman ordered to his vessel and would be automatically be sent the Helmsman from the smaller vessel, thus depriving his original Helmsman of £1.11s.3d. (£1.57) earnings. Taking it to its logical conclusion a Helmsman could lose £4.13s.9d. (£4.69p) in a week or £20.3s.3d. (£20.17p) a month, a King's ransom in the 1900s. How some Pilots delighted in doing this.

The Helmsmen were obviously disturbed and distressed with the Pilots continuance of their odious "Turning Down" practice during the first month of their own Rotary System, so much so that at the January 1920 Pilotage Committee Meeting a letter was read from Mr. W. Langley on behalf of the Helmsmen's Service:

"In April 1919 we requested that a system of pooling the earnings should be arranged. We would like to point out the dissatisfaction this pooling system is likely to cause, owing to the fact that Pilots do not consider certain Helmsmen sufficiently competent to steer large vessels. This has become increasingly clear since the commencement of our Rotary System. Therefore certain Helmsmen will always be allocated the heavy work for only the same remuneration as the Helmsman always steering smaller vessels, shorter distances and in shorter times. Thus there is no tendency for those Helmsmen to endeavour to steer larger ships. Trusting you will give this matter your most urgent and serious consideration."

After a prolonged discussion, during which the Pilots, represented on the Committee by Messrs Hindle and T. Lamey, insisted on retaining their undisputed rights to refuse a Helmsman's service, the Committee resolved not to implement a pooling of earnings system for the Helmsmen until such time as the Helmsmen were fully satisfied that the rotary system was equitable, and fairly distributed the work between all Helmsmen. That was to be over a decade hence.

The first incident of a Pilot refusing the services of a Helmsman was brought to the attention of the Pilotage Committee in April 1920. Mr. Hindle (Pilot) refused to have the services of Mr. P.Morton (Helmsman) to steer the *"Clan MacVicar"* from Eastham to

Manchester. Mr. Bennion (Pilot Clerk) insisted on Mr. Morton going with the vessel. Mr. Hindle demanded an explanation from Mr. Bennion who replied that Mr. Morton had proved to be very reliable and had on several occasions steered large vessels along the Ship Canal. Mr. Hindle when questioned admitted that prior to refusing Mr. Morton's services he had not made enquiries from anyone as to his capabilities nor had Mr. Morton steered a vessel for him before.

The Chairman stated that Mr. Bennion was arranging the Helmsmen's Rotary System, having regard to those who had not been long in the service and consequently only steering small vessels until their qualities had been proved. He told Mr.Hindle he was of the opinion that in this case he was wrong in refusing the services of the Helmsman sent to him. Mr.Hindle steadfastly reserved the right to choose his own Helmsmen as he thought fit. The matter was closed. Mr.Bennion had devised and implemented with the full approval of the Pilotage Committee a system of apprenticeship for Helmsmen:

1)   For the first six months a Helmsman would be restricted to steering vessels up to but not exceeding 1,000 net tons.

2)   The following three months a Helmsman would be restricted to steering vessels up to but not exceeding 1,500 net tons.

[NOTE: In 1935 the limitation was increased to 2,500 net tons. In 1940 the period of the second restricted tonnage was increased to six months and the net tonnage to 3,000].

3)   A Helmsman's competence for steering vessels of unlimited tonnage would then be considered by the Pilotage Committee.

On May 3rd 1920 the Pilots brought to the notice of the Pilotage Committee that Helmsmen were demanding expenses from ship owners and also attempting to charge amounts over and above what they were entitled to under their Schedule for Services. A suggestion was made that perhaps the Pilots would not object to approving accounts before the same were presented to the Masters of vessels for their signature. The Pilots' representatives raised no objections to this proposition, stating that on many occasions Masters of vessels had appealed to Pilots to verify the amount charged by Helmsmen.

The vetting of the Helmsmen's charges was just another way the

Pilots could curtail a Helmsman's earnings because a number of Pilots, especially the Appropriated Pilots, unbelievable as it may seem, did not always charge for extra services they were entitled to e.g. swinging fees, detention etc. They did this to "curry" favour with shipowners or agents in an attempt to induce them to appoint themselves as Pilots for their vessels using the Canal or for the already Appropriated Pilots more proof to the Ship owner and/or Agents of the wisdom of employing them as their Pilots with all the savings in Pilotage Dues they could make, even if it was financially detrimental to his own colleagues, for they were on a Pooling system. One can imagine that this resolution for vetting the Helmsmen's charges was far from popular with them and only served to widen the gulf of antagonism between the two Services.

The Helmsmen's tariff calculations were changed in January 1918 when they decided to incorporate the mileage fee of 6d (2$\frac{1}{2}$p) per mile or portion of a mile, into the initial fee, considering it an easier method of calculating their charges The following are those charges.

FROM EASTHAM TO MANCHESTER AND VICE VERSA.

Vessels up to 1,000 tons Net.	£1.13s 9.	(£1.69p)
Vessels over 1,000 up to 1,500 Net.	£1.17. 6.	(£1.85p)
Vessels over 1,500 up to 2,000 Net.	£2. 1. 3.	(£2.04p)
Vessels over 2,000 up to 2,500 Net.	£2. 5. 0.	(£2.25p)
Vessels over 2,500 up to 3,000 Net.	£2. 8. 9.	(£2.44p)
Vessels over 3,000 up to 3,500 Net.	£2.12.6.	(£2.65p)
Vessels over 3,500 up to 4,000 Net.	£2.16.3.	(£2.82p)
Vessels over 4,000 up to 4,500 Net.	£3. 0. 0.	(£3.00p)
Vessels over 4,500 up to 5,000 Net.	£3. 3. 9.	(£3.18p)
Vessels over 5,000 up to 5,500 Net.	£3. 7. 6.	(£3.37p)
Vessels over 5,500 up to 6,000 Net.	£3.11.3.	(£3.57p)
Vessels over 6,500 up to 7,000 Net.	£3.15.0.	(£3.75p)
Vessels over 7,000 up to 7,500 Net.	£3.18.9.	(£3.94p)
Vessels over 7000	£4. 2. 6.	(£4.12p)

For every mile less than 35 miles, 6d (2$\frac{1}{2}$p) less than the above charged.

There were additional increases in other minor services and a Late Booking Fee of 10/6d (52p) in 1939, (which was increased to £1.1.0d (£1.05p) in 1944) was introduced for vessels booking Helmsmen to vessels outside normal office hours.

The above rates did not change except for certain overall percentages, nor did the method of calculation until January 1947.

A HELMSMANS MONTHLY EARNINGS DECEMBER 1920

Mr. J.H. WARREN.

DATE	VESSEL	NET.TONS.	FROM-TO	PILOT	FEE
1. 12.20.	DELAWARE	2469	Manc.-East.	J.Barnes.	£2.5s.od. (£2.25p)
2. 12.20	WESTERN CHIEF	3505	East-Manc.	F.Hankinson	£2.16s.3d.(£2.82p)
5. 12.20	LEXINGTON	3902	East-Manc.	J.Baxter.	£2.16s.3d.(£2.82p)
8. 12.20.	M/C.MARINER.	2610	Manc.-East.J.Baxter.		£3.5s. 9d.(£3.18p)
11.12.20	SCOTOL	863	Manc.-W/My.J. Lamey.		£1.8s. 9d.(£1.44p)
12.12.20.	ROYAL TRANSPORT.	2927	East-Manc.	J.Inglefie.£2.8s.9d. (£2.44p)	
15.12.20.	SAN ZOTICA	3370	Manc.-East.W.Lamey		£3.12s.6d.(£3.62p)
17.12.20.	WEST CILENA	3838	East.-Manc.J.Baxter.		£2.16s.3d.(£2.82p)
19.12.20.	DUNGANNON.	4485	Manc.-East,T.Lamey.		£3.5s.0d. (£3.25p)
23.12.20.	TELESFORA DE LAR.	3536	Manc.-East.G.Davidson.		£2.16s.3d.(£2.82p)
26.12.20.	AMANDA.	.658	East.-Manc.P.Bennet.		£1.15s.9d.(£1.6dp)
30.12.20	BOVIC.	4229	Manc.-East.T.Lamey.		£3.15s.0d.(£3.75p)

TOTAL EARNINGS FOR MONTH. £32.17s.6d.

TOTAL EARNINGS FOR THE YEAR 1920. £226.15s.3d. (£226.76p)

Mr. Warrens earnings for 1920 came from only six and a half months, he commenced steering on June 14th. He averaged £35 per month. In his first full year of steering 1921 he earned £382 .15s.9d (£382.78p) an average of £32 per month. Considering that a Master of a vessel of 7,000 to 9,000 gross tons would have been earning approximately £30 per month and a Chief officer £23 per month Mr. Warren was indeed on a very good wage especially as he did not pay Income Tax at that time and beer was 3d (1p) a pint and spirits 6d. (2½p) a glass.

By kind permission of the Warren Family

G.P.O. Cable Ship H.M.T.S. "Monarch" GRT: 8056 L. 484'. B. 56'.

*This was the largest Cable Ship in the world seen here loading 39 miles of 138K.V.
submarine power cable at Trafford Wharf via the specially constructed overhead gantry
direct from the factory of W.T. Glover & Co. Ltd. Another Helmsman headache with such
a restricted view from the wheelhouse by the equipment on the bow.*

19.

THE HELMSMENS SERVICE 1920 - 1934

The Pilots were never slow to disparage the Helmsmen whenever they could. At the Pilotage Committee in July 1920 the Pilots representative, M. Hindle, made a complaint on behalf of the Pilots that certain Helmsmen appeared to resent the instructions given to them by Pilots in charge of the vessel on which they were steering. The secretary of the Committee was instructed to write to the Helmsmens Association stating that they should clearly understand that whilst they were to place all their efforts and experience at the services of the Pilots, they were to carry out such duties under the instructions and guidance of the latter, whilst steering vessels up and down the Ship Canal. The Committee also warned that there would be no more complaints about actions or remarks made by Helmsmen in their association with Pilots whilst carrying out their duties.

The truth of the matter was the Helmsmen did not resent the instructions given to them by the Pilots, what they did resent was the completely ungentlemanly manner in which the orders were given, a mannerism that some Pilots perpetuated for the next forty years. A case in point arose in October 1921 during a discussion at Pilotage Committee on a Damage Report submitted by a Pilot, in which the vessel he was in charge of collided with the Barton Aqueduct Bridge. The Pilot placed the entire blame for the accident on the Helmsman's steering actions. The Pilot added that further trouble was experienced on the passage down the Canal because of the Helmsman's inability to steer the vessel, although no further damage occurred. At Latchford Locks the Master dismissed the Helmsman, that service being performed afterwards by a crew member of the crew. The Pilot concluded

1930
Pilot Mr. W. Milsom and Helmsman Mr. M.B. Fisher
compare the bleakness of this steering position with that of the
hi-tec bridge of 1990 at the end of this volume.

Photo courtesy of the Milsom Family

'I could find no fault with the vessel's steering gear or her steering qualities or the view from behind the wheel and cannot account for the Helmsman's inability to give anything like satisfaction on this occasion".

The Chairman reported that having regard to the Pilot's remarks regarding the Helmsman's inability to steer the vessel, he had called for a report from the Helmsman. The Helmsman's statement revealed a number of salient points conveniently omitted in the Pilot's report.

1) The view from behind the wheel was severely obstructed, by being enclosed on three sides, leaving only part of the vessels bow visible to steer by.

2) The Helmsman had drawn the attention of the Pilot in Modewheel Lock, to the slowness of the steering gear when putting helm on and taking helm off. The Pilot tested the steering gear and drew the attention of the Master to its condition.

3) The vessel was in ballast and the wind was blowing very strongly on the Port beam.

The Helmsman stated he did everything he was ordered to as fast as the steering gear would allow him and still this was not satisfactory to the Pilot who knew of the steering conditions. In Latchford Locks in the presence of the Master the Pilot told me in no uncertain terms to leave the vessel and he would steer the vessel to Eastham himself. The Master signed my Bill and I went ashore. The Chairman said that the Helmsman's statement was in complete contradiction to the Pilot's report and appointed a sub-committee to enquire into the case and report back to the full Committee. The result of the subcommittee enquiry was as follows.

That the evidence was so conflicting and the answers given so contradictory that no satisfactory conclusion could be arrived at. However, they considered that some of the blame was attached to both Pilot and Helmsman. It transpired that the Pilot had frequently used strong language to the Helmsman, which in their opinion might have impaired the quality of the Helmsman's steering. It may also have influenced the Master in sanctioning the Pilot's refusal to allow the Helmsman to steer the vessel after reaching Latchford Locks. The sub-committee concluded that they had impressed upon the

The Steering Engine of the S.S. "Allegenhy"
Courtesy of Capt. P. Heyboer - Dutch Marine Surveyor

"Allegenhy"
GRT. 858. L.213' B.32'

Another horror from Esso. The Helmsman stood in front of a small steering wheel steering the vessel with his hands behind his back. The Helm Indicator was also behind him. The steering engine was open in the wheelhouse constantly spraying oil over the Helmsman. The Helmsman was given an oil can to lubricate the steering mechanism from time to time to prevent it from seizing up.

T.S. "Esso Fulham"
GRT. 4352. L.366' B.60'

Ex Lake Maricibo Tankers. There were three such vessels regularly trading to Manchester. They were all twin propellered, under-powered and given the sobriquet "The Ding Bats". They were unquestionably the most awkward vehicles to transit the canal.

Photos courtesy of World Ship Society

Pilot and Helmsman that no ill feeling between them should exist following this conclusion and had cautioned the Pilot as to his future use of obscene language and intimidating conduct towards Helmsmen. It was like asking a snowball not to melt in Hell.

This case was proof enough that it was not the orders a Helmsman resented but the manner in which they were given. It is an unquestionable fact that some Pilots appear to imagine, that because they hold a Ship Canal Licence they can be insulting and tyrannical over all those who do not, when the very fact of their being a Pilot should be an inducement to them to show an example of courtesy and gentlemanly conduct in the execution of their duties, no matter what the circumstances. It was fortunate only some Pilots tried to make themselves feel important by such ungentlemanly conduct, but it did cause a great deal of ill-will and not just to Helmsmen.

It must be appreciated that a Helmsman's working conditions were far from satisfactory, almost primitive by today's standards. From the very beginning of their service almost 90% of steering positions had no cover at all, these vessels were known as "Open Bridge" ships, whilst the Pilots position on the lower bridge did have a modicum of shelter from the elements. The steering mechanism was generally unsuitable for manouvering in narrow waters, such as the Canal and a large proportion of vessels were fitted with the infamous "*Chain and Rod*" steering gear.

With this system the wheel had to be heaved round, for it needed Herculean strength to turn the wheel. The wheel was connected by a system of rods and cogs to the lower bridge, then on stanchions to the boat deck abaft the bridge. The final rod at the end of the boat deck went down to the steam driven steering engine situated on the top of the after end of the engine room. On each side of this steering engine there were attached chains which ran in steel channels on each side of the after deck and then by rising sheaves up to the poop deck. They were then connected by means of a shackle to the quadrant which in turn was connected to the rudder post.

If the steel channels that carried the chains along the after deck became obstructed with debris during the loading or discharging of cargo it made the task of turning the wheel twice as difficult and

THE CHAIN AND ROD STEERING SYSTEM

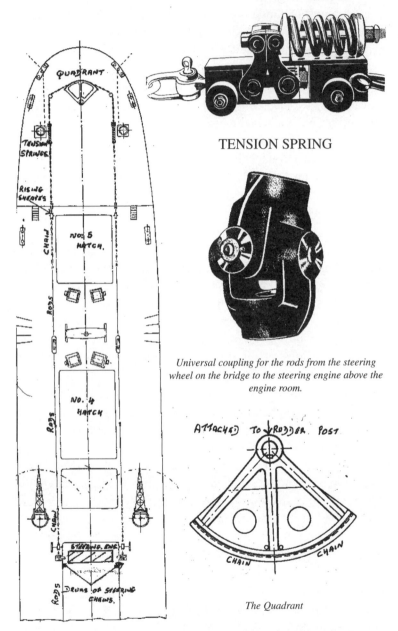

TENSION SPRING

Universal coupling for the rods from the steering
wheel on the bridge to the steering engine above the
engine room.

The Quadrant

Courtesy Capt. P. Heyboer - Dutch Marine Surveyor

184

considering the wheel had to be brought back by hand to amidships, after helm had been applied to port or starboard one can imagine how tired and exhausted a Helmsman would become after six or eight hours behind the wheel. Pilots seldom took into consideration the complexities of these steering systems and if a Helmsman was having difficulty in keeping a vessel in its correct position on the Ship Canal the Pilots would just increase the Helmsman's discomfort by giving more and more helm orders. The introduction of electric steering systems in the latter part of 1940s took the physical effort out of steering but did little to reduce the lot of a Helmsman. This was mainly through its unreliability often due to blown fuses or the heart stopping slowness of the electric motors to move the helm from port to starboard and vice versa. "Open Bridges" were still in use right until the 1970s, indeed many vessels had dual steering positions "open" and "covered". Some Pilots took the greatest sadistic pleasure in insisting the Helmsmen steer always from the "Open" position even if it had a restricted view, especially during the winter months and certainly in inclement weather, whilst they stayed in the comparative comfort of a dry and warm lower wheelhouse.

Another cause of great ill-will between the Helmsmen and Pilots was the continuing practice of a number of Pilots claiming a Helmsman's fee in addition to their own Pilotage fee. One such case occurred on May 10th. 1920 when a Pilot was ordered to the S.S *"Lockee"* 600 net reg tons from Weston Point Dock to Eastham. The Agents of the vessel had not required a Helmsman and had indicated such to the Pilotage Department, but the Pilot however presented a bill for £1.2s.3d. (£1.11$^1/_2$p) for the services of a Helmsman. The Pilot's letter in reply for an explanation of this matter read as follows.

"The vessel had a Helmsman from Eastham to Manchester and from Manchester to Weston Point. It was not my fault there was not a Helmsman from Weston Point to Eastham. I had to steer the vessel myself therefore I consider I am entitled to be paid for same."

The secretary of the Committee wrote to the Pilot informing him of the illegality of this action and should a repetition of such action come to their notice in the future, a more serious view of the matter would be taken even to the suspension of his licence.

The Pilots continued at every opportunity to harass the Helmsmen, and on October 22nd 1922 at the Pilotage Committee, the secretary of the Pilots' Association tabled this resolution:

"The right of Pilots in charge of vessels to refuse the services of Helmsmen who they consider to believe are not competent to steer such a vessel".

The Pilotage Committee said they could not delegate to any Pilot the right to say he would not take any particular Helmsman. If any Pilot had reason to complain of the conduct or inefficiency of a Helmsman he should make a written complaint to the Committee. The Helmsmen's earnings also came under pressure. In December 1923 the Steamship Owners Association lodged a complaint that there was no proper check on the charges made by Helmsmen for their services and a suggestion was made that the Ship Canal Company should take in hand the collection of the Helmsmen's charges in the same manner as those of the Pilots. The Pilots' representatives were not slow in backing this complaint they too agreed that the Helmsmen's conditions and charges should be regularised by the Canal Company. The Chairman said that this matter had been brought to the notice of the Pilotage Committee on previous occasions and he promised this suggestion would receive careful consideration.

From the commencement of the Pilot service in 1896, their fees were collected by the Ship Canal Company but not those of the Helmsmen. The Helmsmen presented a fully documented account of his services to the Master of the vessel, who, after suitable scrutiny would sign it thus agreeing to the amount payable. This account would then be presented to the Shipping Agent or Broker to be settled. It became quite a social occasion for three or four Helmsmen to choose a certain day and go together to collect a week or months fees. They would often make as many calls, if not more, at local taverns in Manchester and Liverpool, than the Shipping Agents offices. In 1925 the Helmsmen, probably because of the inefficiency and expense of collecting their fees in this way changed their system.

They deposited their accounts for every vessel at Eastham Lock

1922

S.S. "Singleton Abbey" GRT.2325. L.303. B.43'

A dreaded sight often seen by Helmsmen. A heavy list, chain and rod steering and the prospect of a 12 hour passage.

1924

"ManO" GRT.1415. L.250. B.38'

An unusual sight to Helmsman a timber ship with no list.

Photos courtesy of Mrs W. Yates

and accepted the services of Mr. James Linded of Bromborough to collect their accounts at Eastham then proceed to have them settled by the Shipping Agents. Mr. Linden would either deliver the monies to the Helmsman's home or they would collect it from him at his home.

The charge for this service was 9d (3^1/$_2$p) in the pound and was collected once a month. This system was in operation until September 1928.

During 1920 - 1923 the Helmsmens Service had increased to seventeen men. Some promotions had been made to Second Class Pilots and most of the new intake held either Master or First mate certificates of competency, a far different breed from that of Helmsmen in the past. This seemed to incense some Pilots and they began to complain bitterly about the ability of individual Helmsmen. This culminated in a letter from the Pilots Association to the Pilotage Committee:

"With reference to the complaints that have been made from time to time regarding the conduct and work of certain Helmsmen, I am instructed to inform you that the Pilots generally report that there is no improvement in the cases of Messrs Callister and Hughes, both of whom are reported to display great indifference towards the orders of the Pilots and fail to appreciate the importance and responsibility of their work, thereby hampering the Pilot in his work. I am also informed that a number of the Pilots refuse to accept the services of these two men and I am to suggest that they be given a serious warning that unless they pay more care and attention to their work you will be asked to dispense with their services."

The Chairman pointed out to the Pilots' representatives (Mr. G. Cartwright and Mr. C.F. Young) that no written complaint had been received from any Pilots in regard to the work of these two Helmsmen. The representatives said it was a difficult problem for specific complaints to be made because in order to avoid accidents in the Canal, Pilots had frequently taken the wheel of the vessel. They were, however, very strongly of the opinion that Messrs Callister and Hughes were not competent. Mr. Browning (Chairman) said he would interview the two Helmsmen in question and report back to a later meeting.

The two Helmsmen who incidentally held Master Mariners Certificates were duly interviewed and it was reported that they seemed genuinely surprised that such complaints had been levelled at them. They both realised the seriousness of the complaints and undertook to take a more serious attitude to their work in future. They also hoped that their future conduct would not give rise to any further complaints against them.

It is interesting to note that Mr. C (Cliff) Callister became one of the most loved and respected Pilots in the service. He became an appropriated Pilot for the United States Line and was a lifelong friend of all Helmsmen. The stories about Mr. Callister and his piloting are legendary and are recounted all over the world. It was indeed a sad day when he retired in September 1961. The Manchester Pilot Service lost one of its most colourful characters. He retired to the Isle of Man, his place of birth, and died in 1966.

During the next decade there is little or nothing recorded in the history of the Helmsmens Service although it was true there was always an undercurrent of discontent between the Helmsmen and Pilots. This never ceased during the ninety years of the existence of the Helmsmans Service. It is still perpetuated even unto this day as you will read in the last chapter. It occasionally surfaced during that decade but it was so trivial and insignificant it is not worthy of recording. The only significant happening was the introduction of a non-compulsory contribution towards a system of sick pay in 1926, whereby a Helmsman off duty through illness (not self inflicted) would receive 5s.0d. (25p) per week from every working Helmsman. Being non-compulsory the amount of sick pay per week varied from one Helmsman to another entirely depending on his popularity within the service and the frequency and length of time he was absent from the rota due to illness.

There had been however an ongoing discussion at Pilotage Committee level during these years, over the merits of introducing a system of setting, collecting and distributing the Helmsmen's fees whereby the Canal Company would become wholly responsible for this undertaking. The Canal Company had vacillated for many years over this subject and had studiously avoided any commitment towards implementing such a system. At the Pilotage Committee in July 1928 the Manchester Shipowners Association and the Pilots' representatives urged the Canal Company to approach the Board of Trade to ascertain their feelings regarding the Canal Company controlling all Helmsmen's fees and the feelings of the Helmsmens Association. Both these bodies replied that they had no objections legally or otherwise and on September 1st 1928 the Canal Company became the responsible authority for all Helmsmen's fees.

Because the Helmsmen were not pooling their earnings (hence no sick pay and no leave either) the Canal Co. charge for administering this service was $2^1/_2$% of each individual Helmsmen's earnings.

This situation remained unchanged until 1933. The Helmsmens Service had now increased to 19 men and in July of that year, at a meeting held in Rock Ferry, a resolution to implement a system of pooling their earnings was proposed and passed by 12 votes for, 5 against with two abstentions. Mr. Browning announced the Helmsmen's decision to pool their earnings at the August Pilotage Committee Meeting. With the minimum of discussion the Committee unanimously agreed to implement this system as from September 1st 1933. This system was to last until September 1st 1947. The success of the Helmsmen in achieving a pooling system was diminished when at the same August Pilotage Committee Meeting the Chairman announced that as from August 1st. all Pilots and Helmsmen's tariffs would be reduced by 10% (See chapter on Pilots tariff, volume III.)

20.

THE HELMSMENS SERVICE 1934 -1939

In the minds of the administrators of the Pilot Service and most certainly in the hearts of all Helmsmen the system of pooling earnings, combined with the Rotary System, would at last see the end of the pernicious practice of "Turning Down", that had plagued the Helmsmens Service from its inception. Sadly, it has to be recorded that this was not to be so. Certain Pilots continued to "turn down" Helmsmen, but knowing they could no longer control a Helmsman's livelihood financially, because of the pooling system, they in their strange and twisted thinking took great delight in reversing their practice of refusing the services of a Helmsman they disliked.

For example:

A Pilot would "turn down" a Helmsman on a vessel he was in charge of from Eastham to Ellesmere Port - distance three miles. Time thirty minutes - knowing that that Helmsman would be sent to a vessel proceeding from Eastham to Manchester - distance thirty five miles, time eight hours or more - thus ensuring he would have to work several hours longer, for the same amount of monthly earnings as the Helmsman steering to Ellesmere Port. It certainly gave some Pilots great satisfaction to pursue this practice, but there were also Pilots who were sufficiently competent and decent not to lower themselves to the odious level of "turning down" a Helmsman for whatever reason. To those Pilots in particular the Helmsmens Service would always be eternally grateful.

Although many years had passed in what seemed like endless negotiations for improving working conditions and equal pay this was not to the exclusion of other aspects of a Helmsman's future. There was great concern, continually expressed during those years, regarding the future prospects of obtaining their Pilots licence before they reached the age limit of forty years mentioned in Pilotage Bye Law No. 2 (8) 1913. At the Pilotage Committee meeting held on October 15th 1934 a letter from the secretary of the Helmsmens Association (Mr. R.D. Richardson) was read out.

"We the undersigned Helmsmen, are desirous of bringing to your notice our present rather anomalous position in the Pilot Service

In as much as the present senior Helmsmen have served for periods in the region of ten years, with the doubtful prospect of promotion at some distant date, it is very evident that in the normal course at least half of the Helmsmen cannot hope to ever become Pilots by virtue of their age. We would point out that whereas the number of Pilots is at present two below full strength, the Helmsmen are 33% in excess of the 1923-24 period. If the number of Pilots were increased by two (the present traffic returns justify this) it would in some small measure alleviate the present stagnant condition of promotion.

We also wish to suggest the issuing of licences to Helmsmen of a given period of service, such Pilot licences to remain inoperative until a vacancy occurs in the usual manner. This system existed prior to the Pilots present Pilots Rota and Pooling system. This would ensure quite half of the Helmsmen a position, which at present, there seems no prospect of attaining."

All nineteen Helmsmen signed the letter. A copy of this letter was sent to the Pilots Association and all the proposals were deferred for consideration, until the next Pilotage Meeting.

The November Pilotage Committee Meeting received the following letter from the Pilots Association, and what a letter it was:

"The letter from the Helmsmen has been considered by the Pilots and it appears to raise the following three questions.

Firstly, that the present number of Pilots should be increased by two. The Pilots are of the opinion that no increase in the present number of Pilots can be justified by the existing traffic figures.

"Bittern" GRT.1527. L.290'. B.43'

Regular Traders to Manchester. This company, British and Continental, had a number of vessels trading to Manchester and were all named after seabirds. They all had open wheelhouses but they steered brilliantly. They also had excellent food.

"Ardetta" GRT.1542. L.289'. B.41'

Note Helmsman on upper open wheelhouse and pilot on lower sheltered bridge on starboard side.

Courtesy of the World Ship Society

Secondly, that some system of granting provisional licences should be instituted. This is of course for the consideration of the Pilotage Authority but so far as the Pilots are concerned it appears to them to be an impractical suggestion.

Thirdly, that the Helmsmen are required to serve for an unduly long period and that some of them cannot hope to ever become Pilots. This is a matter for which the Pilots cannot accept any responsibility and whilst they sympathise with some of the Helmsmen in their predicament they are unable to offer any suggestions for alleviating any hardships that may arise, many of which appear to be due to insufficient regard being given to the ages of the candidates at the date of appointment"

The Pilots' crocodile tears would have filled the whole of the Manchester Ship Canal.

The Pilotage Committee dismissed the suggestion of temporary licences as 'impractible and unworkable' and after further discussion on this matter it was agreed that further consideration must be given to this contentious subject. The deferment lasted until July 1937, almost three years later.

The notorious letter from the Manchester Ship Canal Pilots Service gave rise to such replies always being referred to as, *"Pontius Pilate"* letters and one does not have to be a genius to see the reason why. In subsequent years many letters in a similar vein were to be written by the Pilots Association with regard to the Helmsmen's future. By completely 'washing their hands' of the Helmsmen's problems and thereby abdicating from all responsibility towards the future of the Helmsmens Service, the Pilots could not see, that in point of fact, they were destroying the very future of their own service. It was almost an act of suicide this very blinkered view the Pilots took. The cold and cynical wording of the letter is even more incomprehensible. The 'night of the long knives' was never far away from the Pilots.

Even more puzzling was a complaint placed before the Pilotage Committee the following month. The Pilots' representatives stated that in the opinion of the Pilots some of the Helmsmen who had been appointed in recent years were not as they were required to be for entry into the Pilot Service. Future candidates should be medically examined before being appointed as Helmsmen. This was indeed a strange attitude to take, showing great concern that Helmsmen were medically fit to steer vessels for Pilots, but showing no concern whatsoever over a Helmsman's prospect of ever obtaining a Pilot's Licence.

From 1934 to 1937 very little is recorded regarding the Helmsmens Service but three points of interest did emerge. The Chairman of the Pilotage Committee at a meeting held in October 1935 drew the attention of those present to the fact that some of the Helmsmen had proffered their service to the Masters of vessels, particularly to vessels moving from point to point at Ellesmere Port and from Ellesmere Port to Eastham. It appeared that Helmsmen were only employed on vessels proceeding the whole or some considerable length of the Ship Canal , whereas if they were only moving a short distance a Pilot only was ordered. The Committee agreed that instructions be given to the Helmsmen only to attend vessels when ordered to do so by the Pilotage Clerk and accompanied by a Pilot. An avenue for individual Helmsmen to earn extra money was successfully and firmly closed. The second point of interest was a letter dated 23rd. May 1936 from the Helmsmens Association secretary (Mr. R.D. Richardson) which was read to the June Pilotage Committee Meeting:

"The Helmsmens Committee wish to ask if you could promote new Helmsmen after they have completed six months service to vessels up to and including 3,500 net reg tons instead of 2,500 tons at present in force. The number of vessels under 2,500 net reg tons are very few, consequently the ensuing experience is inadequate. After six months a new Helmsman at present automatically receives the full rate of pay and it seems only just that these Helmsmen should bear their share of the work at the earliest opportunity."

The Helmsmens Service had no room for slackers and hangers on. It appears from this letter certain Helmsmen were rather disgruntled at having to share their earnings with other Helmsmen who were not working as hard. The Pilotage Committee agreed to raise the limit after six months to 3,000 net reg tons.

The third point of interest occurred in March 1934 when Mr. Bennion (Chief Pilot Clerk) in co-operation with the Helmsman Committee formulated the first organised leave rota for the

S.S. "Ellenic Chryssoula" GRT. 3849. L.370' B49'
A typical Greek vessel loading coal at Partington. Open bridge and suspect steering
gear. Food unedible.

S.S. "Ulster Coast" GRT. 774. L. 201'. B. 31'
Another open bridge. Every meal sausage and beans.

Courtesy World Ship Society

Helmsmens Service. They were granted fourteen days leave a year, with pay, such leave to be taken between the months of May and September only. It had taken nearly 40 years for a leave system to be initiated into the Helmsmens Service.

A further example of the Pilots continuing pressure to exert their influence on the Helmsmens Service came at the February Pilotage Committee Meeting in 1937, when it was reported that two Helmsmen, Messrs McIntosh and Shepherd, had completed twelve months steering and from March 1st would be permitted to steer vessels of any tonnage. The Pilots' representatives requested that in future before a Helmsman's name was placed before this Committee in this manner, the Pilots should be asked to state their opinion of the capabilities of any Helmsman being promoted to higher tonnage and voice any objections. The Pilotage Committee agreed that this would be done.

The continuing concern expressed by the Helmsmen regarding their prospects of obtaining their Pilots' licences before they reached the age limit of forty years, once again came before the Pilotage Committee in July 1937. A statement was submitted showing the age at which the Helmsmen at present serving would succeed the twenty senior Pilots, providing the latter remained until they attained the age of sixty five years. From this it proved that apart from the senior Helmsman the remaining nineteen Helmsmen would all be more than forty years and many over fifty before their turn for promotion arrived.

True to form once again the Pilots' and Shipowners' representatives said they would like their associations to have the opportunity of considering this position and it was agreed that the matter be placed on the agenda for the next meeting. At the August Pilotage Committee Meeting the Manchester Steamship Owners Association representatives stated that while they were in sympathy with the aims of the Helmsmen in wishing to assure their future they felt it should be left for the Pilotage Committee to consider how this was to be done. In modern day parlance this would have been known as 'passing the buck'. The Pilots' representatives stated that the matter had been discussed amongst the Pilots, but no suggestion was forthcoming for dealing with the difficulty which appeared likely to arise during the next two or three years unless changes occurred which could not be foreseen. In modern day parlance this would be an 'I'm alright Jack' attitude.

After more discussion it was agreed that further consideration of this matter be deferred. It was deferred for another two and a half years. As previously observed 'the wheels of justice' grind exceedingly slowly at Pilotage Committee. This prickly problem would not go away and was raised once more on December 18th at Pilotage Committee when the following three propositions were put forward:

1) Promote a bye-law to advance the age limit of attaining a licence beyond 40 years.

2) Grant inoperative licences at the age of 40 years.

3) Introduce a Third Class Licence.

With monotonous regularity it was deferred again to the next Pilotage Meeting, in order that the views of the Pilots could be obtained.

At the Pilotage Committee Meeting held on January 10th 1940 a letter from the Pilots Association was read stating:

"That whilst sympathising with the difficulties concerning certain Helmsmen in regard to their prospect of becoming Pilots, the Pilots were unable to offer any suggestions for alleviating the position other than the removal of the age limit . They did not approve the suggestions to grant inoperative licences or introduce a Third Class Licence".

The Committee agreed to promote a bye law to suspend the present age limit of 40 years, at least for the duration of the war. The matter never came before the Pilotage Committee again, the Pilots had seen to that.

As a footnote to this saga of obtaining a licence, a letter from the senior Helmsman, Mr. C.M. Oliver, stating that he understood that First Class Pilot Mr. W.H. Roberts had reached retiring age and he wished to apply for promotion to a Second Class Pilot (after examination) to fill the vacancy that would occur on Mr. Roberts' retirement, Mr. Oliver was informed that the Committee had not considered the desirability or otherwise of renewing the licence at present held by Mr. Roberts nor had they had any intimation that it was his intention to resign. His application was denied. That was September 1940; he was eventually licensed in September 1942.

21.

THE HELMSMENS SERVICE 1940 - 1945

The following decade heralded the beginning of the most bitter and turbulent years in the working relationship between the Helmsmens Service and the Pilots Service ever to be recorded. It divided the two services to such an extent that the rift was never healed. From time immemorial there had been some animosity between certain Pilots and the Helmsmen, but now it broke out into the open with a vengeance, history was about to repeat itself once more. It was during the first World War that the first intimation that acrimony existed between Pilots and Helmsmen came to the notice of the Pilotage Committee. Nearly thirty years later during another World War it was to surface once again but this time with greater vindictiveness.

During 1940 there had been a considerable increase in vessels requiring the services of a Helmsman, especially vessels of small tonnage, which prior to the war would never have considered employing a Helmsman. For some reason a certain number of Pilots objected to having a Helmsman ordered to these smaller vessels. This increase in the Helmsmen's work was due mainly to the War. In order to prevent a collapse of the Helmsmens Service it necessitated the Pilotage Committee appointing new Helmsmen from sea going personnel on a temporary wartime basis. The first four temporary Helmsmen were appointed on September 1st 1940 to steer vessels up to but not exceeding 1,500 net reg tons. On

Typical "Rust Bucket" Helmsmen dreaded.
No shelter, no speed, no food and a liverish Pilot

T.S. "Pacific President" GRT: 7114. L. 450'. B. 61'.

A Helmsman would often steer a vessel of this size for 12 hours or more, with little or no rest. A brief relief from behind the wheel occurred whilst the vessel was in any of the four locks. Another twin propeller vessel.

Photos courtesy of Mrs. W. Yates collection

January 14th 1941 they were promoted to steer vessels not exceeding 3,000 net reg tons but the Pilots demanded, and were granted, the option of refusing any of them if they thought the circumstances necessitated it. [*Author's Note*: This was indeed par for the course].

The temporary Helmsmen were never well received or accepted by the Pilots. This was firstly because of the Pilots' historical distrust of any Helmsman who held a certificate of competency as a sea going officer, which applied to all the temporary Helmsmen and secondly the temporary Helmsmen did not take too kindly to the Pilots' attitudes or conduct towards them. They did not hesitate to inform the Pilots of their own feelings towards them. Over the next two years an uneasy and fragile working relationship existed between the two services. Temporary Helmsmen came and went, either hounded out by the Pilots or under their own volition, preferring to risk the wrath of a Nazi U-Boat commander rather than to continue to live and work with Pilots under such hostile conditions, the same feelings as their predecessors in the 1914-1918 War. Tension was building up to unprecedented proportions because Pilots refused to accept temporary Helmsmen on large vessels transiting the full length of the Ship Canal and some even refused any Helmsman on a small tonnage vessel. The Allan Green and Peter Onion affair added more volatile fuel to an already over heated situation.

At the May Pilotage Committee Meeting in 1943 the Committee's attention was called to the fact that Pilots were refusing the services of Helmsmen and the vessels upon which they were ordered to attend had, in consequence, proceeded without a Helmsman, against the wishes of the Master and /or Owner. This had mainly occurred when the Helmsman concerned had been a temporary Helmsman and in view of the fact that it was the vessel which requisitioned the services of a Helmsman, the Pilot had no authority to refuse these services. A Pilot could only intimate to the Master of the vessel, where such was the case, that the particular Helmsman allocated by the Pilot Clerk was not, in his opinion, competent to steer her. It then remained for the Master to decide whether he would accept the Helmsman's service or not. The Chairman stated they were not questioning the right of any Pilot to refuse a Helmsman and request a more highly qualified man, but this was not the case in any of the instances to which attention had been called and he expressed the hope that it would not be necessary for any further notice to be made of this matter. What a forlorn hope that was to be.

This hope was completely ignored by many Pilots. During the Allan Green and Peter Onion affair they became even more openly abusive to all Helmsmen often refusing their services in a way that was detrimental to the safe navigation of a vessel in enclosed waters. The disruption of the organised Helmsmen's rota caused much distress, not only to Mr Bennion (Pilots' and Helmsmen's Clerk) but also to individual Helmsmen who were being forced to work unacceptably long hours because of the Pilots' intransigent attitude. The family feuds also exacerbated the considerable stress of working and living under wartime conditions which also took its toll, not only on the individual Helmsmen but the Helmsmens Service as a whole. It was an intolerable situation that could not be allowed to continue.

This explosive situation, that had been simmering for so long, finally erupted. At the Pilotage Committee Meeting held in November 1943 Captain Bennet (Harbour Master) submitted a report stating when the S.S. *"Nordest II"* of 329 net reg tons arrived at Eastham on November 14th at high water 0825 hrs, the Pilot and Helmsman duly attended her, but when the Pilot observed the Helmsman he refused to take the vessel informing the Master that he did not need a Helmsman. The Master insisted that he wanted a Helmsman and stated he was satisfied with the capabilities of the Helmsman in question. Captain Bennet spoke to the Master who repeated his satisfaction of the Helmsman and stated as the Pilot would not have this Helmsman he required the services of another Pilot. Another Pilot was ordered and the *"Nordest II"* eventually sailed that evening at 1725 hrs. An explanation had been called for from the Pilot, but although he replied, he did not, in the opinion of the Committee, reply to the question at issue. After discussion it was agreed that the matter be allowed to lie on the table. A classic tactic of the Pilotage Committee.

At the same meeting a letter from the Helmsmens secretary (Mr. R. Southwood) was read referring to a meeting of all Helmsmen, when it was decided that they would not steer or accept orders to steer vessels for certain Pilots. They said their action was due to the unwillingness of these Pilots to co-operate with the Helmsmens Service and the unreasonable attitude adopted towards Helmsmen with regard to the question of meals, their conduct towards them and failing to provide a relief at the wheel for any reason at all, as was the procedure with some of the other Pilots.

They concluded that while these reasons may appear to be trivial, the conduct and attitudes of these Pilots made it impossible for the Helmsmen to continue working with them and the wartime conditions which Helmsmen were enduring were such as to keep them working at full capacity and left them with no time to cope with personal differences and grievances, real or imaginary, that particular Pilots wished to incorporate in their piloting. It was left in the hands of the Chairman (Mr. Leslie Roberts, later Sir Leslie) to deal with this matter.

A genuine attempt was made by the Chairman to try and diffuse this situation, but at the December Pilotage Committee he reported that he had interviewed certain Pilots in connection with this matter and as a result of those interviews he had hoped to hear in due course that everything was in order, but unfortunately his hopes had not materialised. Did the Chairman really think they would have ever materialised? The Pilots in question had written to the Minister of War Transport who had referred their complaint and recommendations to the Regional Port Director, and the latter would probably wish to make some enquiries as to what the position really was.. It appeared to the Chairman that these Pilots considered it incumbent upon the authority to take strong disciplinary action *against* the Helmsmen. It was quite incongruous for these Pilots to demand that the Helmsmen should be disciplined, when it was their own truly abhorrent conduct that had given rise to this situation in the first instance. That they considered themselves totally blameless was a monumental piece of self-righteousness.

Mr. F. Davenport (Pilot's representative) stated a recent case when there was only one Helmsman available at Eastham and that Helmsman had been requested by the Pilotage Clerk to hold himself in readiness to steer the first large vessel to enter Eastham Locks on the tide. The first vessel to enter was the S.S *"Stephanos"* a small coaster of 306 tons, and one of these Pilots had insisted on the services of a Helmsman, although he was fully aware of the position regarding Helmsmen at Eastham on that tide. The same Pilot had refused the service of a Helmsman on the previous tide for a vessel of similar size. Mr. Davenport said that this Pilot's action was solely to inconvenience himself (Mr. Davenport) knowing full well that he would not be able to proceed to Manchester with his larger vessel, with vital war supplies, due to no Helmsman being available. The reason for this was because of the animosity that existed between them due to a personal dispute the Pilotage Committee were well aware of.

The Chairman said that under present war conditions the services of Helmsmen familiar with the Ship Canal was vital. This must have been the first acknowledgement of the value of a Helmsmens Service.

The Chairman continued by saying that there should be a special meeting in connection with this whole matter, with the Pilots' representatives present to speak for the whole body of the Pilots. The date was improbably fixed for December 24th 1944. The Helmsmen's representatives had not been invited to place their side of the dispute before this specially convened meeting. One must draw the conclusion from this very biased investigating Committee that the Helmsmen's views were considered totally inconsequential. The meeting was, suprisingly enough, duly convened on Christmas Eve. The committee members were as follows:

> Mr. Leslie Roberts (Chairman)
>
> Mr. M. Kissane   (Secretary Pilotage Committee)
>
> Captain L.G. Richardson (Harbour Master)
>
> Mr. F. Davenport   } (Pilots' representatives)
>
> Mr. R. Lloyd   }
>
> Mr. Letch   (Regional Port Director)

The main subject for discussion was the necessity to employ a Helmsman on any vessel below 600 net reg tons, under the guise of saving manpower. The Pilots over the years had many dubious reasons for their inherent resentment towards a Helmsman steering small vessels that they piloted and in some cases it led to the objectionable behaviour of certain Pilots towards the Helmsmens

Service. The Helmsmens Service could only see it as an unwarranted curtailment in their earning capacity. A proposal was made in relation to saving manpower, namely vessels under 600 net reg tons need not, except in exceptional circumstances, engage the service of a Helmsman. The meeting was in general agreement with this proposal subject to confirmation from the full Pilotage Committee. There was no reference recorded whatsoever regarding the dispute between certain Pilots and Helmsmen.

At the Pilotage Committee Meeting on January 7th. 1943 a draft letter was proposed which was to be sent to all Shipowners, Agents, Pilots, and Helmsmen and read as follows:

"As the strength of the Helmsmens Service has been reduced and is liable to be still further reduced owing to the priority , of the manning requirements of the Merchant Navy, the Pilotage Committee consider that the larger vessels should have first claim on the Helmsmen available. Accordingly Owners, Masters and Agents are requested to refrain from requisitioning the services of a Helmsman to a vessel under 600 net reg tons unless there is a good reason for doing so in any particular case. The Master of inward bound vessels will have the benefit of the advice of the Pilots as to the necessity for a Helmsman (the Pilots would revel in that situation) and outward bound vessels, the Shipping Agents can seek the advice of Pilots if in any doubt as to the requisition of the services of a Helmsman. The Pilots have been requested to co-operate with this proposal."

The Chairman said that was the position until this morning, but a letter stating that a special meeting of Pilots was held to consider the report of the meeting held on December 24th and the 17 Pilots present repudiated the statements made by certain Pilots concerned in this dispute. Special reference was made, and objection taken to, the suggestion that there was no necessity for Helmsmen on vessels under 600 net reg tons. They said this would have a tendency to slow down the turn-around of vessels during the War, because inexperienced Helmsmen would not allow the Pilots to navigate vessels up and down the Ship Canal as quickly as was done at present. They concluded that a further meeting of the Pilots' Association had been arranged for January 12th and requested the Pilotage Committee to defer from taking any action in the meantime.

"Trigga"
GRT: 761. L.197'. B.29'

"Shell Brit"
GRT: 460. L.157'. B.27'
These are the type of vessels that Pilots were so adamant did not require Helmsmen

Photos courtesy of Mrs. W. Yates

The Chairman said it appeared that under present day conditions, having regard to the necessity of dispatch and bearing in mind the built up bridges which restricted the view from the steering position, and particularly the poor crews available for steering, the proposal put forward at the December 24th meeting and the draft letter should be reconsidered.

The Pilots' representatives cited a case were a Pilot had used four of a vessels crew to steer the vessel between Moedwheel Lock and Barton Lock, but as they were all a failure the ship was detained until the services of a Helmsman was obtained. They stated that it was not uncommon at the the present time for a vessel to have only one "qualified" seaman on deck and he might have limited experience. Furthermore, even if a member of the ship's crew did steer, his spell at the wheel was limited to two hours and therefore if there were not sufficient qualified crew to relieve him the vessel could well be delayed. A Ship Canal Helmsman's spell at the wheel was unlimited and they often steered vessels for eight, ten, twelve or more hours. After further discussion the Committee agreed to the Pilots' representatives' request for a deferment of a final decision until after the Pilots' Association meeting on January 12th.

Quite suddenly there appeared to be a complete reversal of Pilots' attitudes towards the Helmsmen's Service, and it became almost supportive. It was quite possible that the majority of the Pilots were tired of the constant friction between the services and wished, once and for all, to put an end to these self-destructive disputes. It was also quite possible the Pilots were at last beginning to appreciate the value of a skilled Helmsman and his contribution towards the safe navigation of a vessel of which they were in charge. This latter possibility appeared to be more likely when at the Pilotage Committee Meeting held on January 17th 1944 the Pilots' representative (Mr. Davenport) said he wished to express very definite opinions on the question of the necessity of employing specialised Helmsmen on vessels navigating the Ship Canal. They did not consider it could be denied that the very short period of training undergone at present by seamen, could ever qualify him to act as a Helmsman in narrow waters. A Pilot after trying several members of the crew at the wheel often had to take over in order to ensure the vessel's safe arrival at her destination. This was neither reasonable nor desirable in their opinion.

The Pilots said that it had been proved by experience that the employing of a regular Helmsman resulted in safer navigation, reduced passage times and risk of accidents. The advisability of employing specialised Helmsmen in the Ship Canal must be fully recognised, on all classes and all tonnages of vessels. The Chairman stated the draft letter under consideration was only an exhortation to Shipowners, Agents and Pilots not to take Helmsmen unnecessarily, having due regard to the saving of manpower in these difficult times. The Pilots' representatives said they realised how important it was to save manpower but not at the expense of safe navigation and for the reasons already given could not agree to the proposed letter being sent. This was the very first time, and the last, in nearly 50 years of the Helmsmens Service, that the Pilots had openly recognised the true value of a Helmsmens Service.

An exchange of letters between the Manchester, Liverpool, London, and Small Shipowners Associations and the Chamber of Commerce (Maritime Division) all concluded that the decision as to whether a Pilot or Helmsman should be engaged on a vessel must remain with the Master. One firm, Messrs Everard and Sons, even stated "They did not consider that the employment of a Ship Canal Pilot or Helmsman resulted in the quicker or safer navigation of their vessels". A view shared by the Chamber of Commerce (Maritime Division).

Mr. L. Roberts (Chairman) of the February Pilotage Committee Meeting said he thought that the difficulties in the service, and he referred particularly to those connected with certain Pilots whom Helmsmen refused to steer for, had been resolved and that they were to enter into a period of co-operation, but the Helmsmen still continued to operate their ban on one particular Pilot. That being so the Committee thought it wise to write to the Helmsmen's Secretary to the effect that they would not tolerate the withholding of essential services on what appeared to be purely personal grounds. An assurance was asked at the earliest possible moment that this practice would be discontinued.

The Helmsmen's secretary replied that having been in consultation with his Association he was unable to furnish the assurance requested but would be glad of an interview in regard to the matter. Mr. Roberts continued by saying four representatives of the Helmsmens Service attended at Ship Canal House, Manchester and after a long discussion they maintained their refusal to steer vessels for that one Pilot until they received an apology from that Pilot for his totally uncalled for remark made to a Helmsman, just prior to the meeting on the 24th December; to the effect that "All Helmsmen should be put up against a wall and shot". The expletives had been removed from this remark. The Helmsmen said that rather than steer for this Pilot they were prepared to join' the Royal Navy or enter the Pool for the Merchant Navy, which would mean there would be no Helmsmen on the Ship Canal. The Chairman said presumably other Helmsmen could be obtained to take their places but they would have to be trained and this would require the goodwill of all the Pilots, to ensure that their training was effective and would also take a considerable time. No further discussion was able to shake the Helmsmen in their decision not to steer for this Pilot.

The continuing distress and the formidable strength of the feelings of the Helmsmens Service is amply illustrated in their statement that rather than steer for this Pilot they were prepared to face all the horrors of war at sea. The Chairman said that the next step taken was to interview the Pilot in question with Mr Kissane (Secretary Pilotage Committee). This having been done that morning it appeared that the Pilot had quite genuinely thought the hatchet had been buried after the December 24th meeting. The Pilot felt that he was going to have the full co-operation of the Helmsmen and he in turn was going to co-operate. He did not regard the point of telling Mr. Bennion (Pilot Clerk) he did not want Helmsmen, as unfriendly for one moment and regarded it as a proper course to adopt in wartime when manpower had to be conserved. He stated other Pilots acted in this way to conserve manpower. The Pilot went on to say that the Helmsmen did not look upon his actions as saving manpower but as a vendetta against them. He declined to write a letter to this Committee withdrawing the expression he had used about Helmsmen but said if he had an approach from the Helmsmen that they would accept conciliation he would then probably take a different attitude.

This was a complete tissue of lies, and the most hypocritical cover-up for his personal attacks on Helmsmen. Hiding behind the "saving of manpower" reasoning was typical of this Pilot's whole attitude towards the Helmsmen. The Pilot's statement that *he* would take a different attitude if the Helmsmen approached *him* and asked for reconciliation - they who had done nothing wrong - was the most cynical attitude that could have been taken in the whole of this sordid affair. He maintained this attitude and continued to refuse Helmsmen services on various vessels and treat Helmsmen abominably until the day he retired, ten years later, a most despised man. That was how genuine his statement was towards reconciliation with Helmsmen.

Mr. Kissane asked the Pilots' representatives if they could do something to smooth over these difficulties and they agreed to get in touch immediately with the Helmsmen and, if possible, get them to come to some arrangement with the Pilot for a resumption of normal working. The Helmsmen eventually agreed, after much heart searching, to resume steering vessels for this Pilot whose conduct they had so strongly objected to. Some of the Pilots, however, continued to be antagonistic and disruptive towards the Helmsmens Service. One such Pilot went as far as to write to the Regional Port Director (Mr. Letch) stating that the employment of Helmsmen on vessels of the Coaster Class still continued in contravention of his mandate of December 24th 1943 meeting. The Pilot recalled to Mr.Letch's notice the fact that Helmsmen were not employed before the War on this type of vessel and he further stated that although the Helmsmen had capitulated - not the best choice of wording- in regard to steering for certain Pilots, including himself, they still were reluctant to steer for one Pilot. He thought it was a disgraceful state of affairs when important vessels were navigating the Ship Canal without the services of a Helmsman, whilst in the case of small vessels they were being forced to take Helmsmen.

Although the Helmsmen had made all the advances in trying to heal the rift between the two services the Pilot in question earlier in this chapter, was involved in another incident shortly after his hypocritical assurances he would co-operate with all Helmsmen.

The Master of of the S.S. *"Shellbrit 3"*, 322 net reg tons inward bound for Stanlow Oil Dock requested the services of a Pilot and Helmsman. The Helmsman boarded the vessel but when the Pilot

The art of steering past another vessel on the Moore Lane Straight. Not for a faint hearted Master.

Courtesy of Captain P. Dunbavand

subsequently arrived on board he informed the Master that he did not require a Helmsman. As a result of the Pilot's attitude towards the Master and Helmsman, the Master dismissed both Pilot and Helmsman and proceeded to Stanlow without the services of any Pilot or Helmsman. This case was reported to the Pilotage Committee in March 1944 and they agreed that consideration of this matter should be deferred. This case was never resolved and at their April meeting it was unanimously agreed to let the matter lapse. It was a constant source of wonder that the Pilot Service themselves never attempted to discipline or financially punish their own Pilots. Here was a case where the share of this pilotage fee was lost to all Pilots through no fault of their own, because of a Pilot's selfish prejudices. It was not the first case nor would it be the last, but those Pilots who caused so much anguish would for ever remain unrepentant.

Certain Pilots continued to press for a meeting with the Regional Port Director but had no success until they eventually met Mr. Letch without having previously arranged an appointment. Mr. Letch regretted that he could only spare a few minutes because he was to preside at another meeting. The Pilots enquired what progress had been made in regard to the difficulties between Pilots and Helmsmen and he pointed out that the matter must be kept on constitutional lines and was for the Pilotage Committee to consider. He was anxious that the differences should be resolved as soon as possible. Mr. Letch then made reference to a complaint against one of the Pilots present connected with the S.S.*"Vliestroom"*.

The circumstances of the case referred to by Mr. Letch were that when the *"Vliestroom"* entered Eastham Locks inward bound the Helmsman on duty for that vessel was informed by the Pilot that he would not accept his services.The Pilot emphatically denied this.

 Mr. Letch thought that that particular Helmsman should have been quite capable of taking a small vessel like her, only 289 net reg tons, and thereby left a more experienced Helmsman to attend a larger vessel docking later. He did not know what the Pilots' grievances were, but he assumed it was mainly concerning Helmsmen attending small vessels. He promised the Pilots that he would take up this matter again with the Chairman of Pilotage Committee.

The Pilots concluded by saying there was a definite waste of manpower, especially in regard to Helmsmen and if the Pilots did not get satisfaction they were prepared to raise the matter again with the Ministry of War, Transport or even through a Member of Parliament.

The Pilotage Committee received a report on that meeting and it was agreed that there should be a further meeting at which the views of all concerned could be properly expressed in regard to the utilisation of the Helmsmens Service. At the same time at that Pilotage meeting, the question of the differences between Helmsmen and one particular Pilot was resolved. Mr. Kissane announced he had received a telephone message from Mr. J. Patterson (Helmsmen's secretary) who stated that because of work commitments it had not been possible to get the Helmsmen together for the purpose of a meeting. He had therefore spoken to a number of them on the telephone and the general concensus was that they should from now on attend vessels with that Pilot.

Thankfully, this contentious matter was at last allowed to rest, at least till the end of the war. What was never reconciled was the working relationship between certain Pilots and the Helmsmens Service. All the promises of a more considerate attitude towards Helmemen were not worth the paper they were written on. Hardly had the Helmsmen agreed to commence steering vessels for certain Pilots than the Pilotage Committee received a memorandum from the Harbour Master giving details of the number of occasions, since the Helmsmen's agreement, when his attention had been drawn to that one particular Pilot's lack of co-operation. The most recent of the cases related to the passage of the S.S. *"Actinia"* from Partington to Eastham, when the Master remonstrated with the Pilot over his unreasonable conduct and criticism of the Helmsman. The Pilot proceeded to make himself so objectionable to the Master of the vessel - because of the Master's defence of the Helmsman that he ordered the Pilot to leave his vessel on at least two occasions. The Pilot refused to go.

What credence can one give to a Pilot's integrity when in February he states that he "genuinely thought the hatchet was buried between Helmsmen and Pilots". He "was not acting unfriendly to Helmsmen for one moment" and "if the Helmsmen accepted conciliation he would take a different attitude" and then in May he behaved in the way described. The Helmsmen feared that if this Pilot's conduct was allowed to continue it may precipitate other Pilots into similar conduct. There is always a number of 'sheep' in every profession and this Pilot Service was no exception. The Helmsmen requested a meeting with the Pilotage Committee in order to present their grievances. Their request was granted and at the July Pilotage Committee Meeting all parties in this dispute were present.

From the very outset the Pilot was abrasive and contemptuous towards the Helmsmen. When the Pilot was asked if he wished the Helmsmen who were in attendance to be called singly, he replied that he took exception to the witnesses being called at all and thought the Helmsmen's specific complaints should be put in writing and copies supplied to him. The Chairman told the Pilot that if this was his idea he should have said so when he received notification of the meeting. The Helmsmen's secretary was called in. Addressing the Chairman, Mr. Patterson said he had been instructed by all Helmsmen to protest very strongly against the continued lack of co-operation on the part of the Pilot. His conduct towards the Helmsmen both regarding meals and general demeanour, had shown no sign of improvement as expected.

Mr. Patterson said it would be remembered the Pilotage Committee recommended very strongly to the Helmsmen to resume duty with this Pilot. The Helmsmen did not agree to do so immediately but they had decided that for the good of the service in general they would do so, and they had hoped there would be no further trouble. During the first month after they had resumed work with this Pilot, he had received a number of complaints regarding the failure of this Pilot to co-operate with the Helmsmen. Mr. Patterson then read extracts from letters he had received from Helmsmen and he thought the complaints they contained, some of which had been submitted to the Pilotage Committee, constituted sufficient evidence to prove their point. He then related that on the first occasion he attended a vessel with this Pilot, after the Helmsmen had agreed to resume working with him, the Pilot asked him why the Helmsmen had come back to work with him as he had not gone round to ask them to work with him. The Pilot told him his own tail was not down, it was the Helmsmen's tails that were between their legs. The expletives once again have been removed from this report. The Pilot admitted he did say this to the Helmsman and the Chairman remarked that he thought he would have been wiser not to have mentioned the subject.

Mr Patterson also referred to a later occasion when he was steering the S.S. *"Asbjorn"* when this Pilot never spoke to him the whole time he was on board the vessel and never gave him any helm orders or meal reliefs. To this charge the Pilot replied that on this occasion the Helmsman took his berth (bed) when the vessel tied up for the night. Mr. Patterson replied that the berth was given to him by the Third Officer of the vessel.

The Pilot went on to say it was not necessary to give helm orders as it was a twin-screw (two propellers one on each side of the vessel) vessel which steered almost automatically and anyhow he was not in the habit of fraternising with Helmsmen. The childlike and querulous complaint, "the Helmsman took my berth" was not worthy of ones position as a Pilot nor was the statement "a twin-screw vessel steered automatically". It is a well known and proven fact, hydrodynamically, twin-screw vessels are the most unmanageable vessels in enclosed waters especially the Manchester Ship Canal. Mr. Patterson left the meeting and Mr. G. Young was called to the meeting

Mr. Young said the cause of his complaint was the failure of this Pilot to do what all other Pilots did, and that was to see that he got a meal. He had been steering for six hours when the Chief Officer asked if he wanted dinner. The Master thereupon remarked that the Pilot had informed him that the Helmsman did not want anything to eat which was not correct.

The Master then spoke to the Pilot who was outside on the wing of the bridge but he was unable to hear the conversation, but later on the Captain arranged for a cup of tea and sandwiches to be sent up to him which were placed close to the wheel. This was far from a satisfactory way of trying to eat a meal and steer a large vessel at the same time. I therefore asked the Chief Officer to ask the Pilot for a relief for a few minutes. The Pilot stormed into the wheelhouse and said "Certainly not". I then asked the Chief Officer to ask the Master if I could have a relief and to release me at the next lock. The Master sent the Third Officer to the wheel.

The Pilot tried to explain to the Master that the vessel had not been steering very well and he did not feel justified in releasing the Helmsman for his dinner. The Pilot commented to the Committee that the vessel handled better during the time the Third Officer was at the wheel than during the whole of the remainder of the passage. He also stated that it was he that had arranged for the tea and sandwiches to be supplied.

Mr. Young contradicted this by saying he had distinctly heard the Master order the Third Mate to go below and inform the steward to make a tray up for the bridge. Mr. Young concluded that Pilots usually helped the Helmsman to get their meals, not necessarily always at the particular meal time but when a suitable opportunity presented itself. The Pilot said, Mr. G. Young was one of the Helmsmen who expected the Pilots to go on what he termed "pub crawling" and said he was one of the Pilots who did not believe in this "hob nobbing" with Helmsmen. This was a totally uncalled for and unjustified accusation and not the last this Pilot would make.

Mr. Young was always regarded as a most abstemious Helmsman and of such a nature he would certainly not consider going "Pub Crawling". This attempt at character annihilation was typical between feuding pilot families and these two families were piloting in 1895. Both these Pilots had fathers who were Canal Pilots.

Mr. Young left the meeting and Mr. Clugston was called in.

The Chairman then asked Mr. Clugston about his complaint against the Pilot relating to the S.S. *"Actinia"*. Mr. Clugston said as soon as the Pilot came into the wheelhouse he commenced to abuse him. His first remark was "Fancy a .... Helmsman on a ship of this size".

The Master of the vessel was very upset at the Pilot's attitude. The Pilot also caused him (Mr. Clugston) a great deal of annoyance when he accused him of dodging the army. I had served the first three years of the war - they were the worst years of the war at sea - in coasters in the North Sea and I took great exception to this snide remark. During the passage the Master and the Pilot were constantly quarrelling so much, that eventually the Master ordered the Pilot ashore, but he refused to leave. Among other remarks the Pilot made was that the Helmsmen were getting money under false

1968
*A group of Helmsmen pesenting a Stevenson Screen to the sailing vessel
"Malcolm Miller"*
*Left-Right: D. Snowden, J. Southwood, A. Cooke, J. Davis, A. Watts
J.J. Pierpoint, B. Edwards, and presenting gift D.J. Edwards.*

By kind permission of The Helmsmans Association

pretences and he himself was ashamed to take the Pilotage fees. The Pilot remarked about the steering of the vessel and alleged that the Master had to take the wheel on one occasion when they were meeting and passing another vessel. The Committee informed the Pilot they would endeavour to contact the Master to substantiate that statement. None of these allegations regarding Mr. H. Clugston's steering abilities were substantiated by the Master at a later date - Mr. Clugston left the meeting.

The Chairman informed the Pilot that it was the general opinion of this Committee, that he was bringing the Pilot Service into disrepute. After giving consideration to the complaints it was apparent he was suffering under a sense of grievance and he knew what it was about, and he must forget it. The Committee required a new attitude to be shown by him in his conduct in the service. The Chairman emphasised that this was the very last time a warning would be given. He must have due respect for the Master of a vessel and show a more co-operative spirit towards the Helmsmen. If he continued as he had done in the past he would be bringing the Pilot Service and the Port into disrepute that the Pilotage Committee would not stand for. The chairman said that he hoped that was made perfectly clear to him. Mr. L. Roberts concluded by saying if the Pilot wished he could make life much happier by doing his job in a happier manner and that was the way he should go about his piloting in future.

The Pilot stated he did his job properly and was second to none in the service (what pomposity). He would not take a reprimand and if there was a penalty provided for him by the Pilotage Act he would pay it.

The Chairman told the Pilot if he would not change his attitude it would have to be changed for him and if he was a sensible man, and the Committee hoped that he was, he would act on the advice given him.

The Pilotage Committee was far from happy with the Pilot's manner and response to their findings and they had every right to be so. The Pilot had left the meeting totally unrepentant and clearly thinking ha had done no wrong. Six days later a letter was received in which a complaint was made against this Pilot for his conduct

The type of vessel's Mr. W. yates would have steered in 1940.
Note the lovely mast rigging

"HJalmar Wessel"
GRT. 1769 L.253' B.40'
This Norwegian coaster built in 1930 was still sailing in 1965.

Courtesy of World Ship Society

219

towards a Helmsman. Mr. R. Southwood steering the S.S. *"Salmon P. Chase"*, complained of his aggressive attitude towards him and abusive language. The following month, August, a fellow Pilot sent a complaint to the Pilotage Committee because of the manner in which this Pilot handled his vessel when meeting and passing him. It had led him to the conclusion that in the future he would moor his vessel to a quay rather than meet a vessel under the pilotage of this man. This Pilot so heavily criticised and reprimanded by the Pilotage Committee and his fellow Pilots, never ever changed his attitude towards Helmsmen or Pilots until the day he retired. Can a leopard ever change its spots? The mediaeval philosopher, St. Thomas Aquinas, stated "Prejudice is thinking ill of someone without sufficient warrant". Where was the warrant for these scurrilous and unsubstantiated accusations against Helmsmen. There is none, of course, none that would stand any scrutiny in any Pilot Service that took pride on being founded on the principles of truth, honour and comradeship. Most Pilot Services are based on these foundations.

22.

THE HELMSMENS SERVICE 1946 - 1950

The summer of 1945 had seen the cessation of hostilities in Europe and the Far East, but the war of attrition between the Pilots and the Helmsmen still continued in various degrees of intensity and insanity. Old scores real or imagined were still to be settled. Sadly this animosity continued for the next 45 years. Over the years the Helmsmens' Service had never greatly fluctuated in numbers, averaging fourteen men from as early as 1900. By 1939 it had risen to seventeen men and during the war, the temporary Helmsmen employed to ease the pressure and stress on the Service, brought the total to twenty five men. In 1946 most of the temporary Helmsmen had been dismissed.

Messrs Harrington and Cheshire had returned from war service and the Helmsmens Service read as follows:

A. Almond	W. McIntosh
H. Clugston	S. Willis
G. Cartwright	J. Patterson
J. Clarke	R. Robinson
E. Clare	A.L. Shepherd
R.C. Cheshire	R. Southwood
R.T. Green	J. Warren Jnr
H. Gibson	W. Walker
H.H. Harrington	H. Whitehead
S.P. Jones	W. Yates

The Helmsmens Association had calculated that a service of twenty men would be sufficient to meet the demands of all vessels requiring a Helmsman. They had also quite correctly anticipated that Ship owners and Pilots would revert to their pre-war practice of regarding Helmsmen as superfluous to their requirements and an unnecessary expense. They had not, however, anticipated the boom in traffic using the Ship Canal. In the twelve months from 1947 to 1948 the tonnage using the Ship Canal increased by over one and a quarter million tons the biggest increase in the Ship Canal's history. It continued to increase at a rate of over half a million tons per year.

On September 1st 1947 the Helmsmens Service abolished the pooling system of earnings and of course their sick pay and leave system. Many still regard this as the most retrograde step ever taken by the Helmsmens Association. This momentous decision, for indeed momentous it was, as the future was to disclose, was not taken lightly. The prevailing conditions that existed at the time precipitated this action. The unprecedented and wholly unexpected increase in shipping coupled with the advent of sickness to certain Helmsmen which rose proportionally with the extra work, had placed an intolerable strain on the Helmsmen who did not seek refuge from work behind a dubious sick note. The Pilots "turning down" practice was back in full sway now the war was over, placed an even greater strain on the senior Helmsmen. Negotiations with the Pilotage Committee had failed to increase their complement and they saw the abolishment of pooling earnings as their only recourse. It is interesting to note the incidents of sickness in the Winter of 1947-48 was considerable reduced and it was one of the worst winters for fifty years.

What the Helmsmen failed to see was the resurrection of that pernicious and most loathsome of practices, used indiscriminately by certain Pilots, the practice of "turning down". It is with the utmost regret that it must be recorded that quite a number of Pilots reverted to this practice with a vengeance. The Helmsmen suffered the greatest privations and humiliations from this odious behaviour, which at times knew no bounds. What is even more sad is that some Pilots who had suffered greatly under the "turning down" system when they were Helmsmen, indulged in this practice now. It is indeed hard to understand how the human mind works.

In 1947 the secretary of the Helmsmens Association, Mr. R. Southwood, with the assistance of two other Helmsmen, conducted a survey of a typical working month for Helmsmen. A brief resume of that survey can be found in Appendix III. It was abundantly clear from this survey that the Helmsmen were working exceptionally long hours. The travelling time, which has always been recognised as an inherent factor of each service performed also constituted an important item of expenditure. This was the beginning of the hardest working schedule the Helmsmen were ever to experience. At the April Pilotage Committee 1947, Mr. Southwood presented the results of their survey to the Chairman. Mr. Southwood pointed out the irregularity of the Helmsmen's working hours and the uncertainty of their disposition over the thirty six miles of the Ship Canal, had repercussions on their home life. He requested that these facts should be borne in mind and receive appropriate consideration when deliberating on the Helmsmens survey. To substantiate their claim for fourteen services per month, Mr. Southwood stated that for the figures tabled before them, the proportionate time worked would be as follows:

Steering Time	96 hours
Stand by Time	64 hours
Attending Tide	33 hours
Travelling Time	25 hours
TOTAL	218 hours

He went on to say that this represented a $9^1/_2$ hour day based on a 24-day month or a $7^1/_2$ hour day based on a 30 day month, which the Helmsmen had agreed to accept as a reasonable working rate. Mr. Southwood informed the Committee that an increase of nine Helmsmen was required to achieve this goal with the corresponding increase in the percentage on the Helmsmen's basic tariff from 35% to 49%. The Chairman stated that the Helmsmens survey and their requests to implement its findings must be fully discussed by the Manchester Shipowners Association and the Directors of the Ship Canal Company. When this had been done a further meeting would be arranged to discuss the matter.

"Golden Hind"
A Helmsmen was expected to steer every conceivable type of vessel.
Mr J. Wainwright (Pilot) at the Helm.

Courtesy of the Wainwright Family

1986

Steering towards the Weaver Bend a turn of 90° to port, the navigation light below the two white domes in the background was the first navigation light to be built in the canal. M.S.C. Grab Hopper "Donald Redford" being passd on the port side.

Approaching the notorious Runcorn Bend. A Helmsmans ability was judged on his steering through this narrow bridge hole, and rounding the Weaver Bend.

Courtesy of Mrs. J.J. Pierpoint

Mr. A.L. Shepherd
1936 - 1950

Mr. G. Kitchen
1960 - 1977

Mr. G. Collins
1960 - 1990
And still able to raise a smile

Tragically, no such meetings were arranged. Negotiations had commenced between the Pilots Association and the Pilotage Committee regarding the measure of their work and notional complement. This totally overshadowed and eventually nullified any further progress in the Helmsmans negotiations. In March 1949 the severest of set-backs occurred to the Helmsmen's negotiations, from which they never recovered. Five of the senior Helmsmen (Messrs Southwood, McIntosh, Cartwright, Patterson and Walker) were examined and promoted to Second Class Pilots. A loss so important as that of their five senior men, amongst whom was the principal architect of their new working system, could not fail to be generally and severely felt. The final blow came in June 1950 when Messrs Harrington and Sheppherd were examined and promoted to second class pilots. The consequences of these promotions was that the negotiations for a new working system, so satisfactorily prepared and diligently pursued, was allowed by the new Helmsmen's representatives to lie on file. The matter was never raised again at Pilotage Committee. Indeed a great tragedy.

On a historical note, when Mr. A.L. Shepherd was promoted to Second Class Pilot in 1950 he had been a Helmsman for 14 years. He became the holder of the unenviablé record of the longest steering time before obtaining a Pilot's licence. He held that record for 27 years when in 1977 Mr. G. Kitchen reluctantly claimed the new record of 17 years, which he held for 23 years. The all time record for the longest steering time, which will never be surpassed, was set by Mr. G. Collins who was promoted to Second Class Pilot on October 1st 1990 after a mind bending 30 years. How he retained his sanity the Author is at a loss to explain.

A HELMSMANS MONTHLY EARNINGS DECEMBER 1940
(COURTESY OF MRS. W. YATES)
Mr.W. Yates.

FRI & SAT:29th,30th NOV:1940.
S/S "SARDINIAN PRINCE".   BRITISH(PRINCE LINE)   1871 REG TON.
EASTHAM TO MANCHESTER FROM DUNDEE.PILOT:-RHODES.   £2-1-3. (£2.06)
TUGS:-"EASTHAM"&"BARTON".

SUN:1st DEC:1940.
S/S "GREGALIA".   DONALDSON LINE.   3580.
PARTINGTON TO EASTHAM FOR ST JOHNS & HALIFAX.
                                       PILOT:-KILLENDER.   £3-8-6. (£3.43p)
TUGS:-"STANLOW"&"MERLIN".

WED:4th DEC:1940.
M/V "BIRMINGHAM".   DUTCH.   257.
RUNCORN TO PARTINGTON.   PILOT:-DAVENPORT.   £1-3-9.(£1.19)

THURS:5th DEC:1940.
S/S "LOM".   NORWAY.   719.
PARTINGTON TO EASTHAM,COAL FOR DARTMOUTH.
                                       PILOT:-J.LAMEY.   £1-9-9.(£1.48)

SAT:7th DEC:1940.
S/S "SELBO".   NORWAY.   1027.
ELLESMERE PORT DRY DOCK JETTIES TO EASTHAM.
BALLAST FOR HALIFAX.   PILOT:-COLVIN.   £1-1-6.(£1.08p)

TUES & WED:10th,11th DEC:1940.
M/ "BRITISH HONOUR".   B.T.C.   4174.
EASTHAM TO MANCHESTER.   PILOT:-GREEN.   £3-0-0. (£3.00p)
BALLAST FROM GREENOCK.
TUGS:-"STANLOW"&"BARTON".

THURS:12th DEC:1940.
S/S "GLOXINIA".   STAG LINE.   1961.
WEASTE TO PARTINGTON IN BALLAST.PILOT:-HUGHES.   £1-12-3.(£1.61p)
TUGS:-"MOUNT MANISTY"&"MERLIN".

FRI:13th DEC:1940.
S/S "GLOXINIA".   STAG LINE.   1961.
PARTINGTON TO EASTHAM.   PILOT:-HUGHES.   £1-17-3.(£1.87p)
TUGS:-"LORD STALBRIDGE"&"BARTON".

SUN & MON:15th,16th DEC:1940.
S/S "AKERHUS".   NORWAY.   368 REG TON.
ESTHAM TO MANCHESTER.   PILOT:-COLVIN.   £1-13-9. (£1.68p)

TUES:17th DEC:1940.
M/V "LIBERTY".   DUTCH.   148.
PARTINGTON TO ELLESMERE PORT PONTOON JETTIES WITH COAL.
                                 PILOT:-STOTT.   £1-8-9. (£1.43p)

TURS & FRI:19th,20th DEC:1940.
S/S "OSTREVENT".   BRITISH(EX FRENCH)   916.
PARTINGTON TO EASTHAM,FOR DARTMOUTH WITH COAL.
                                 PILOT:-STOTT.   £2-9-4. (£2.47p)

---

nb 23rd DEC:1940.
S/S "MARIANNE II".   BRITISH(EX NORWAY)   715.
EASTHAM TO PARTINGTON,FROM CLYDE WITH TEA.
                                 PILOT:-LAMBY.   £2-15-3.(£2.76p)

THURS:26th DEC:1940.
M/V "SHELBRIT 3".   BRITISH.   193.
STANLOW TO EASTHAM WITH SPIRIT FOR DOUGLAS.
                                 PILOT:-LLOYD.   £-18-9. (96p)

SAT:28th DEC:1940.
S/S "SAN DARIO".   BRITISH.   583.
S LOW TO WEASTE WITH CRUDE OIL.PILOT:-ONION.   £1-10-9.(£1.54p)

MON:30th DEC:1940.
M/V "ATT S".   DUTCH.   252.
ACTON GRANGE TO ELLESMERE PORT CEMENT WHARF VIA LATCHFORD.
                                 PILOT:-OLIVER.   £1-16-9. (£1.84p)

TUES:31st DEC:1940.
BRITISH SCOUT".   BRITISH TANKER Co.   836.
STANLOW TO EASTHAM WITH SPIRIT FOR AVONMOUTH.
                                 PILOT:-HUGHES.   £-18-9. (93p)
                    TOTAL EARNINGS FOR DECEMBER 1940 £27.3s.1d. (£27.17p)

Mr. Yates total earnings for the year 1941 was £460.8s.2d. (£460.43p) an

average of £38.per month. A pint of beer cost 10d.(4p) and Income Tax was

6s.6d. (32p) in the pound. A Master of a deep sea vessel between 7,000 -9,000

tons was ~~also~~ earning £38.per month.

23.

THE HELMSMENS SERVICE 1950 - 1990

The failure of the Helmsmens Association to negotiate a new measure of work and notional complement for their service in 1949 was a severe setback. It caused so much disillusionment and despair that they never attempted to approach the Manchester Pilotage Committee ever again with any radical schemes to alter their service. From that moment in 1949 until the Helmsmens Service ceased to exist in October 1990, they stoically accepted a percentage of any increases the Pilot Service managed to negotiate with the Manchester Pilotage Committee. Between 1950 and 1956 three very significant changes occurred - which for once were undeniably for the betterment of the whole service - that was to change the whole image and conditions of the Helmsmen. It had always been the Manchester Ship Canal Company policy as the ruling Licensing Body, to issue a standard typed letter of authority giving permission for any person to steer vessels in the Manchester Ship Canal. On 25 March 1955, this letter was replaced by a Helmsman's Permit - the author held the Number One Permit - couched in the legal terminology of a Pilot's Licence and printed on vellum. It was a far more suitable document to produce on the request of a Pilot or Master for their inspection.

On 1 February 1956 the most significant change of all took place, when the Helmsmen's Association voted unanimously to re-introduce the pooling system of earnings after a lapse of over 10 years.

(265)

THE MANCHESTER SHIP CANAL COMPANY

Harbour Master's Office

DOCK OFFICE   MANCHESTER 17

Telegrams: "WATERWAY, MANCHESTER."   *Telephone:* TRAFFORD PARK 2411

REFERENCE No. ....HM/H.................................

Any reply should bear this Reference and should be addressed
to The Harbour Master.   *Extn.*......232.

13th January, 1950.

Mr. P. K. Ralli,
30, Knowsley Road,
WALLASEY,
Cheshire.

Dear Sir,

      I am pleased to be able to inform you that
on the 16th instant you will have completed six months steering
vessels up to 4,500 tons gross, and authority has been granted for
you to steer vessels of all tonnages on and from the 17th idem.
This permission is, of course, subject for the time being to the
usual proviso that your services may be refused for a particular
vessel if the pilot does not consider your experience warrants
his accepting your services.

      The necessary authority is attached.

      Yours faithfully,

Captain, R.N.(Retd.).

This was the standard letter issued to all Helmsmen as proof they
were full tonnage to be produced on demand by a Pilot or Master of a Vessel
It was replaced by the Helmsmans Permit in 1955.

THE MANCHESTER SHIP CANAL COMPANY

Helmsman's Permit No. 1.

The Manchester Ship Canal Company having found:

M R.   D E R E K   A V E R E L L   C L U L O W

of 1, Kingsville Road, Bebington, Wirral.

to be a fit and competent person duly skilled to act as a Helmsman on the Manchester Ship Canal do hereby authorise and permit him to steer vessels of any tonnage on the said Canal and to act as Helmsman in the manner, and at the rates, from time to time appointed or approved by the Company.

This Permit (unless it shall have been suspended or revoked by the Company in the meantime) is to continue in force up to and until the Thirty-first day of December next after which it shall be subject to renewal from time to time by endorsement hereon.

Granted this 25th *day of* M a r c h, *19* 55.

~~HARBOUR MASTER~~

for MANCHESTER SHIP CANAL COMPANY.

Concurrent with the pooling system, a rota for an organised leave system was instituted giving Helmsmen three weeks leave between June and September and three separate weeks leave between October and May; all with pay.

Without doubt the greatest benefit of all with the introduction of pooling earnings was the immediate establishment of a Sick Pay Scheme, based on the well founded rules and regulations drawn up by the Pilot Service. All these changes made for a healthier and certainly happier Helmsmens Service and it reflected in their attitude towards their profession.

The percentage increase on the basic tariff, between these years, had increased from 35% to 49%. This gave the Helmsman an average monthly income for the Tax year 1955/56 of £80 gross. With the introduction of the pooling system this figure increased to £90 gross. During this period a Chief Officer of an ocean going vessel of 9,000 tons gross, holding a Master's Certificate, was earning £83.17.6d (£83.88) gross per month; beer was ls.5d ($7^1/_2$p) a pint; whiskey 10d (4p) a tot and the rate of Income Tax on the first £60 was 2s.3d ($11^1/_2$p); on the next £150 it was 4s.9d (24p) and 6s.9d (34p) on the next £150. The remainder was charged at 8s.9d ($42^1/_2$p) in the pound. With all the allowances received from the Inland Revenue, as a self-employed person, the Helmsman's Tax bill averaged out at £20 p.a.

From 1956 to 1963 the Manchester Pilot Service and therefore the Helmsmens Service was beset, once again, with diverse problems. In May 1963 the Manchester Pilotage Committee produced a comprehensive review of those problems in conjunction with positive and constructive recommendations to resolve them. There had always been an inherent fear in the Helmsmens Service that one day they would become the sacrificial lamb on the altar of the Pilots' negotiations for an increase in the pilots' tariff. This fear became a reality during these negotiations. The Helmsmens Service had now increased to 44 men and their gross earnings per month had risen to £108.

The Manchester Pilotage Committee had stated that because of the Helmsmen's close interest in many of the issues to be considered, they should whenever possible be brought into the negotiations from

A HELMSMANS MONTHLY EARNINGS DECEMBER 1954

Mr. D.A.CLULOW

BASED ON SCHEDULE OF CHARGES FROM FEBRUARY 1st 1954 (SEE APPENDICES)

DATE OF SERVICE		VESSEL	AMOUNT £	s.	d.	TRAVELLING EXPENSES £ s. d.	NATIONAL INSURANCE £ s. d.	
December	1	Ingeborg	3	9	9	7 0		East.-Manc.
"	3	Gem	4	9	7	7 0		East.-Manc.
"	8	Kilwa	1	5	11	14 0	5 0	Shift in Manc.
"	9	"	4	2	11	7 0		Manc.-East.
"	13	Shell Director	1	13	4		5 0	East.-Stanlow.
"	13	" "	1	15	6			Stanlow.-East.
"	15	Hemsley 1	3	7	2	7 0		East.-Manc.
"	16	Pass of Glenogle	3	12	8	7 0		Barton.-East.
"	18	Hemsley 1	2	19	2	7 0		Stanlow.-East.
"	20/21	Pass of Drumochter	4	10	0	7 0	5 0	East.-Barton.
"	22	Marie Boettcher	1	13	9			East.-Ince.
"	22	" "	1	13	6			Ince.-East.
"	21	Inverpriot	3	13	1	7 0		Manc.-East.
"	30	"	1	5	4	14 0	5 0	
"	30	"	1	15	6			Cancellation
"	25	Hoheweg	3	14	2	7 0		East.-Manc.
		DEDUCTIONS £ s d	45	5	9	4 11 0	1 0 0	
		N.H. Contributions 1 3 0						
		Collection Expenses 1 2 8						
		General Expenses 13 11	2	19	7			
			42	6	2	4 11 0	1 0 0	

Mr. Clulow had started as a Helmsman in October Of 1954 and the above earnings represented work done on vessels all under 1,500 gross tons. There was no pooling of earnings in those days, therefore no leave system or sick pay. In that year 1955 to 1956 his gross earnings totaled £933 and after Income Tax allowances for a Helmsman the assessable Tax for that year was £752. Income tax was 2s.3d (11p) in the pound and his Tax bill was £4.3s.3d. (£4.16p). A pint of bitter was 1s.5d. (7p) and a glass of whiskey 10d (4p). A Master of a 7,000 to 9,000 tons deep sea vessel would have been earning £95 per month approximately. MR. CLULOW WAS EARNING APPROXIMATELY £77 PER MONTH.

the earliest stage. The Pilots' representatives vetoed this proposal and the Helmsmen were only considered and presented with a virtual fait accompli in the very latter stages of these negotiations. The Pilots' total disregard for the Helmsmens Service and the unfeeling approach to the Helmsmen's livelihood still continued to exist.

It had always been a prerequisite in all negotiations - past and present - regarding changes in the Schedule of Charges for Services, that the Manchester Steamship Owners Association should be entirely satisfied that any increase had been kept to a bare minimum. With this precept, much in the forefront of their minds, the Manchester Pilotage Committee in collusion with the Manchester Pilot Service for the first time, used the Helmsmens Service as a strong bargaining point to assist the Pilots in their negotiations for a successful increase in their tariff. It is sad to record that this incident would not be the last time the Helmsmens Service would be used in such a deplorable manner by the Manchester Pilot Service.

The following motion was tabled at the Manchester Pilotage Committee Meeting in June 1963:

"The Helmsmen's complement will be reduced to 43 men. This will be attained by the Helmsmen withdrawing their services from Shifting Duties at Eastham and on vessels of 500 net reg tons and under, if such a vessel is proceeding only 13 miles or under.

(Author's Note: There is a certain amount of irony in this edict because it was so near and dear to the hearts of many Pilots and caused so much animosity within the service over 40 years ago. Now in what was supposedly enlightened times, it had come to fruition. It also deprived the Helmsmen of over 90% of their individual remuneration from Runcorn and Weston Point Docking Fees.)

"The Helmsmen's gross earnings will be £1,485 a year and as there is a surplus of £442 p.a. on the earnings to support 44.3 men the Helmsman's gross receipts will be reduced by £6,827. The total reduction due to Helmsmen not being employed on Shifting Duties and vessels under 500 net reg tons will amount to £8,057 a year. To recover this difference the Helmsmen's rates will have to be increased by 2%. The additional cost to the Steamship Owners, taking into consideration the 4.33% increase in Pilotage Rates and

1988
"No room for a steering error".
A Helmsmans modern day view of approaching Barton Aqueduct and Road Bridge outward bound from Manchester.

1988
A Helmsman stll has to have skill in steering past another vessel in the canal.

Courtesy of Mrs. J.J. Pierpoint

Helmsmen's representatives to be included in the negotiations for a more secure future for the Pilots in the Port of Manchester - the Helmsmen's livelihood was even more at risk than that of the Pilots - was either summarily dismissed or totally disregarded. The prevailing attitude was that the Manchester Pilot Service looked upon the Helmsmen's Service as a disruptive presence and a serious stumbling block to their negotiations for a secure future. The Manchester Pilot Service knew only too well that without their support to negotiate on the Helmsmen's future the service would cease to exist. The Pilots were prepared to sacrifice the Helmsmens Service if it would gain security for their future, such was the manner in which the Manchester Pilot Service would repay the Helmsmens Service for over three-quarters of a century of loyal service.

During the next 14 years the decline of the Port of Manchester reflected the irreversible decline of the Helmsmens Service and with the policy adopted by the Manchester Pilot Service of not automatically replacing Pilots who retired or died in service, 36 Licences became available through these years and only 23 Licences issued. The last 2nd Class Licence was issued on 1 March 1977 to Mr G.H. Kitchen who had been a Helmsman for 17 years; the prospects of promotion to a Pilot was very remote to new entrants into the Helmsmen's Service.

Consequently, many of the later entrants all of whom held a Master's Certificate of Competency, left the service and successfully made a career as Pilots in other United Kingdom ports.

By the year 1982, the complement of Helmsmen had been reduced to 19 men. The yearly increases in their basic rates relating to National Maritime Board awards, inflation adjustments, etc, coupled with the reduction in their complement led to the level of their earnings for that year reaching a record high of £1,151 gross per month. The increasing rapidity at which the decline of the Port of Manchester was taking place is clearly shown in the following table of Helmsmen's earnings, but it must be recorded that all the "ills" that beset the Helmsmens Service could not be contributed solely to the decline of the Manchester Ship Canal. More and more Pilots were proceeding on vessels without employing a Helmsman for various self interests.

LEVEL OF A HELMSMAN'S GROSS MONTHLY EARNINGS

1983	:	£1,057
1984	:	£ 814
1985	:	£ 804
1986	:	£ 833

Between 1983 and 1986, some Helmsmen sought a second self-employed occupation to enable them to keep the standard of living they had achieved over the years. Their new ventures covered a wide variety of employment, proving what versatile and talented men they were - a point that Pilots could never acknowledge. They became postmasters, insurance brokers, a tenant of a country inn, owner of a chauffeur service company and a landscape gardener. A number of these new occupations, much to their own surprise, eventually became their main source of income and the income derived from being a Helmsman was relegated to a supporting role, a complete turn-about.

At about this time, two long serving Helmsmen, Messrs J. Southwood and G.H. Harrington - whose fathers and grandfathers had been Pilots in the Manchester Pilot Service - resigned from the service and were successfully examined and appointed Licensed River Dee Pilots, covering such ports as Mostyn and Shotton. It is a pleasure to report they have carried out their duties as Pilots with great acumen and distinction, much to the surprise of the majority of the Manchester Pilots. Mr G.H. Harrington had the added distinction of being the last Trinity House Pilot to be appointed by that august body before they too ceased to exist, after being the controlling Pilotage Authority of the majority of the United Kingdom ports for 350 years.

From 1986 the level of earnings gradually increased until the final tax year of their existence 1989/90. In that year they grossed per month £1,204, a record figure and one that was indeed fully justified and deserved. Their complement had been reduced to 14 men. Mr J.G. Taylor, Secretary of the Helmsmens Association, had been keeping a very close observation on all the machinations on the

1962 - 1988

Mr. J.J. Pierpoint

Mr. Pierpoint was the only member of the Manchester Pilot Service to be a Captain of a golf club (Wallasey G.C.) Handicap 9. Tragically he was also the only Helmsman ever to die in service, February 1988 aged 49 years.

By kind permission of Mrs. J.J. Pierpoint

6.

MANCHESTER SHIP CANAL HELMSMEN SERVICE (APPRENTICE PILOTS)

AUGUST   1961.

The Rota below -in seniority- is the largest rota of Helmsmen ever
to be in service,it was never surpassed and commenced to decline
from 1963,until the rota had 8 men on the list ~~only~~, in 1988.

Emberton. J. S.	Southport.
Foster.D.J.	Manchester.
Russell.J.E.	Liverpool.
Golsby.R.A.	Wirral.
Ball.R.J.	Frodsham.
Davies. M.J.	Wirral.
Avery. E.	Wirral.
Appleton.F.K.	Liverpool.
Barber.A.W.	Stockport.
Gannicliffe. J.	Liverpool.
Keys.J.T.	Wirral.
Neck.D.T.	Wirral.
Lightfoot. M.G.	Warrington.
Foulkes.R.	Blackburn.
Maycock.R.	Liverpool.
Smith. G.H.	Wirral.
Gray.G.R.	Wirral.
Wood. B.D.	Wirral.
Mackinnon.I.C.	Wirral.
Bell. B.	Chester.
Boyles. R.S.	Wirral..
Woodhead.P.F.	Wirral.
Winchester.B.	Liverpool.
Hopkins. W.	Warrington.
Law. J.H..	Warrington.
Baines.J.P.E.	Altrincham.
Hopkinson..D.W.	Wirral.
Andrews. G.	Lymn.
Williams. D.G.	Mold.
Lloyd. J.M.	Warrington.
Cahill.J.	Wirral.
Jarvis.J.W.	Liverpool.
Bartleet.F.M.	Wirral.
Brown. D.R.	Wirral.
Astles. J.	Wirral.
Davis.J.F.	Chester.
Watts.M.D.	Wirral.
Snowden.D.A.	Wirral.
Edwards.D.J.	Liverpool.
Bernard.D.H.	Wirral.
Kitchen.G.H.	Wirral.
Rolph.D.C.	Liverpool.
Jones. B.H.	Wirral.
Collings.W.G.	Wirral.
Hulse.R.O.	Liverpool
Taylor.J.G.	Wirral.
Cooke. A.E.	Wirral.
Higgins.D.E.	Chester.
Elliot. A.A.	Liverpool.

future of the Manchester Pilot Service which took place between the Pilots and the new owners of the Manchester Ship Canal Company. As these negotiations progressed, it became abundantly clear to the Helmsmen's representatives that they had no alternative but to negotiate entirely separately for their own survival, on a self financing early release scheme. This was due to the total rejection by the Manchester Pilot Service for the Helmsmen to become part of their organisation and the Pilots being oblivious of the Helmsmen's plight) coupled with the complete refusal of the Manchester Ship Canal Company's new owners to recognise their responsibility towards the future of the Helmsmens Service.

In the past, Mr Julian Taylor (Secretary of the Pilotage Committee) and Mr R S Boyles, Pilot Manager, had gone on record to state that the Manchester Pilotage Committee would always recognise a moral responsibility for the future of the Helmsmens Service. The new owners were not prepared to honour this commitment.

These negotiations ended on 1 September 1989 when the following early release scheme was agreed :

1)   The Manchester Ship Canal Company would fund the Helmsmen's Early Release Scheme.

2)   The Helmsmen's Service to be reduced to 8 men.

3)   The six Helmsmen released to receive a one time only payment of £9,000.

4)   The Helmsmen's gross earnings per month would be fixed at £1,250.

5)   All excess from Schedule of Earnings to repay the Early Release Scheme.

6)   The funding to be repaid within 12 months @ 1% interest above Bank Standard Rate at that time.

7)   The Early Release Scheme to be implemented immediately.

8)   This offer not repeatable or negotiable.

The six Helmsmen who accepted an early release from the service - everyone had over 20 years service - realistically had no alternative. They had been informed that their prospects of ever becoming a Licensed Pilot either in the Port of Manchester or any other district in the United Kingdom was non-existent. Fortunately they had already established themselves as successful entrepreneurs in their new occupations, but nevertheless, the paltry payment of £9,000 for over 20 years of dedicated service was utterly derisory to say the least. It was the maximum amount the Helmsmen's representative could extract from a miserly Manchester Ship Canal Company, to fund the early release scheme. The funding was repaid by the Helmsmens Service in 8 months.

At this same time in 1989, the remaining 8 Helmsmen, as an association, applied to become members of the now newly named Manchester Pilots Limited Co-operative. On 1 August 1989, their application was approved and an appropriate agreement was entered into to preserve the value of the respective Reserve Funds of the Pilots and the Helmsmen. A resolution was passed to issue shares to the new entrants into the co-operative. It had taken an unbelievable 93 years for the Helmsman's Service to be accepted and recognised as part of the Manchester Pilot Service. It has to be recorded as an everlasting tribute to the tenacity and unswerving dedication of numerous representatives over the years and an everlasting shame to the Manchester Pilots Service intractable and intransigent attitude.

On 1 October 1990, the 8 Helmsmen were examined and passed to 2nd Class Pilots. The Helmsmans Service which had given itself so unstintingly for the betterment of a Pilotage Service for nearly a century, ceased to exist. The final Helmsmen's Rota read as follows, with service record:

W.G. COLLINGS	HOYLAKE	30 years
A.E. COOKE	THORNTON HOUGH	30 years
D.J. EDWARDS	FORMBY	20 years
A.A. ELLIOTT	NORTHOP	16 years
D.E. HIGGINS	CHESTER	29 years
D.H. JACKSON	WREXHAM	23 years
J.D. REYNOLDS	WARRINGTON	21 years
J.G. TAYLOR	BROMBOROUGH	30 years

1990
The hi-tec wheelhouse of today.
Mr. G. Taylor Helmsman

Mr. R. Maycox
Sec. Helmsmans Association
1960 - 1965

Mr. G. Taylor
The last Secretary of the Helmsmans
Association

EPILOGUE

During the whole of their 93 years in existence, the Helmsmens Service never had any real support or received much appreciation or were ever acknowledged for their expertise in steering a vessel through narrow channels, by anyone connected with the Manchester Ship Canal Pilotage District. The shipowners and shipping agents from time immemorial always observed the Helmsmens Service as an unnecessary expense and unwanted presence and continually did their uttermost to dispense with their services on any type of vessel.

The Manchester Pilotage Committee observed them as an additional expense that could deter trade coming into the Ship Canal if pilotage dues became increasingly expensive. No other port in the United Kingdom had Helmsmen, but to their everlasting credit they did acknowledge that the Helmsmens Service was an integral part of the Pilot service as the only means of recruiting future Pilots.

The Masters of vessels of every size and nationality, viewed the Helmsmen with great suspicion - having been suitably "wound up" by a previous Pilot - because 99 times out of 100, someone, somewhere, would attempt to blame the Helmsman for any damage to his beloved vessel or if he missed a tide, thus incurring extra expense or missed cargo.

The Tug Masters had seen it all before; they were a different breed and knew the predicament a Helmsman would be in by the very virtue of the Pilot who was in charge of the vessel. They did, on more than one occasion, proffer kindly words of advice on how to appease a ranting Pilot, but even they were prone to bouts of uncontrollable criticism of Helmsmen for their inability to steer a straight and narrow course.

The Pilots, their traditional antagonists, had a hatred of Helmsmen bordering on the pathological. They fumed if a Helmsman acquired a new car or even a car at all; they created if a Helmsman's holidays were abroad. To certain Pilots, this sort of living diminished the Helmsman's ability to steer correctly and they were promptly placed on the "Turn Down" list. That some Helmsmen survived to become Pilots was a miracle in itself. In the new and supposedly magnanimous Manchester Pilots Ltd Co-operative of total equality, there still remains a very noticeable distinction syndrome between 1st and 2nd Class Pilots. The following clauses have been applied by the ruling 1st Class Pilots.

1)   If a 2nd Class Pilot having been ordered to pilot a vessel, on boarding that vessel finds he requires a helmsman to assist him, the next Pilot on his rota will be sent to that vessel BUT if the Pilot sent to steer the vessel is a 1st Class Pilot, he will immediately assume the role as Pilot and the 2nd Class Pilot originally ordered as the Pilot, will assume the role of Helmsman.

2)   The promotion from 2nd Class to 1st Class Pilot must not be considered as automatic on the retirement or death of a 1st Class Pilot. Such promotions will be at the entire discretion of the Manchester Pilots Limited Co-operative senior 1st Class Pilots.

3)   The duty pilot at Eastham responsible for the receiving and issuing of pilotage orders, shall always be a 1st Class Pilot.

The second clause is clearly understandable from a 1st Class Pilot's point of view, that any promotions would reduce their portion of the earnings. By increasing the 2nd Class Pilots - who are licensed to pilot 95% of the vessels now using the Port of Manchester - and decreasing the 1st Class Pilots, their 1st Class share of the pooled earnings must increase. A 2nd Class Pilot on 1 October 1990, has every possibility of remaining as such until his retirement, on a reduced pension, of which the present 1st Class Pilots do not appear to care one whit. The third clause was promoted because certain

Pilots refused to accept orders from a 2nd Class Pilot who they still considered as Helmsmen. The very thought that a Helmsman would be giving THEM orders filled these Pilots with horror.

THE LEOPARDS NEVER CHANGE THEIR SPOTS!

EPITAPH TO THE HELMSMAN

When the last wheel has been turned
And the Helmsman laid to rest,
His body all weary and worn
Talk between you, what you think was best.

No open bridges or Pilots' whims
Will there, the Helmsman annoy,
But in robes of white, a shining light
Somebody's fair haired boy.

No compass to swing, no spokes to turn
Nor Chain and Rods to tighten,
No Pilots to pander, no canal to meander
Nor passing ships to frighten.

But on that bright and happy shore
Beyond this vale of tears,
Where Pilots' cease from moaning
A Helmsman has no fears.

So leave him alone in God's Heaven
He's gone, doing best for his Camelot,
Let Heaven be reserved for the Helmsman -
And Hell set apart for the Pilot.

ONE OF THE LAST RETURNS OF A HELMSMAN EARNINGS

THE PORT CF MANCHESTER

THE   MANCHESTER   SHIP   CANAL   COMPANY

MR A E COOKE   142   SUMMARY OF EARNINGS.
4C ETON DRIVE   ---------------------
THORNTON HOUGH   HELMSMAN
WIRRAL MERSEYSIDE   MONTH MARCH   1990
L63 1JS

SCHEDULE OF CHARGES FROM JANUARY 1st 1988. APPENDIX NO. VII

VESSEL	REFERENCE	DATE	EARNINGS	TRAVEL EXPENSES
ILSE	ACC831	2 MAR	267.61	EASTHAM TO STANLOW
ESSO CLYDE	ACC872	1 MAR	359.65	EASTHAM TO STANLOW
MARAMOZZA	JCG910	6 MAR	222.03	ELLS.PORT TO EASTHAM
THUNTANK 9	ACC945	8 MAR	257.29	STANLOW TO EASTHAM
CITY OF PLYM	JC1087	17 MAR	147.79	ELLS.PORT TO EASTHAM
ARGENTUM	JC1092	18 MAR	176.62	EASTHAM TO ELLS.PORT
AGRENTUM	JC1097	19 MAR	183.50	ELLS.PORT TO EASTHAM
SHELLTRANS	JC1147	21 MAR	281.46	EASTHAM TO STANLOW
VELAZGUEZ	AC1170	22 MAR	103.21	OGWATERS TO EASTHAM
ILSE	JC1207	23 MAR	193.76	STANLOW TO EASTHAM
THUNTANK 9	JC1239	25 MAR	194.91	STANLOW TO EASTHAM
CITY OF ATHE	JC1271	29 MAR	150.34	EASTHAM TO ELLS.PORT
		TOTALS	2538.17	

It makes interesting reading to compare the work schedule of Mr. Thomas Lamey in 1902 and Mr. Alec Cooke in 1990 nearly 90 years later.

DATE	NAME	VESSELS No.	MILES STEAMED.	TIME	EARNINGS	EARNINGS PER TIDE.
DEC.1902.	T.LAMEY	16	481	168 Hours	£22.80p.	1.70p.
MAR.1990.	A.COOKE.	12	46	12 Hours	£2538.17p	£211.51p

In 1990 a pint of beer was £1, 20p (1p) and a glass of whiskey £1 (1½p). Income tax was 25p in the pound (6p). The prices in the brackets are Mr. Lameys costs in 1902. A Master of a ship and vessel would be earning approximately £2,188   per month, a Chief officer £1,700. *N 1990*.

Appendix I

Name of Pilot	Commence holiday (12 noon)	Resume Duty (12 noon)	Name of Pilot
Robinson A.L.	April 18th	May 9th	Lamey J.E.
Green R.	"	"	Postlethwaite A.E.
Bennett A.P.	May 9th	May 30th	Lamey W.
Southwood E.	-do-	-do-	Green M.
Heath J.W.	May 30th	June 20th	Harvey W.L.
Baxter J.G.	-do-	-do-	Roberts W.H.
Onion W.	June 20th	July 11th	Dudley W.P.
Cartwright G	-do-	-do-	Lamey T.
Davidson G.	July 11th	August 1st	Young C.F.
Lloyd R.	-do-	-do-	Onion F.
Hindle J.A.	August 1st	August 22nd	Southwood R.
Hankinson R.	-do-	-do-	Langley W.H.
Inglesfield J.	Septr. 12th		
Richardson G.	August 22nd	Septr. 12th	Barnes J.
Green G.	-do-	-do-	Shaw J.D.
Inglesfield J.	Septr 12th	Octr. 3rd	Southwood W.D
Marker W.	-doᴮ	-do-	

1923

The first Pilots Leave Rota

Appendix II

For each ship entering or leaving and navigating the Ship Canal requiring the services of a Helmsman an initial fee shall be payable (except where otherwise herein provided) according to the net. reg. tonnage of the vessel:

1) For a vessel:

Not Exceeding 1,000 tons	15s.0d.	(75p.)
Exceeding 1,000 tons but not exceeding 2,000 tons	£1.0s.0d.	(£1.00)
Exceeding 2,000 tons but not exceeding 3,000 tons	£1.15s.0d.	(£1.75)
Exceeding 3,000 tons but not exceeding 4,000 tons	£1.15s.0d.	(£1.75)
Exceeding 4,000 tons but not exceeding 5,000 tons	£2.0s.0d.	(£2.00)
Exceeding 5,000 tons but not exceeding 6,000 tons	£2.10s.0d.	(£2.25)
Exceeding 6,000 tons and upwards	£2.10s.0d.	(£2.50)

In addition there shall be payable a sum of 9d (4p) a mile or portion of a mile for the distance the vessel has been steered. A vessel in ballast shall pay only half the mileage rate but the full initial fee.

2) For each vessel requiring the services of a helmsman when moving from point to point in the Canal but without leaving or entering the Canal one half of the initial fee shall be payable in addition to the mileage rate.

3) For a vessel requiring the services of a Helmsman when moving:

      a. Point to point within the Manchester Docks.

      b. Between Manchester Docks and Barton Locks.

      c. At Partington Coaling Basin.

The following charges shall be payable on their net reg tons:

For a vessel not exceeding 1,000 tons 5s.0d (25p)

For a vessel exceeding 1,000 tons and upwards £1.1s.0d. (£1.05p)

d. When moving a vessel from Eastham Lock to a berth in Eastham Basin or vice versa:

For a vessel not exceeding 1,000 tons .... 2s.6d (12^1/$_2$p)

Exceeding 1,000 tons and upwards .... 10s.6d (52^1/$_2$p)

4) If a vessel is detained on her voyage on her passage up or down the Canal for the purpose of discharging or loading cargo, bunkering or otherwise a fee of 7s.0d (35p) will be payable if the vessel proceeds on her journey within twelve hours. An additional fee of ls.0d (5p) shall be payable in respect of each hour or part therof the vessel is detained in excess of twelve hours.

5) When a vessel is detained in excess of two hours from the time the Helmsman is ordered a fee of 5s.0d. (25p) shall be payable provided the vessel is not delayed by weather. (This fee was increased to 7s.6d. (37^1/$_2$p) in 1940)

6) Where a vessel is swung in the Canal at any point a fee of 5s.0d. (25p) shall be payable in addition to the Schedule Helmsman's Dues.

7) When a Helmsman has been ordered to a vessel and the sailing of that vessel is cancelled and he is not required a fee of 7s.6d. (37^1/$_2$p) shall be payable. (This fee was increased to l0s.0d. (50p) in 1940 as it was not sufficient to cover out of pocket expenses).

March 17th 1913.

Appendix III

HELMSMAN	RESIDENCY	NO. OF DAYS	NO. OF SERVICES	MILES MILEAGE	STEERING TIME (H M)	STANDBY FOR ORDERS (H M)	ASCENDING TIME (H M)	TRAVEL TIME (H M)	TOTAL TIME (H M)
R. SOUTHWOOD	LITTLE SUTTON	30	19	400	129 57	72 16	56 12	50 20	307 45
A. SHEPHERD	EASTHAM	30	23	422	124 35	120 45	64 40	31 50	341 50
H. WHITEHEAD	PSYTON-U-LYME	30	22	463	180 27	96 16	29 25	76 33	382 41
	TOTALS	90	64	1,285	433 59	289 17	150 17	108 43	1,032 16
AVERAGE PER MAN		30	21·3	428	144 40	96 26	50 05	52 54	344 05
" PER MAN	7 DAY WEEK.	7	4·97	160	33 43	22 24	11 40	12 22	80 09
" " "	PER DAY	1		14·2	4 49	3 12	1 40	1 46	11 27

THE HELMSMAN SURVEY OF 1947 — APPENDICES NO. III

EXCLUDING TRAVEL TIME:- AVGR. HR. PER DAY PER 7 DAY WEEK. 9hrs 41m.

AVERAGE MANS NORMAL WORKING MONTH. 24 DAYS, AVERAGE HR PER DAY FOR

HELMSMAN WOULD BE. 14HRS. 20min.

Appendix IV
HELMSMEN - ADMINISTRATION

a)   The single Service to have two distinct categories licensed Pilots engaged solely on pilotage and Apprentice Pilots (not necessarily so-called) engaged solely on steering with a view to their becoming licensed Pilots.

b)   The whole Service to be under the jurisdiction of the Pilotage Committee to the same extent as Pilots themselves are. Subject to this overall jurisdiction Apprentice Pilots' affairs to be the responsibility of a subcommittee of the Pilotage Committee.

c)   Schemes for graduated earnings, improved status of senior men, amalgamation of pension arrangements and for overcoming the age limit problem to be considered after the new constitution is established. Such schemes are not however to put present Helmemen in a worse position than now in terms of promotion, prospects, earnings or security of employment.

d)   Byelaws to be made for the good government of apprentices under Section 17(c) of the Pilotage Act. Such Bye-laws to give present Helmsmen in the Service protections, rights and duties (where consistent) equivalent to those applied to Pilots under the Pilotage Act, to the extent that this is legally possible and acceptable to the Board of Trade.

e)   Representation. Apprentice Pilots not to be directly represented on the Pilotage Committee or in the election of representatives of that Committee. The Pilots' representatives not to be regarded as representatives of the Apprentices but as members of the Pilotage Committee in their dealings with Apprentices' affairs. One or more

Pilots' representatives to serve on the Apprentice Pilots' sub-committee. Helmsmen's representatives to be elected by the Helmsmen only. Procedure for election to be agreed. Shipowners and Authority also to be represented on the subcommittee.

f) No decision to be made by the Pilotage Committee in connection with the terms of service and working conditions of Apprentices without full consultation with the Apprentices through the sub-committee.:

g) Apprentices may have a separate identity in the form of their own association and the management of their association affairs - subject to the overall jurisdiction of the Pilotage Committee on matters connected with the working system, through the sub-committee.

h) The special sub-committee established by the Pilotage Committee on July 11, 1966 to have these heads of agreement referred to them and to submit draft Byelaws with a detailed scheme for amalgamation. This sub-committee also to deal with the other matters raised in Part 4 of the Report.

The Company are well aware of the Helmsmen's anxiety that the future position, particularly with regard to the distribution of earnings to new entrants and senior Helmsmen, should be settled within twelve months of the commencement of the Agreement so that if for example it is eventually agreed to revert to the present system of a full share after 12 months the new entrants will not have suffered any loss.

This is one of the reasons why the Company have thought it best to keep the shares for the first 12 months at the levels provided in the past rather than to adopt the smaller shares suggested in the Agreement. Whilst no guarantee can be given with regard to the timing or content of any settlement the Helmsmen have been assured that the Company, the Ship owners and the Pilots appreciate the Helmsmen's point and will use their best endeavours to reach an early settlement in full consultation with the Helmsmen.

It would not be appropriate, under the terms of the Agreement, to take any decision at this stage which would anticipate the outcome of the discussions on status and earnings and the special sub-committee have stressed the importance of keeping the options open until the discussions have taken place. The Company fully endorse this view and believe that the best results can only be achieved if all the parties maintain an open mind in the first instance.

The following additional assurances have been given to the Helmsmen, through their representatives, on behalf of the Company and of the special sub-committee.

(1)   It is the firm intention of all the parties to do everything within their power to settle the whole question of the Helmsmen's future status and conditions as soon as possible within the first three years of the Agreement.

(2)   With regard to the distribution and levels of earnings all the possible alternatives are still open to be explored. These alternative possibilities might include an increase for senior Helmsmen in one form or another, or a return to the system of one level for all Helmsmen after the first year, or any other system which may be considered to be the right one in all the circumstances. In other words all the options are quite genuinely still open and the Company hope as always that whatever is finally adopted will be agreed as the right and proper course by the representatives of all the parties including the Helmsmen.

(a)   Administration

The parties agree in principle to the administrative amalgamation of the Pilots' and Helmsmen's Service as soon as convenient, under the jurisdiction of the Pilotage Committee, according to the heads of agreement set our in Appendix hereto. The special sub-committee is to be given new terms of reference accordingly.

(b)   Status

The future status of Helmsmen is to be determined within the framework of the heads set out in Appendix 3 but the following are now agreed as provisional measures:

(i)   From the commencement of this Agreement new entrants to the Helmsmen's Service shall be granted permits on the following conditions:

(A)   Subject to the following paragraph (b) their permits shall be liable to termination at reasonable notice and entirely at the discretion of the Company (or Pilotage Committee as appropriate).

(B)   In the case of redundancy, however, their permits will be terminated on the "last to come - first to go" principle, entirely at the discretion of the Company (or Pilotage Committee as appropriate) only after consultation with the Pilots and Helmsmen, and only on strong evidence of a permanent state of overmanning in the Service.

(C) The share of earnings to be as follows:

First 6 months	- $^2/_3$ share (small tonnage ships)
Second 6 months	- $^3/_4$ share (intermediate tonnage)
Next 3 years	- $^3/_4$ share (full tonnage)
After 4 years	- Full share

(D)   "The question of the status of Helmsmen being under consideration, no time limit can at this stage be specified within which the permits of new entrants will be subject to the same conditions, with regard to termination, as those of Helmsmen now in the Service"

The above mentioned conditions attached to new permits and to promotions within the Service may be reviewed by the Pilotage Committee under the new administration arrangements, but it is thought advisable that in the meantime new entrants should not be brought in on the same terms with regard to level of earnings and status as the present members of the Service. The Company reserve the right to vary the above mentioned provisional conditions after consulting the special sub-committee established by the Pilotage Committee on July 11, 1966, and the Helmsmen.

(ii)   The position of Senior Helmsmen in the service is to be examined, in the light of suggestions made in the Report, within the first adjustments in the levels of earnings (whether made within the three years or not) can then be taken into account in a review at the end of three years.

(E)   "New entrants are to serve a satisfactory probationary period prior to appointment, as has been the practice in the past".

ROUGH DRAFT OF COMBINED PILOT'S
AND HELMSMAN'S SERVICE CARD.

Pilots Signature P	Tolls a/c Ref.
H Helmsmen's Signature	Date of Service
Vessel	Nationality
Owner or Agent	

Tonnages		Maximum draught at start of service
Gross	Net	
From		
To		
Initial Fee	Mileage	
Extra Services, Detentions, Cancellations etc.		
Signature of Master		

National Insurance	Travelling Expenses	
	Pilot	Helmsman
F.W.E.	Attendance No.	

Appendix V

THE MANCHESTER SHIP CANAL COMPANY.

SCHEDULE OF CHARGES FOR THE SERVICES OF HELMSMEN

OPERATING ON AND FROM 1ST FEBRUARY, 1954.

1 (a) For each vessel entering or leaving and navigating the Ship Canal and requiring a Helmsman, an initial fee shall be payable according to the gross registered tonnage of the vessel, as follows:-

							£	s	d.
For a vessel -									
Not exceeding 1,500 tons	...	...	...	-	15.	0.			
Exceeding 1,500 tons but not exceeding 2,000 tons				-	17.	6.			
"	2,000	"	"	"	2,500	"	1.	0.	0.
"	2,500	"	"	"	3,000	"	1.	2.	6.
"	3,000	"	"	"	4,000	"	1.	7.	6.
"	4,000	"	"	"	5,000	"	1.12.	6.	
"	5,000	"	"	"	6,000	"	1.17.	6.	
"	6,000	"	"	"	7,000	"	2. 2.	6.	
"	7,000	"	"	"	8,000	"	2. 7.	6.	
"	8,000	"	"	"	9,000	"	2.12.	6.	
"	9,000	"	"	"	10,000	"	2.17.	6.	

Exceeding 10,000 tons, 5/-d for every additional 1,000 tons.

(margin note: Initial Fees.)

In addition there shall be payable a sum based on a rate of ¾d per foot draft per mile or portion of a mile for the distance the vessel has been steered. Draft to be based on the maximum draft at the commencement of the service, and to be taken to the nearest foot (six inches and over to be charged to the higher foot).

Minimum charge for services under
            Clause 1 (a) to be   £1. 0. 0.

(margin note: Minimum Charge.)

1 (b) For each vessel moving from point to point in the Ship Canal with a Helmsman (except as otherwise provided) but without entering or leaving the Canal there shall be payable:-

(margin note: Moving from point to point in the Canal.)

(i) An initial fee calculated as follows:-
If the Helmsman's service is less than 8 miles, fee at half the appropriate rate set out in Clause 1 (a) above.
If the Helmsman's service is over 8 miles, at two-thirds of the appropriate rate set out in Clause 1 (a) above.

and (ii) A rate of ¾d per foot draft per mile or portion of a mile for the distance the vessel has been steered.

- 1 -

- 2 -

Provided that if a vessel is moved from point to
point as aforesaid after loading in the Canal for
a destination within the Port, the charges payable
shall be at the rates provided in Clause 1 (a).

Minimum charge for services under Clause 1 (b) to
be £1. 0. 0.   Minimum.

1 (c)   For a vessel shifted in the Manchester Docks, or   Dock
between Manchester Docks and a berth below Mode   Shifting.
Wheel but not below Barton Bridge, or (except as
hereinafter otherwise provided) in any part of
the Canal where the distance of the shift does
not exceed one mile, a fee of £1.0.0. shall be
payable, together with an additional sum of 9/-d
if the vessel is passed through Mode Wheel Locks.

1 (d)   For a vessel shifted from the entrance lock of   Eastham
the Oil Dock at Eastham to a berth in the Dock,   Oil Dock
or vice versa, or from one berth to another within   Shifting.
the Dock, the following dues according to gross
registered tonnage shall be payable in respect of
the services rendered:-

	£	s	d.
Vessels not exceeding 500 tons	-	7.	6.
Exceeding 500 tons but not exceeding 1,000 tons..	-	15.	0.
" 1,000 " " " 3,000 " ..	1.10.	0.	
" 3,000 tons	2. 5.	0.	

2 (a)   For a vessel moved at Eastham from the Locks to   Eastham
the dolphins or sheer legs, or vice versa, or   Shifting.
between the sheer legs and the dolphins, the
following fee according to the gross registered
tonnage of the vessel shall be payable in respect
of each such service:-

	£	s	d.
Not exceeding 2,500 tons	-	9.	0.
Exceeding 2,500 tons...	-	17.	0.

Provided that no such fee shall be payable for an
inward bound vessel which is ready to proceed up
the Canal.

2 (b)   For a vessel moved into or out of a Dry Dock, the   Drydocking
following fee according to the gross registered   Fee.
tonnage of the vessel shall be payable in addition to any other dues which may be applicable:-

	£	s	d.
For a vessel:-			
Not exceeding 2,500 tons	-	9.	0.
Exceeding 2,500 tons...	-	17.	0.

2 (c)   When a Helmsman is detained on board a vessel on   Detention
passage up or down the Canal which may be berthed   up to
at any intermediate point short of her destina-   4 hours.
tion in the Port for any reason other than stress
of weather or other circumstances affecting the
safe navigation of the vessel a fee of 10/-d shall
be payable on each occasion for the first 4 hours
or part thereof.

- 3 -

If the detention at any such intermediate point exceeds in all 4 hours, but does not exceed 8 hours, an additional fee of 5/-d shall be payable. In respect of detention exceeding 8 hours a further fee of 2/-d shall be payable for every hour or part thereof in excess of 8 hours.

(d) If a Helmsman is detained on a vessel through stress of weather a detention fee shall be payable after the first 12 hours at the rate of 2/-d per hour or part thereof in excess of 12 hours. In reckoning detention under this clause time shall not run during the hours of darkness, that is to say from half-an-hour after sunset till half-an-hour before sunrise.

Detention stress of weather.

(e) When an inward bound vessel is berthed at a temporary berth in the Manchester Dock area for the purpose of waiting until her appointed berth is available, the Helmsmen's service shall be deemed to be completed if the vessel is not moved within one hour, and a fee of £1.0.0. shall then be payable, when the vessel is shifted to the appointed berth.

Berthing at temporary berth.

If a Helmsman is detained on board for more than one hour at the temporary berth a detention fee of 2/-d per hour or part of an hour after the first hour shall be paid, unless the vessel is delayed through stress of weather or other circumstances affecting her safe navigation.

(f) When a Helmsman is ordered to and attends upon a vessel about to sail or shift, and the vessel is not ready to move within two hours after the time for which the Helmsman is ordered, a detention fee of 5/-d shall be payable. If the vessel is not ready within 3 hours after the time for which the Helmsman is ordered a further fee shall be payable at the rate of 2/-d each subsequent hour or part thereof. Provided that these fees shall not be payable if the vessel is delayed by stress of weather or other circumstances affecting her safe navigation.

Detention prior to sailing.

(g) When a Helmsman has been ordered to attend a vessel, and, on attending, is not then required, a fee of 15/-d shall be payable.

Cancellati Fee on attendance

(h) When a vessel inward bound for a point below Mode Wheel and not below Barton Bridge is brought to the Manchester Docks for the purpose of swinging, the Helmsman's service shall be deemed to be completed when the vessel has arrived at the Manchester Docks.

Swinging vessels inward bound for berth not below Barton Bridge.

For steering the vessel back to the berth below Mode Wheel and not below Barton Bridge, a fee of £1.0.0. shall be payable.

- 4 -

2 (i)   When a vessel inward bound for a point below
        Barton Bridge is brought to the Manchester
        Docks for the purpose of swinging, the Helms-
        man's service shall be deemed to be completed
        when the vessel has arrived at the Manchester
        Docks.

        For steering the vessel back to the berth
        below Barton Bridge, an initial fee together
        with the draft mileage rate shall be payable
        under Clause 1 (b).

Swinging inward bound vessel for berth below Barton Bridge.

2 (j)   When a vessel outward bound from a point below
        Mode Wheel and not below Barton Bridge is
        brought to the Manchester Docks for the pur-
        pose of swinging, a fee of £1.0.0. shall be
        payable for the service to the Manchester
        Docks, and the steering of the vessel from
        the Manchester Docks shall be treated as a
        separate service.

Swinging outward bound vessel from berth not below Barton Bridge.

2 (k)   When a vessel outward bound from a point below
        Barton Bridge is brought to the Manchester
        Docks for the purpose of swinging, a fee together
        with the draft mileage rate, under Clause 1 (b)
        shall be payable for the service to the
        Manchester Docks, and the steering of the vessel
        from the Manchester Docks shall be treated as
        a separate service.

Swinging outward bound vessel from berth below Barton Bridge.

2 (l)   For a vessel brought to any place other than
        the Manchester Docks for the purpose of swing-
        ing, the following fees according to the gross
        registered tonnage of the vessel shall be paya-
        ble in addition to the charges provided either
        in Clause 1 (a) or 1 (b) as the case may be:-

Vessel swinging at other point than Manchester Docks.

	£	s.	d.
Not exceeding 2,500 tons	-	9.	0.
Exceeding 2,500 tons	-	17.	0.

2 (m)   For a vessel (exceeding 2,000 tons gross regis-
        ter) swinging at Stanlow a fee of 17/-d shall be
        payable in addition to the charges provided
        either in Clause 1 (a) or 1 (b) as the case may
        be.

Vessel swinging at Stanlow.

2 (n)   When a vessel is booked for a Helmsman out of
        office hours (before 9 a.m. and after 5 p.m.
        from Monday to Friday, and before 9 a.m. and
        after 1 p.m. on Saturday, or on Sundays, or
        Bank or National Holidays) an additional late
        booking fee of £1.1.0. shall be payable to
        the individual Helmsman concerned.

Late Booking Fee.

- 5 -

2 (o) When a Helmsman has commenced a particular service and his attendance on the vessel is not required for the completion of that service a cancellation fee of 15/-d shall be payable in addition to such other charges as may be applicable to the service rendered, provided that the cancellation fee shall not be payable if the Helmsman is not required for the completion of the service through a breakdown of the vessel or through stress of weather or another Helmsman is later engaged for the completion of the service.

Dismissal of Helmsman before Contract completed.

2 (p) The charge for any exceptional services not covered by this Schedule shall be fixed by the Manchester Ship Canal Company and the Manchester Steamship Owners' Association.

Charges for special services.

All the above charges are subject to 49 per cent increase which came into operation on and from 1st August, 1953.

In addition to the steering fees, and to cover expenses which may be incurred by a Helmsman in travelling from Eastham (reckoned as from the Eastham Pilot Station) to join a vessel above Latchford, or returning from a vessel above Latchford to Eastham, a sum of 7/-d shall be payable to the Helmsman.

Travelling Expenses.

Unusual travelling expenses incurred shall be settled by agreement between the Steamship Owner and the Helmsman concerned.

Harbour Master's Office,
Dock Office,
Manchester, 17.

27th January, 1954.

Appendix VI

This reprint is in substitution of page 20 of the Schedule of Ship Dues and Other Charges payable by Shipowners, Reference No. S.C.S. 4, and operates on and from September 4, 1968, until further notice.

1968
CHARGES FOR
PILOTAGE AND HELMSMEN'S SERVICES

The Company collect all charges for pilotage on the Canal. They also collect all charges in connection with Helmsmen's services.

The services of Pilots and Helmsmen are not compulsory, but when a Pilot and/or Helmsman is requisitioned the Pilotage Dues* and/or Helmsman's charges§ for the Pilotage District shall be as follows:—

1. (*a*) **Vessels entering or leaving the Canal**

(i) Initial fee (Service Code 001)
For each vessel entering or leaving and navigating the Ship Canal under pilotage and/or with a helmsman, an initial fee shall be payable according to the gross registered tonnage of the vessel of:—

							PILOT			HELMSMAN		
							£	s.	d.	£	s.	d.
Vessels not exceeding 500 tons	...	...	...	...	...	7	3	7			
Exceeding	500 tons but not exceeding	1,000 tons	...	8	19	6	5	3	4
„	1,000 „	„	„	„	1,500	„	...	10	15	5		
„	1,500 „	„	„	„	2,000	„	...	12	11	4	6	0	7
„	2,000 „	„	„	„	2,500	„	...	14	7	2	6	17	10
„	2,500 „	„	„	„	3,000	„	...	16	3	1	7	15	0
„	3,000 „	„	„	„	4,000	„	...	19	14	11	9	9	6
„	4,000 „	„	„	„	5,000	„	...	23	6	8	11	3	11
„	5,000 „	„	„	„	6,000	„	...	26	18	6	12	18	5
„	6,000 „	„	„	„	7,000	„	...	30	10	4	14	12	10
„	7,000 „	„	„	„	8,000	„	...	34	2	1	16	7	3
„	8,000 „	„	„	„	9,000	„	...	37	13	11	18	1	9
„	9,000 „	„	„	„	10,000	„	...	41	5	8	19	16	2
For every additional 1,000 tons in excess of 10,000 tons	...	3	11	10	1	14	6

(ii) Mileage fee (Service Code 010)
In addition there shall be payable a sum computed at a rate, as shown below, per foot draught for each mile (or portion of a mile) over which the vessel has been piloted or steered. For the purposes of such computation the draught of a vessel shall be her maximum draught at the commencement of the service taken to the nearest foot (six inches and over to be charged as a foot):—

> PILOT .... 8·975d.
> HELMSMAN .... 5·168d.

(iii) Minimum charge under Clause 1 (*a*). (Service Code 020)
> PILOT .... £10 15s. 5d.
> HELMSMAN ...... £6 17s. 10d.

(*b*) **Vessels moving from point to point in the Canal**
(i) Initial fee (Service Code 002 or 003)
For each vessel moving from point to point in the Ship Canal under pilotage and/or with a helmsman (except as otherwise provided) but without entering or leaving the Canal there shall be payable an initial fee calculated as follows:—

Calculated on the basic rates with a Surcharge of *618% §589%

262

This reprint is in substitution of page 21 of the Schedule of Ship Dues and Other Charges payable by Shipowners, Reference No. S.C.S. 4, and operates on and from September 4, 1968, until further notice.

Charges for Pilotage and Helmsmen's Services

8 miles or over (Service Code 002)
If the pilotage or helmsman's service is 8 miles or over, at two-thirds of the appropriate rate set out in Clause 1(*a*)

Less than 8 miles (Service Code 003)
If the pilotage or helmsman's service is less than 8 miles, at half the appropriate rate set out in Clause 1(*a*);

(ii) Mileage fee (Service Code 010)
In addition a rate per foot draught per mile or portion of a mile of:—

> PILOT .... 8·975d.
> HELMSMAN .... 5·168d.

(iii) Minimum charge under Clause 1(*b*) (Service Code 020)
> PILOT ....£10 15s. 5d.
> HELMSMAN .... £6 17s. 10d.

Provided that if a vessel is moved from point to point as aforesaid after loading cargo in the Canal for a destination within the Port, the Pilotage dues and/or Helmsman's charges payable shall be at the rates provided in Clause 1(*a*).

(*c*) **Vessels shifting at Manchester** (Service Code 030) **and elsewhere in Canal** (Service Code 035)
For a vessel shifted in the Manchester Docks, or between Manchester Docks and a berth below Mode Wheel but not below Barton Bridge or (except as hereinafter otherwise provided) in any part of the Canal where the distance of the shift does not exceed one mile, the following charges according to the gross registered tonnage shall be payable in respect of the services rendered:—

	PILOT £ s. d.	HELMSMAN £ s. d.
Vessels not exceeding 500 tons	3 11 10	
Exceeding 500 tons, but not exceeding 1,000 tons ...	7 3 7	6 17 10
„ 1,000 „ „ „ „ 3,000 „ ...	14 7 2	
„ 3,000 „	21 10 10	
Additional charge if vessel is passed through Mode Wheel Locks (Service Code 031)	3 15 5	3 2 0

(*d*) **Vessels shifting at Queen Elizabeth II Dock, Eastham** (Service Code 032 or 033)
For a vessel shifted from the entrance lock of Queen Elizabeth II Dock, Eastham, to a berth in the Dock or vice versa or from one berth to another within the Dock the following dues according to gross registered tonnage shall be payable in respect of the services rendered:—

	PILOT £ s. d.	HELMSMAN £ s. d.
Vessels not exceeding 500 tons	5 7 8	2 11 8
Exceeding 500 tons but not exceeding 1,000 tons ...	10 15 5	5 3 4
„ 1,000 tons but not exceeding 3,000 tons ...	21 10 10	10 6 8
„ 3,000 tons	32 6 2	15 10 1

21

This reprint is in substitution of page 22 of the Schedule of Ship Dues and Other Charges payable by Shipowners, Reference No. S.C.S. 4, and operates on and from September 4, 1968, until further notice.

Charges for Pilotage and Helmsmen's Services

EXTRA SERVICES

2 (a) Eastham Shifting (Service Code 034)

For a vessel moved at Eastham from the locks to the dolphins or masting crane, or vice versa, or between the masting crane and the dolphins, the following fees according to the gross registered tonnage of the vessel shall be payable in respect of each such service:—

	PILOT			HELMSMAN		
	£	s.	d.	£	s.	d.
Vessels not exceeding 2,500 tons	3	15	5	3	2	0
Exceeding 2,500 tons	7	10	9	5	17	2

Provided that no such fees shall be payable for an inward bound vessel which is ready to proceed up the Canal.

(b) Drydocking Fee (Service Code 040)

For a vessel moved into or out of a Dry Dock, the following fees according to the gross registered tonnage of the vessel shall be payable in addition to any other dues which may be applicable:—

	PILOT			HELMSMAN		
	£	s.	d.	£	s.	d.
Vessels not exceeding 2,500 tons	3	15	5	3	2	0
Exceeding 2,500 tons	7	10	9	5	17	2

(c) Detention (Service Code 050)

If during her passage up or down the Canal a vessel is berthed at an intermediate point short of her destination in the Port for any reason other than stress of weather or other circumstances affecting the safe navigation of the vessel (except circumstances arising out of an obstruction in or over the Canal which does not permit the vessel to be navigated with safety beyond such obstruction) and the pilot and/or helmsman is detained on board at such intermediate point at the request of the Master, a fee shall be payable on each occasion for the first four hours or part thereof as under:—

> PILOT .... £5 7s. 8d.
> HELMSMAN ... £3 8s. 11d.

If the detention at any such intermediate point exceeds in all four hours, but does not exceed eight hours, an additional fee shall be payable of:—

> PILOT .... £1 15s. 11d.
> HELMSMAN ... £1 14s. 6d.

In respect of detention exceeding eight hours a further fee shall be payable for every hour or part thereof in excess of eight hours as under:—

> PILOT .... £1 1s. 7d.
> HELMSMAN ... 13s. 9d.

This reprint is in substitution of page 23 of the Schedule of Ship Dues and Other Charges payable by Shipowners, Reference No. S.C.S. 4, and operates on and from September 4, 1968, until further notice.

Charges for Pilotage and Helmsmen's Services

(*d*) **Detention due to stress of weather** (Service Code 051)

If a pilot or helmsman is detained on a vessel through stress of weather, a detention fee shall be payable after the first 12 hours at a rate per hour or part thereof in excess of 12 hours as under:—

PILOT .... £1   1s.   7d.
HELMSMAN ......   13s.   9d.

In reckoning detention under this clause, time shall not run during the hours of darkness, that is to say from half an hour after sunset till half an hour before sunrise.

(*e*) **Berthing at a temporary berth** (Service Code 053)

When an inward bound vessel is berthed at a temporary berth in the Manchester Docks area for the purpose of waiting until her appointed berth is available, the service shall be deemed to be completed if the vessel is not moved within one hour, and a shifting fee under Clause 1(*c*) shall then be payable when the vessel is shifted to the appointed berth.

If a pilot or helmsman is detained on board for more than one hour at the temporary berth a detention fee per hour or part of an hour after the first hour shall be paid as follows, unless the vessel is delayed through stress of weather or other circumstances affecting her safe navigation:—

PILOT .... £1   1s.   7d.
HELMSMAN ......   13s.   9d.

(*f*) **Detention prior to sailing** (Service Code 052)

When a pilot or helmsman is ordered to and attends upon a vessel about to sail or shift (which expression does not include shifting from Eastham Locks to the dolphins or to the masting crane) and the vessel is not ready to move within two hours after the time for which the pilot or helmsman has been ordered, a detention fee shall be payable of:—

PILOT .... £3   11s.   10d.
HELMSMAN ...... £2   8s.   3d.

If the vessel is not ready to sail within three hours after the time the pilot or helmsman is ordered, a further fee shall be payable for each subsequent hour or part thereof as under:—

PILOT .... £1   1s.   7d.
HELMSMAN ......   13s.   9d.

The detention fees under this clause shall not be payable if the vessel is delayed by stress of weather or other circumstances affecting her safe navigation.

(*g*) **Cancellation Fee** (Service Code 071)

When a pilot or helmsman has been ordered to attend a vessel (other than an inward bound vessel at Eastham Locks or at the Entrance Lock to Queen Elizabeth II Dock) and, on attending, is not then required, a fee shall be payable of:—

PILOT .... £5   7s.   8d.
HELMSMAN ...... £5   3s.   4d.

This reprint is in substitution of page 24 of the Schedule of Ship Dues and Other Charges payable by Shipowners, Reference No. S.C.S. 4, and operates on and from September 4, 1968, until further notice.

Charges for Pilotage and Helmsmen's Services

(h) Swinging vessels inward bound for berth not below Barton Bridge

When a vessel inward bound for a point below Mode Wheel and not below Barton Bridge is brought to the Manchester Docks for the purpose of swinging, the pilotage and/or helmsman's service shall be deemed to be completed when the vessel has arrived at the Manchester Docks.

For the service of piloting and/or steering the vessel back to the berth below Mode Wheel and not below Barton Bridge, a shifting fee under clause 1(c) shall be payable.

(i) Swinging vessels inward bound for berth below Barton Bridge

When a vessel inward bound for a point below Barton Bridge is brought to the Manchester Docks for the purpose of swinging, the pilotage and/or helmsman's service shall be deemed to be completed when the vessel has arrived at the Manchester Docks.

For the service of piloting and/or steering the vessel back to the berth below Barton Bridge, an initial fee together with the draught mileage rate shall be payable under clause 1(b).

(j) Swinging vessels outward bound from berth not below Barton Bridge

When a vessel outward bound from a point below Mode Wheel and not below Barton Bridge is brought to the Manchester Docks for the purpose of swinging, the shifting fees under clause 1(c) shall be payable for the service to the Manchester Docks, and the pilotage and/or steering of the vessel from the Manchester Docks shall be treated as a separate service.

(k) Swinging vessels outward bound from berth below Barton Bridge

When a vessel outward bound from a point below Barton Bridge is brought to the Manchester Docks for the purpose of swinging, the initial fee together with the draught mileage under clause 1(b) shall be payable for the service to the Manchester Docks, and the pilotage and/or steering of the vessel from the Manchester Docks, shall be treated as a separate service.

(l) Swinging vessels at points other than the Manchester Docks or Stanlow
(Service Code 061)

For a vessel brought to any place other than the Manchester Docks or Stanlow for the purpose of swinging, the following fees according to the gross registered tonnage of the vessel shall be payable in addition to the charges provided either in clause 1(a) or 1(b) as the case may be:—

	PILOT £ s. d.	HELMSMAN £ s. d.
Vessels not exceeding 2,500 tons	3 15 5	3 2 0
„ exceeding 2,500 tons	7 10 9	5 17 2

This reprint is in substitution of page 25 of the Schedule of Ship Dues and Other Charges payable by Shipowners, Reference No. S.C.S. 4, and operates on and from September 4, 1968, until further notice.

Charges for Pilotage and Helmsmen's Services

(m) **Swinging vessels at Stanlow** (Service Code 060)

For a vessel (exceeding 2,000 tons gross registered tonnage) swinging at Stanlow, the fee shown below shall be payable in addition to the charges provided either in clause 1(a) or 1(b) as the case may be:—

```
PILOT  .................. £7 10s.  9d.
HELMSMAN  ......... £5 17s.  2d.
```

(n) **Disappointment Fee** (Service Code 072)

When a pilot or helmsman is ordered to attend a vessel on entering the Pilotage District at Eastham on a specified tide, and does in fact attend at Eastham for the purpose of boarding such vessel and the vessel does not arrive on that tide, or upon arrival on that tide does not require the service of a pilot or helmsman, a disappointment fee (together with travelling expenses as set out on Page 26 where appropriate) shall be payable of:—

```
PILOT  .................. £8 1s.  7d.
HELMSMAN  ......... £6 17s.  10d.
```

Such fee shall not, however, be payable:—

(i) If the pilot or helmsman is notified that the order is cancelled before he has commenced his journey to Eastham, or

(ii) If the vessel arrives prior to the commencement of the specified tide, but is nevertheless attended by the pilot or helmsman who was originally ordered to attend her on that tide, or

(iii) If the vessel is known in advance to require shifting from Eastham Locks to the dolphins or the masting crane at Eastham and arrangements have accordingly been made for a pilot or helmsman to attend her solely for the purpose of performing such shift.

For the purpose of the provisions set out under this head a tide shall be deemed to commence four hours before and to finish four hours after the time of high water at Liverpool, and a vessel shall be deemed to have arrived when her stern has passed the outer lock gates at Eastham Locks or at the entrance to Queen Elizabeth II Dock as the case may be.

(o) **Dismissal of Pilot and/or Helmsman before contract completed** (Service Code 070)

When a pilot and/or helmsman has commenced a service but is not required to complete it, a cancellation fee shall be payable (in addition to any other dues payable for the service rendered), unless the dismissal of the pilot and/or helmsman before completion of the service was occasioned by a breakdown of the vessel or stress of weather or another pilot was later engaged for the completion of the service:—

```
PILOT  .................. £5 7s.  8d.
HELMSMAN  ......... £5 3s.  4d.
```

(p) **Charges for special services** (Service Code 073)

The charges for any exceptional Pilotage services not covered by this Schedule shall be determined by the Pilotage Authority. The charges for any exceptional Helmsman's services shall be determined by the Manchester Ship Canal Company and the Manchester Steamship Owners' Association.

Charges for Pilotage and Helmsmen's Services

Travelling Expenses. (Service Code 180)

In addition to the pilotage dues and/or helmsman's charges, a pilot and/or helmsman shall be paid a sum of 15s. 0d. to cover any expenses he may incur in travelling in either direction between Eastham and a vessel at or above Latchford or between Manchester and a vessel at or below Latchford.

Unusual travelling expenses incurred shall be settled by agreement between the Shipowner and the pilot and/or helmsman concerned.

The Master's signature on the pilot's and/or helmsman's certificate of services rendered is accepted by the Company as binding upon the Master, Owner or Ship's Agent to pay the scheduled charges incurred.

Relief at Latchford.

The following provisions are contained in the Pilotage Bye-laws. A similar arrangement applies to Helmsmen.

(a) For the purpose of providing for the relief at Latchford of the Pilots of such vessels as they may from time to time approve the Pilotage Committee may introduce a scheme wherein such vessels are specified and whereby the pilotage service on such vessels is deemed to be completed at Latchford so that separate pilotage charges are payable in respect of the passages to Latchford and beyond Latchford. Such charges shall be calculated in accordance with the Schedule annexed to the Pilotage Bye-laws, subject to the special provisions hereinafter mentioned.

(b) Such a vessel shall in respect of the service immediately above Latchford be exempted from the payment of the initial fee provided for under Clause 1 (b) of the said Schedule.

(c) A Pilot who attends at Latchford for the purpose of performing the service beyond Latchford shall in no circumstances be entitled to a cancellation fee or a fee for detention in respect of such attendance.

(d) A Pilot attending such a vessel for either service shall, where appropriate under the said Schedule, be entitled to travelling expenses, subject to any special provisions which the Pilotage Committee may make in connection with the said scheme.

(e) No scheme introduced in accordance with this Bye-law shall have the effect of requiring the compulsory relief of a Choice Pilot performing a service on a vessel to which he is appropriated.

MOORING SERVICES

The services of Mooring and Unmooring vessels at most points within the Canal are performed by Boatmen licensed by the Company. Where such Boatmen are not in attendance, these services may be performed by the Company's Tugmen or Lockgatemen, but the Company accept no liability therefor.

Details of the charges for such services will be furnished on application.

Appendix VII

CHARGES FOR
PILOTAGE AND HELMSMEN'S SERVICES
1988

The Company collect all charges for pilotage on the Canal. They also collect all charges in connection with Helmsmen's services.

When a Pilot and/or Helmsman is requisitioned the Pilotage Dues and/or Helmsmen's charges for the Pilotage District shall be as follows:-

PART I

1. *(a)* **Vessels entering or leaving the Canal**

(i) Initial fee

For each vessel entering or leaving and navigating the Ship Canal under pilotage and/or with a helmsman, an initial fee shall be payable according to the gross registered tonnage of the vessel of:-

	PILOT £	HELMSMAN £
Vessels not exceeding 500 tons	80.63	
Exceeding 500 tons but not exceeding 1,000 tons	100.78	68.74
Exceeding 1,000 tons but not exceeding 1,500 tons	120.93	
Exceeding 1,500 tons but not exceeding 2,000 tons	141.10	80.27
Exceeding 2,000 tons but not exceeding 2,500 tons	161.25	91.77
Exceeding 2,500 tons but not exceeding 3,000 tons	181.41	103.18
Exceeding 3,000 tons but not exceeding 4,000 tons	221.72	126.25
Exceeding 4,000 tons but not exceeding 5,000 tons	262.03	149.11
Exceeding 5,000 tons but not exceeding 6,000 tons	302.33	172.05
Exceeding 6,000 tons but not exceeding 7,000 tons	342.66	194.96
Exceeding 7,000 tons but not exceeding 8,000 tons	382.97	217.83
Exceeding 8,000 tons but not exceeding 9,000 tons	423.28	240.87
Exceeding 9,000 tons but not exceeding 10,000 tons	463.58	263.82
For every additional 1,000 tons in excess of 10,000 tons	40.31	23.02

(ii) Mileage fee

In addition there shall be payable a sum computed at a rate, as shown below, per foot draught for each mile (or portion of a mile) over which the vessel has been piloted or steered. For the purposes of such a computation the draught of the vessel shall be her maximum draught at the commencement of the service taken to the nearest foot (six inches or over to be charged as a foot):-

> PILOT 41.993p
> HELMSMAN 28.673p

(iii) Minimum charge under Clause 1 (a)

> PILOT £120.93
> HELMSMAN .... £ 91.77

CHARGES FOR PILOTAGE AND HELMSMEN'S SERVICES

(b) Vessels moving from point to point in the Canal

(i) Initial fee

For each vessel moved from point to point in the Ship Canal under pilotage and/or with a helmsman (except as otherwise provided) but without entering or leaving the Canal there shall be payable an initial fee calculated as follows:-

8 miles or over

If the pilotage or helmsman's service is 8 miles or over, at two-thirds of the appropriate rate set out in Clause 1 *(a)*.

Less than 8 miles

If the pilotage or helmsman's service is less than 8 miles, at half the appropriate rate set out in Clause 1 *(a)*.

(ii) Mileage fee

In addition a rate per foot draught per mile or portion of a mile of:-

PILOT 41.993p
HELMSMAN 28.673p

(iii) Minimum charge under Clause 1 *(b)*

PILOT £120.93
HELMSMAN .... £ 91.77

Provided that if a vessel is moved from point to point as aforesaid after loading cargo in the Canal for a destination within the Port, the Pilotage dues and/or Helmsman's charges payable shall be at the rates provided in Clause 1 *(a)*.

(c) Vessels shifting at Manchester and elsewhere in Canal

For a vessel shifted in the Manchester Docks, or between Manchester Docks and a berth below Mode Wheel but not below Barton Bridge or (except as hereinafter otherwise provided) in any part of the Canal where the distance of the shift does not exceed one mile, the following charges according to the gross registered tonnage shall be payable in respect of the services rendered:-

	PILOT £	HELMSMAN £
Vessels not exceeding 500 tons	40.31	
Exceeding 500 tons,but not exceeding 1,000 tons	80.63	
Exceeding 1,000 tons,but not exceeding 3,000tons	161.25	91.77
Exceeding 3,000 tons	241.88	
Additional charge if vessel is passed through Mode Wheel Locks	42.31	41.37

CHARGES FOR PILOTAGE AND HELMSMEN'S SERVICES

(d) Vessels shifting at Queen Elizabeth II Dock, Eastham

For a vessel shifted from the entrance lock of Queen Elizabeth II Dock, Eastham, to a berth in the Dock or vice versa or from one berth to another within the Dock the following dues according to the gross registered tonnage shall be payable in respect of the services rendered:-

	PILOT £	HELMSMAN £
Vessels not exceeding 500 tons	60.46	34.40
Exceeding 500 tons but not exceeding 1.000 tons	120.93	68.74
Exceeding 1,000 tons but not exceeding 3,000 tons	241.88	137.54
Exceeding 3,000 tons	362.81	206.61

EXTRA SERVICES

2. (a) Eastham Shifting

For a vessel moved at Eastham from the locks to the dolphins or masting crane, or vice versa, or between the masting crane and the dolphins, the following fees according to the gross registered tonnage of the vessel shall be payable in respect of each such service:-

	PILOT £	HELMSMAN £
Vessels not exceeding 2,500 tons	42.31	41.37
Vessels exceeding 2,500 tons	84.66	77.98

Provided that no such fees shall be payable for an inward bound vessel which is ready to proceed up the Canal.

(b) Drydocking Fee

For a vessel moved into or out of a Dry Dock, the following fees according to the gross registered tonnage of the vessel shall be payable in addition to any other dues which may be applicable:-

	PILOT £	HELMSMAN £
Vessels not exceeding 2,500 tons	42.31	41.37
Exceeding 2,500 tons	84.66	77.98

(c) Detention on passage

If during her passage up or down the Canal a vessel is berthed at an intermediate point short of her destination in the Port for any reason other than stress of weather or other circumstances affecting the safe navigation of the vessel (except circumstances arising out of an obstruction in or over the Canal which does not permit the vessel to be navigated with safety beyond such obstruction) and the pilot and/or helmsman is detained on board at such intermediate point at the request of the Master, a fee shall be payable for the first four hours or part thereof as under:-

CHARGES FOR PILOTAGE AND HELMSMEN'S SERVICES

PILOT £60.46
HELMSMAN £45.99

If the detention at such intermediate point exceeds in all four hours, but does not exceed eight hours, an additional fee shall be payable of:-

PILOT £20.17
HELMSMAN £23.02

In respect of detention exceeding eight hours a further fee shall be payable for every hour or part thereof in excess of eight hours as under:-

PILOT £12.10
HELMSMAN .... £ 9.14

(d)   Detention due to stress of weather

If a pilot or helmsman is detained on a vessel through stress of weather, a detention fee shall be payable after the first 12 hours at a rate per hour or part thereof in excess of 12 hours as under:

PILOT £12.10
HELMSMAN ....£ 9.14

In reckoning detention under this clause, time shall not run during the hours of darkness, that is to say from half an hour after sunset till half an hour before sunrise.

(e)   Berthing at a temporary berth

When an inward bound vessel is berthed at a temporary berth in the Manchester Docks area for the purpose of waiting until her appointed berth is available, the service shall be deemed to be completed if the vessel is not moved within one hour, and a shifting fee under Clause 1 (c) shall then be payable when the vessel is shifted to the appointed berth.

If a pilot or helmsman is detained on board for more than one hour at the temporary berth a detention fee per hour or part of an hour after the first hour shall be paid as follows, unless the vessel is delayed through stress of weather or other circumstances affecting her safe navigation:-

PILOT £12.10
HELMSMAN .... £ 9.14

(f)   Detention prior to sailing

When a pilot or helmsman is ordered to and attends upon a vessel about to sail or shift (which expression does not include shifting from Eastham Locks to the dolphins or to the masting crane) and the vessel is not ready to move within two hours after the time for which the pilot or helmsman is ordered, a detention fee shall be payable of:-

PILOT £40.31
HELMSMAN £32.15

6

CHARGES FOR PILOTAGE AND HELMSMEN'S SERVICES

If the vessel is not ready within three hours after the time for which the pilot or helmsman is ordered, a further fee shall be payable for each subsequent hour or part thereof as under:-

PILOT £12.10
HELMSMAN .... £ 9.14

Provided that the detention fees under this clause shall not be payable if the vessel is delayed by stress of weather or other circumstances affecting her safe navigation.

(g) Swinging vessels inward bound for berth not below Barton Bridge

When a vessel inward bound for a point below Mode Wheel and not below Barton Bridge is brought to the Manchester Docks for the purpose of swinging, the pilotage and/or helmsman's service shall be deemed to be completed when the vessel has arrived at the Manchester Docks.

For the service of piloting and/or steering the vessel back to the berth below Mode Wheel and not below Barton Bridge, a shifting fee under clause 1 *(c)* shall be payable.

(h) Swinging vessels inward bound for berth below Barton Bridge

When a vessel inward bound for a point below Barton Bridge is brought to the Manchester Docks for the purpose of swinging, the pilotage and/or helmsman's service shall be deemed to be completed when the vessel has arrived at the Manchester Docks.

For the service of piloting and/or steering the vessel back to the berth below Barton Bridge, an initial fee together with the draught mileage rate shall be payable under clause 1 *(b)*.

(i) Swinging vessels outward bound from berth not below Barton Bridge

When a vessel outward bound from a point below Mode Wheel and not below Barton Bridge is brought to the Manchester Docks for the purpose of swinging, the shifting fees under clause 1 *(c)* shall be payable for the service to the Manchester Docks, and the pilotage and/or steering of the vessel from the Manchester Docks shall be treated as a separate service.

(j) Swinging vessels outward bound from berth below Barton Bridge

When a vessel outward bound from a point below Barton Bridge is brought to the Manchester Docks for the purpose of swinging, the initial fee together with the draught mileage under clause 1 *(b)* shall be payable for the service to the Manchester Docks, and the pilotage and/or steering of the vessel from the Manchester Docks, shall be treated as a separate service.

7

CHARGES FOR PILOTAGE AND HELMSMEN'S SERVICES

(k) Swinging vessels at points other than the Manchester Docks

For a vessel brought to any place other than the Manchester Docks for the purpose of swinging, the following fees according to the gross registered tonnage of the vessel shall be payable in addition to the charges provided either in clause **1** *(a)* or **1** *(b)* as the case may be:-

	PILOT £	HELMSMAN £
Vessels not exceeding 2,500 tons	42.31	41.37
Vessels exceeding 2,500 tons	84.66	77.98

(l) Swinging vessels at Stanlow

For a vessel (exceeding 2,000 tons gross registered tonnage) swinging at Stanlow, the fee shown below shall be payable in addition to the charges provided either in clause **1** *(a)* or **1** *(b)* as the case may be:-

PILOT £84.66
HELMSMAN £77.98

(m) Cancellation Fee

When a pilot or helmsman has been ordered to attend a vessel (other than an inward bound vessel at Eastham Locks or at the Entrance Lock to Queen Elizabeth II Dock) and, on attending, is not then required, a fee shall be payable of:-

PILOT £60.46
HELMSMAN £53.34

(n) Disappointment Fee

When a pilot or helmsman is ordered to attend a vessel on entering the Pilotage District at Eastham on a specified tide, and does in fact attend at Eastham for the purpose of boarding such vessel and the vessel does not arrive on that tide, or upon arrival on that tide does not require the service of a pilot or helmsman, a disappointment fee (together with travelling expenses as set out on Page 9 where appropriate) shall be payable of:-

PILOT £90.72
HELMSMAN £77.05

Such fee shall not, however, be payable:-

(i) If the pilot or helmsman is notified that the order is cancelled before he has commenced his journey fo Eastham, or

(ii) If the vessel arrives prior to the commencement of the specified tide, but is nevertheless attended by the pilot or helmsman who was originally ordered to attend her on that tide, or

(iii) If the vessel is known in advance to require shifting from Eastham Locks to the dolphins or the masting crane at Eastham and arrangements have accordingly been made for a pilot or helmsman to attend her solely for the purpose of performing such shift.

8

CHARGES FOR PILOTAGE AND HELMSMEN'S SERVICES

For the purpose of the provisions set out under this heading a tide shall be deemed to commence four hours before and to finish four hours after the time of high water at Liverpool, and a vessel shall be deemed to have arrived when her stern has passed the outer lock gates at Eastham Locks or at the entrance to Queen Elizabeth II Dock as the case may be.

(o) Dismissal of Pilot and/or Helmsman before contract completed

When a pilot and/or helmsman has commenced a service but is not required to complete it, a cancellation fee shall be payable (in addition to any other dues payable for the service rendered), unless the dismissal of the pilot and/or helmsman before completion of the service was occassioned by a breakdown of the vessel or stress of weather or another pilot or helmsman was later engaged for the completion of the service:-

> PILOT £60.46
> HELMSMAN £53.34

(p) Charges for special services

The charges for any exceptional Pilotage services not covered by this Schedule shall be determined by the Pilotage Authority. The charges for any exceptional Helmsman's services shall be determined by the Manchester Ship Canal Company and the Ship Canal Users' and Shipowners' Association.

Travelling Expenses

In addition to the dues, pilots are paid travelling allowances at rates agreed by the Pilotage Committee. For the purpose of meeting these allowances and any unusual travelling expenses each vessel is required to pay a surcharge at a rate approved from time to time by the Pilotage Committee. A similar arrangement applies to helmsmen.

The Master's signature on the pilot's and/or helmsman's certificate of services rendered is accepted by the Company as binding upon the Master, Owner or Ship's agent to pay the scheduled charges incurred.

Relief of Latchford

The following provisions are contained in the pilotage bye-laws. A similar arrangement applies to Helmsmen.

(a) For the purpose of providing for the relief at Latchford of the Pilots of such vessels as they may from time to time approve the Pilotage Committee may introduce a scheme wherein such vessels are specified and whereby the pilotage service on such vessels is deemed to be completed at Latchford so that separate pilotage charges are payable in respect of the passages to Latchford and beyond Latchford. Such charges shall be calculated in accordance with the published List of Charges, subject to the special provisions hereinafter mentioned.

9

CHARGES FOR PILOTAGE AND HELMSMEN'S SERVICES

(b)   Such a vessel shall in respect of the service immediately above Latchford be exempted from the payment of the initial fee provided for under clause **1** *(b)* of the said List of Charges.

(c)   A pilot who attends at Latchford for the purpose of performing the service beyond Latchford shall in no circumstances be entitled to a cancellation fee or a fee for detention in respect of such attendance.

(d)   A pilot attending such a vessel for either service shall, where appropriate under the said List of Charges, be entitled to travelling expenses, subject to any special provisions which the pilotage Committee may make in connection with the said scheme.

(e)   No scheme introduced in accordance with this bye-law shall have the effect of requiring the compulsory relief of a Choice Pilot performing a service on a vessel to which he is appropriated